Beyond Peterloo

Beyond Peterloo

Elijah Dixon and Manchester's Forgotten Reformers

Robert Hargreaves

Alan Hampson

PEN & SWORD
HISTORY

AN IMPRINT OF PEN & SWORD BOOKS LTD.
YORKSHIRE – PHILADELPHIA

First published in Great Britain in 2018 by
Pen & Sword History
An imprint of
Pen & Sword Books Ltd
Yorkshire - Philadelphia

ISBN 9781526725097

Typeset in INDIA By Geniies IT & Services Private Limited

Printed and bound in the UK by CPI Group (UK) Ltd., Croydon. CR0 4YY

Pen & Sword Books Ltd incorporates the Imprints of Pen & Sword Books
Archaeology, Atlas, Aviation, Battleground, Discovery, Family History,
History, Maritime, Military, Naval, Politics, Railways, Select, Transport, True
Crime, Fiction, Frontline Books, Leo Cooper, Praetorian Press, Seaforth
Publishing, Wharncliffe and White Owl.

For a complete list of Pen & Sword titles please contact

PEN & SWORD BOOKS LIMITED
47 Church Street, Barnsley, South Yorkshire, S70 2AS, England
E-mail: enquiries@pen-and-sword.co.uk
Website: www.pen-and-sword.co.uk

or

PEN AND SWORD BOOKS
1950 Lawrence Rd, Havertown, PA 19083, USA
E-mail: Uspen-and-sword@casematepublishers.com
Website: www.penandswordbooks.com

To the memory of

Bernard Claude Savage (1913–2011)

whose passion for local history, especially
that of New Moston and its founder, was
the inspiration for this work.

Contents

Acknowledgements

The authors are grateful for the ready and willing help of the following individuals and organisations (listed alphabetically) and to those retiring and anonymous informants whose quiet shoulder-work is no less appreciated.

Chetham's Library, Manchester; Co-operative Archive, Holyoake House, Manchester; Rebecca Coughlan (42nd Street); Karen Cunningham; Philip Dunne; Failsworth Library; Rod Fairbrother; General Register Office, UK; Hackney Archives, Dalston Square, London; Steven Little; Holmfirth Library; Manchester Central Library Archives, St Peter's Square, Manchester; Manchester & Lancashire Family History Society; Julie McCarthy (42nd Street); New Moston Local History Society; Newton Heath Library; Maxine Peake; Jennifer Reid; Salford Local Studies Library; Jackie Settle; Steven Smith; Mr and Mrs J Stephenson, Holmfirth; Swedish Match, Stockholm; Michael Thorpe; David Tomlinson; Stephanie Turner; Stephen P Wilson; Working Class Movement Library, Salford; Deborah Wyles (Holme Valley Civic Society).

The following websites have also provided useful background information or source locations:-

Academia; Ancestry UK; British Newspaper Archive; Family Search (Latter Day Saints); Find My Past; FreeBMD; Gerald Massey; Google Books; Guardian and Observer Archive; Hathi Trust; Historical Directories (Leicester University); JSTOR; Lancashire BMD; Lancashire Online Parish Clerks; London Gazette Archive; Manchester Evening News; Mancuniensis; National Archives (Discovery); National Library of Scotland (Map Archive); Spartacus Educational; The Genealogist; Whaley Bridge Photos; Wikipedia

Foreword

HOW MANY among the residents of Manchester's burgeoning and fashionable Northern Quarter are aware of the poverty and despair that once pervaded their neighbourhood? How many know of Elijah Dixon and his colleagues – men like James Wroe, impoverished journalist and bookseller, or James Scholefield, minister of religion, who once lived in the shadow of the mills now converted into luxury apartments? Who now remembers the sacrifices they made for their beliefs, the imprisonment and persecution suffered by them and their families?

The answer, I fear, is very few. The history of this brave band of foot soldiers has been eclipsed by that of dazzling orators, prominent politicians, and heroes of empire. Only determined digging and delving into the small print of history by Rob Hargreaves and Alan Hampson has unearthed this fascinating tale of ordinary men who, for the most part, lived and died in obscurity, and lie in unmarked graves.

Elijah Dixon arrived in Manchester as an impoverished refugee, worked as a little piecer in a cotton mill, and rose to become a successful manufacturer. Yet the authors show that it was not the pursuit of wealth that energised Dixon's extraordinary life - rather his passionate commitment to reform and the relief of poverty.

No respecter of rank – and mocked by his enemies as a 'cart orator' – Dixon pitched fearlessly into agitation for voting rights. By the time of Peterloo he had already been arrested, clapped in irons, and imprisoned without trial. He was among the first supporters of women's rights, co-operation, and internationalism and would not compromise his views to impress Manchester's 'respectable' reformers like Cobden and Bright.

The authors show how Dixon operated at the grass roots – if that is not a contradiction in terms – to describe the mean streets and crowded slums of nineteenth century Ancoats and New Cross.

Away from the drawing rooms in which The Manchester School of privileged politicians held sway, Dixon was at the hub of a network of street-level demonstrators and pamphleteers, forever organising meetings and protests. They risked arrest daily, and their families bore the brunt of poverty, infant-mortality, and oppression.

And yet their story is not all doom and gloom. The authors also illuminate the human side of their subjects - their family scandals, mistakes and comic confrontations.

We read that once, under pressure at a rowdy meeting, Dixon modestly insisted: 'Mine has been chiefly shoulder-work. I am a friend of freedom.' Not a bad epitaph, and one that any man or woman could be proud of. I recommend this book not only to the young and striving population of the Northern Quarter but to all who have an instinct to better understand our common heritage, and the quiet contributions made to it by our unsung heroes.

Maxine Peake

Introduction

The long life of Elijah Dixon, beginning on 23 October 1790, coincided with a period during which Britain underwent the most profound change it has ever experienced before or since. The change was heralded by revolutions in technology, social mobility and politics, overwhelming the staid structures of society that had held sway for centuries.

Scientific advances, begun in the eighteenth century, culminated in an entirely new phenomenon; huge towns and cities situated not around castle, manor house, abbey or market cross, but in the shadow of industry. And nowhere were these changes so dramatically manifested than in Manchester, as it expanded from a small satellite township bordering Salford to a sprawling city-sized conglomerate in less than fifty years.

With mass migration into these workshop towns, came the realisation that aristocratic governance and parochial administration were inadequate. As transport and communications improved, especially following the defeat of Napoleon at Waterloo, hitherto mainly servile workers developed a sense of awareness that they were not sharing in the new wealth created from the sweat of their brows. Rather, this new class of industrial worker was being treated no better, and often worse, than hereditary landowners had treated their peasantry.

These imbalances and injustices provoked a wave of discontent and a new political dimension, inspired by writers of the 'Enlightenment', and encouraged by revolutionary events in France and the American colonies. Ordinary people began to question the age-old hierarchy, and demanded human rights long denied them.

So it came about that shortly after two o'clock on 16 August 1819, under a cloudless Manchester sky, troopers of the Manchester and Salford Yeomanry, their work done, dismounted, in order to ease their horses' girths, to adjust their accoutrements, and to wipe the blood from their sabres.

The meeting on St Peter's Field was organised by the Manchester Patriotic Union Society, in which Elijah Dixon was a leading light. Then an Ancoats shopkeeper, it was not the first time, nor the would it be the last, that he and his Radical comrades faced military might as a means of suppressing their demands for reform. Another of that disparate, awkward, and irascible brotherhood of Manchester malcontents was Dixon's friend and neighbour, James Wroe, an impoverished journalist and bookseller, who, in a parody of complacent post-war patriotism, coined a word to encapsulate the nation's guilt; Peterloo.

England shuddered with shame. It was a seminal moment in the nation's history.

As well as Wroe, Dixon lived, worked alongside, and befriended many of Manchester's foremost Radicals, including James Scholefield, Edward Nightingale, Reginald Richardson, John Knight, Abel Heywood and William Willis. More moderate reformers, such as Archibald Prentice, did not always see eye to eye with Elijah and his friends. Radical weaver Samuel Bamford scathingly referred to them as 'the contemptible Elijah Dixon set'. At the height of the Reform Act crisis in 1832, a prominent Whig supporter described Elijah and fellow members of a Radical deputation as 'ill-looking conceited fellows'. So too, there were fierce disagreements between Elijah and Richard Cobden, notably over the activities of the Anti-Corn Law League, but their relationship matured into mutual respect.

Ever-present in the tumults of Manchester politics for more than sixty years, Elijah spoke at meetings alongside William Cobbett, Henry Hunt, Feargus O'Connor, and Ernest Jones. A practical politician, Elijah stood alongside Tory reformer Richard Oastler to secure reform of child labour and factory conditions. Not always the most prominent or flamboyant speaker, Elijah characterised his own contribution as 'shoulder work'. Later in life, he befriended reforming Liberal campaigners, such as Jacob Bright and Richard Pankhurst, whose awareness that working people lacked proper representation portended the formation of the Labour Party.

Elijah did not belong by birth to the landless masses who huddled together round the mean streets of Ancoats, seeking work. Like Cobden, he hailed from yeoman stock fallen on hard times. Yet, growing up in deprived and polluted Manchester, he was able to witness, and to contribute to, hard-won improvements in working conditions and education, and eventually a gradual growth in prosperity. From Co-operation and free education, to building societies and utopian land schemes, he pushed for political reform and explored every means of betterment for industrial workers. He was a member of Manchester's first Hampden Club, dedicated to voting reform, along with John Knight and life-long friend David Ridgway. As an organiser of the ill-fated Blanketeers march of 1817, he was arrested, transported to London in chains and imprisoned for eight months without trial or charge.

Elijah lived to see immense technological change – steam-powered factories, mechanised textile processes, the building of canals, macadamised roads, the coming of the railway age, the birth of photography, pharmaceutical chemistry, coal-gas for lighting and heating, electricity, and the introduction of the telegraph. At the Great Exhibition of 1851, these and many other wonders of the age showed off Victorian Britain as the workshop of the world. Among the proud exhibitors was the firm of Dixon, Son & Company, market leaders in match manufacturing. An idealist, yes, but Elijah Dixon the entrepreneur progressed by a combination of shrewdness and hard work from mill hand to mass-production. Along the way, he tried his hand at milk-selling, as a co-operative baker, and making and selling sundries for the growing druggist market. Match-making and an off-shoot timber business made him a fortune.

But success did not dilute his commitment to reform and social justice. To Elijah Dixon wealth was an opportunity to do good – to put Christian beliefs into action – enabling him to progress long-cherished schemes such as land reclamation at Chat Moss, the setting up of mechanics' institutes, and the development of a model suburb at New Moston. He remained a campaigner for the rights of ordinary men and women to the end of his life.

For a short time after his death in 1876, Elijah Dixon was remembered as a Peterloo veteran and 'Father of English reformers'. Yet within a generation or so he and most of his Radical comrades had been forgotten, even by the people of Manchester. In August 2019, democracies all over the world will commemorate the bi-centenary of events on St Peter's Field. It would also be fitting, especially for Mancunians, to reflect on the shoulder work for freedom put in by Elijah Dixon.

Chapter One

Holmfirth

What beauteous visions filled this spot!
What dreams of pleasure long forgot!
Nor hope, nor joy, nor love, nor fear
Have left one trace of record here.

Anonymous (c.1820), *Lines to a Skeleton*

She left the room without a word, and did not return. Her husband, alerted to the sound of his children crying, began searching, only to find her lifeless – strangled by her own silk handkerchief, in the dye-house. Such, according to family legend, was the violent death of genteel Betty Dixon, aged 32, on the 2 September 1798.[1]

Job Dixon, four years her senior, was left to pick up the pieces of a life – a dynasty – in ruins. It was said that a Dixon had formed and led a cavalry troop for Parliament in the Civil War. Down the centuries, the family prospered as clothiers, putting out yarn to cottage weavers in the royds and hamlets of the Yorkshire Pennines, taking in and selling the finished cloth. These clothiers were, before the coming of factories, kingpins of the domestic system, enjoying superior social status. Betty herself, said to be a celebrated Yorkshire beauty, and by all accounts an imperious woman, came from a well-off family of clothiers, in nearby Almondbury. Even so, when she married Job at All Hallows church, Kirkburton, in 1787, she was unable to sign her name, having to resort to the usual formality of making her mark by way of a cross.

Of the seven children Betty (nee Tattersall) bore to Job over ten years, five survived at the time of her death. The eldest of these was Elijah, not yet eight when his mother died, born on 23 October 1790 at Hey End in Wooldale, Holmfirth, and baptised on 7 November at Holy Trinity church, a chapel of ease within Kirkburton parish. It might be supposed, and perhaps inferred from later events, that even as a young boy Elijah Dixon felt the call of duty. Business failing, his father Job now faced the supreme crisis of his life. As the eldest son, Elijah was bound to help care for his younger brothers – Isaiah (6), twins Abner and Hezekiah (3), and Asa (16 months). Elijah's elder brother Nehemiah, Betty's first-born, had died aged four. Asa's twin, Oded, had died on 29 June 1798, aged fourteen months.

Two factors ensured the end of the clothiers' golden age and the downfall of Job Dixon. First was the development of factories powered by water and steam that could out-produce small-scale cottage weavers, and second was war with France and Napoleon, which destroyed ancient trading patterns in Europe. Bitter poverty, universally euphemised as distress, became widespread amongst weaving communities, although some held out longer than others. The weavers and clothiers of Holmfirth, and indeed most of west Yorkshire, were especially hard hit. The mutual blockades of the French and English Navies cut them off from established markets, particularly in France and the Low Countries. Job Dixon was an early victim. His trade with Antwerp collapsed when Napoleon invaded that city in 1794, and the prosperity the Dixons had enjoyed never recovered.

Job's ruin was abetted by a duplicitous agent along the chain of bills of exchange which stretched to Antwerp via London. It is said that ruin comes slowly at first, then quickly. Perhaps, after this disaster, Job was able to stay in business by relying on the family name, help from friends, borrowing, and selling off assets. He struggled on for another seven years, under the threat of peremptory enforcement by creditors, hoping to get their money when trade picked up. Indeed, when the end came, the ultimate humiliations of insolvency – bankruptcy and debtor's prison – were avoided. Instead, Job's creditors permitted him to use the relatively benign legal device of assignment, eschewing bankruptcy proceedings in the hope of recovering losses from his debtors.

A year earlier, at the time of the birth of Oded and Asa, the Dixons appear to have been hanging on to Hey End, their hill-side family home with its handy cellar space for warehousing, and its impressive views south across the valley to Black Hill and Holme Moss. At least, Job's address is so recorded in the baptismal register for the twins at Holy Trinity church. The christening was the last event at which the family was able to keep up appearances, the last occasion shared by the family before tragedy and upheaval changed everything. Perhaps contemplating the moorland grandeur all around him, or playing with friends, six-year-old Elijah had resented the abrupt summons from his mother to be scrubbed and suited, along with younger brother Isaiah and toddler twins Abner and Hezekiah. As Betty gathered the fortnight-old twins into her shawl, and Job led the raggle-taggle procession down the steep twisting lane to the town, Elijah may have picked up enough from their worried looks and hushed conversation to realise that all was not well; that an occasion for thankful celebration was overshadowed by uncertainty and fear of the future. Only eight days later, on 12 May 1797, Job's mother, Mary, died aged 77.

Soon afterwards, Hey End was vacated and the family literally and visibly went down in the world – down the hillside a quarter of a mile to Hey Gap, a terrace of dwellings behind the church, just high enough to catch smoke rising from the fires of houses and shops at river level in the centre of the town. It is easy to imagine Betty's deteriorating state of mind during the summer of 1798, as, on top of the loss of her son, her husband faced bankruptcy.

Betty was laid to rest in the churchyard at Holmfirth, where Oded had been buried barely nine weeks before. Her burial there seems to establish that whatever the true circumstances of her death, there was no formal finding of suicide. Had there been, she could have been denied interment in consecrated ground. But in the light of Elijah's account of his mother's death, fifty years later, it is hard to resist the conclusion that Betty's suicide was covered up.

Job stayed on at Hey Gap for two more years, hoping his fortunes might recover, and while there, as a widower with five young sons, he evidently sought solace in the company of a neighbour, Mary Chatterton. Almost twenty years Job's junior, Mary may initially have merely helped with the children, but then came another child, John Chatterton, born out of wedlock in September 1800. Job and Mary married at All Hallows church on 10 May 1801. Mary could hardly have married for money. Soon there followed the ignominy of a meeting of Job's creditors at the Fleece Hotel, Huddersfield, preceded by publication on 20 July of a legal notice in the *Leeds Intelligencer.*

On the 24 August 1801, a notice of assignment appeared in the same journal, optimistically inviting Job's debtors to pay up on pain of legal action. Naturally, these brief legal notices in the press gave no clue as to the family tragedy which had preceded them. Job's assignees, Titus Tate and James Hollingsworth, respectively in business as wool-stapler and clothier, are likely to have been known to him and Betty, latterly as creditors, but once as socialising members of a clothier elite. Though an assignment was not the same as bankruptcy, it marked the end of Job's business and was undoubtedly terminal to social aspiration and status around the Holme Valley. The celebrated beauty had been spared what she could not face.

A year later, the relieved burghers of Holmfirth would rush to commemorate the temporary cessation of hostilities with France by building 'Owd Genn', a fifteen-foot memorial stone, on the banks of the River Holme. But the Peace of Amiens was a false dawn. Not until after Bonaparte was finally beaten at Waterloo were the clothiers able to trade with Europe again. And by then it was too late for the Dixons.

It is unlikely that Job was destitute, but he must have been desperate to leave Holmfirth to make a new life for himself, Mary and the children. Inevitably he would look to business contacts made on both sides of the Pennines. If he had been among the Yorkshire clothiers who regularly attended the September textile fair in Salford, he could have made contacts in the Manchester area. Even the legal process of Job's assignment straddled the Pennines; joint trustee, and fellow clothier, James Hollingworth, was based in Micklehurst, at the north east extremity of Cheshire, a few miles from Oldham. Crucially, any opportunity on the other side of the great moorland divide would mean a fresh start, leaving behind the shame of business failure and the tragedy of Betty's death.

In any event, the Dixons crossed the Pennines in the autumn of 1801, either together, or with Mary and the children following on after Job had secured accommodation. However they travelled – on foot, by horse-drawn cart or coach – the shortest route was over the moorland road to Oldham, via the hamlet of Greenfield. It is hard to resist the thought that, as our little party of refugees neared the pennine divide at Wessenden Head below the sombre sheep pastures of Black Hill, they may have glanced back ruefully down the valley towards Holmfirth and the world they were leaving forever.

Descending the hills into Lancashire, the children, who had probably never ventured so far from home, would not at first have seen anything very different from the familiar moorland landscape behind them. Until they reached Springhead, a cockstride from Oldham, they were still in the West Riding of the County of York and the stone-built cottages along the road, with multiple mullioned windows on their upper floors, differed little from the handloom weavers' cottages to the east of the watershed.

Just beyond the summit, however, they may, had the weather been fine, have glimpsed a distant and hazy view of the Welsh mountains across the Cheshire plain. At Greenfield, the Dixons would cross the line of the new canal being built to link Manchester and Huddersfield, and then, nearing Oldham, catch glimpses of a different world – the world of the factory, and of spinning mules powered by water or steam, springing up in the towns of Lancashire and Cheshire, and Manchester itself. Elijah and his brothers would see mill chimneys smoking from coal-fired boilers, collieries in Oldham and Werneth, and, as the road descended towards the great town before them, more and more new cottages, built not of stone, but of brick. They might have shared the turnpike with carters taking coal to the new canal basin at Hollinwood, or on into the mills of Manchester and beyond. Although the manufacturers of Lancashire were also feeling the effects of the war against the French, Elijah would see that the Dixons were arriving in a world of bigger horizons, darker skies, and a pace of life that reflected the fact that they had come to the fastest growing town in the kingdom.

Chapter Two

New Cross

Why from the Cart, ye busy elves,
For others' 'mendment waste your breath?
Let me advise - Reform yourselves,
Lest from a Cart you get your death.

Verse in *The Manchester Mercury*, 18 March 1817

In Manchester, Job obtained whatever work he could find in the cotton mills, first as a fustian-cutter, and later as a dyer and labourer. He settled his family in Ancoats at the industrial heart of the town. Nearby was the new Murray Mill, credited with being the first great cotton mill, standing alongside the line of new Rochdale Canal, still under construction.

The mills were hungry for cheap child labour, and Elijah and his older brothers were like as not put to work as soon as Job could find places for them. Long hours and exposure to dirt and dangerous machinery was their lot. Within a few months, Isaiah Dixon died, aged eight. He was the third brother lost to Elijah. Although he never spoke of the cause of death – it might easily have been an accident – Elijah was deeply affected. In the mean streets, overcrowded slums, and mills of New Cross and Ancoats the Dixon brothers were exposed to all the horrors of the industrial revolution, all the brutalities of the unregulated factory system.

Isaiah's burial in December 1801, at the Collegiate church of St Mary, St Denys and St George (later to become Manchester Cathedral), marked the sombre beginning of a new chapter in the lives of Job and Mary and the children. Holmfirth was behind them, but a tenuous link remained; a stately saraband of proceedings in the court of Chancery, by which Job hoped to establish his right to the considerable estate of an ancestor who had died intestate. It was a ray of hope.

There was work, but what else? It is impossible to read of the later achievements of Elijah without believing that somehow or other, in spite of poverty and long hours of work, his education continued. In Holmfirth, despite the shadow of ruin which hung over them, Job had probably done his best to educate his children or to arrange some kind of schooling. Likewise, once in Manchester, Job himself may have continued his children's education. Whatever the circumstances, Elijah acquired the habit of reading widely.

Manchester was expanding at a phenomenal rate as the revolution in textile manufacture generated the building of steam-powered cotton mills. Vast sums of money were being invested and from all over the British Isles, refugees from rural poverty streamed into the city looking for work and livelihood. The wars with France continued, but while they may have slowed the growth of Manchester they did not stop it. Indeed, some there were who did very well out of the wars – manufacturers of uniforms, bandages and patches for muskets, for example.

Close to the Dixons' home, the Rochdale Canal opened on 20 December 1804. The event was marked by two boat loads of dignitaries being towed into town, to the accompaniment of the band of the 1st Battalion of the Manchester and Salford Volunteers. A fully-laden boat – which next day arrived in Liverpool via the Bridgewater canal and the navigable rivers Irwell and Mersey – followed in the wake of the VIPs. It would have been quite a spectacle for the Dixon children if they were able to see it. In times gone by, when Job was a prosperous clothier, they might have expected to see their father in the official party of celebrants, or even to have accompanied him. Now, as child labourers, they would be kept well away from official proceedings, fortunate even to glimpse the pomp and ceremony so removed from the grind of their everyday lives. For the Dixon boys, smoky Manchester was a far cry from the rural wilds of Yorkshire and the moorland air of childhood. The privileges they had once enjoyed belonged to a lost world.

It is therefore easy to understand how an educated boy from a poor home might have viewed the tumults of his adopted town; poverty, and the injustice to men and women denied remedy for their ills. Of these, Elijah Dixon had a worm's eye view. In later life, he told how he started in the mill as a 'scavenger', work well-suited to the small frame of a child, able to crawl under machinery to retrieve waste. Later he became a 'piecer', where a child's thin and nimble fingers were suitable for the vital work of rejoining cotton threads broken in the spinning process. Both jobs carried the risk of injury from moving machinery. Conditions endured by children in mills and factories were to become notorious, and in the early years of the nineteenth century they were dangerous, unhealthy and completely unregulated. Much depended on the attitude of the individual mill owner, or the 'overlooker', who was supposed to ensure that before anyone went under, the machine was stopped. But overlookers, too, were under pressure, and there was always the temptation to risk minor adjustments being made while machinery was still in motion. Long hours, lack of ventilation, and frequent accidents were often concealed, falsified, or justified, by owners, to whom exploitation was as unremarkable and inoffensive as the slavery which produced raw cotton for their mills. For many employers, labour was simply a factor of production, human capital.

At the age of 13 or 14, around 1804, Elijah obtained an apprenticeship as a spinner. Later, he referred to his employer as a 'pious Methodist', and to this being one of the happiest periods of his life. Where the Dixons first resided is not known, but in 1811 they were at 1, Back Gun Street and four years later at 16, Great Ancoats Street. By 1817, Elijah was working as a spinner at the mill of Thomas Houldsworth, known for his Tory sympathies, in Newton Street, Ancoats. Later events suggest that he earned the respect of his employer, which was probably reciprocated. Whatever the conditions at Houldsworth mill, in Ancoats and New Cross, poverty, disease, infant mortality and injustice were everyday facts of life. It is fair to surmise that during these years, Elijah became politicised. Nowhere in England were the writings of William Cobbett read more keenly than in Manchester. Tom Paine's *The Rights of Man* would also have circulated among the growing body of Radical reformers to which Elijah was attracted, as well as a proliferation of pamphlets designed to circumvent the government tax on newspapers.

Indeed, there was injustice, inequality and want across the land. The Tory government of William Pitt, fearful of revolution spreading from France, went on the attack with a series of measures designed to stop working people organising to achieve better wages and conditions. In 1795 the government had issued a series of proclamations respecting seditious meetings, followed by the Seditious Assemblies Act, and the Treasonable and Seditious Practices Act. Other measures enacted by Parliament after 1799, and which became known as the Combination Laws, struck at the principle of trade unions, leaving workers little choice but to organise in secret. The price of wheat, which before the war had been 6s (six shillings) a bushel, rose to 16s 8d. There were bread riots. At the same time, Lancashire gentry and mill owners, encouraged by Lord Derby, as Lord Lieutenant of the county, contributed to a public subscription to raise funds and troops for the war. Workers and anti-war Radicals alike had their noses rubbed in it.

The government's policy was driven by fear of contagion from France. Writers and politicians influenced by the Enlightenment, aided by articulate and prolific pamphleteers, had supported rebellion in the American colonies, and so had the French. Most Tories and many Whigs, as well as the new men of property produced by the industrial revolution, viewed sympathy with the French, opposition to the war and dissent from the Anglican church as challenges to the established social order at home. Likewise, any form of agitation for the relief of poverty and distress, or for political enfranchisement, was seen as potentially revolutionary and treasonable. In Manchester, from the outbreak of war in 1793, this reactionary view was fervently encouraged, and men who had most to lose from continuation of the wars with France, were subject to a campaign of propaganda and persecution from the 'Church-and-King' party. Not really a party as such, this was a nickname for a reactionary, pro-monarchy, pro-Anglican faction, crossing both mainstream political parties, active from the beginning of the Napoleonic wars onwards. However, as a boy growing to maturity, Elijah would have become aware that on occasions these reactionaries suffered reverses. In particular, in what the government had intended to be a show trial, a jury at Lancaster assizes acquitted seven Manchester men on an indictment to overthrow the constitution.

But the Church-and-King party remained active. Organised mobs attacked Radical bookshops and public houses frequented by those opposed to the war and who favoured reform. As the wars dragged on, the employment of spies to obtain dubious evidence against agitators became systematic. The authorities flexed their muscles at every opportunity.

Events in 1808 and 1812 gave them victories of a sort. A meeting of weavers was held on 24 May 1808, in St George's Fields, Manchester, to demonstrate in favour of a Bill to fix a minimum rate of wages. When the meeting resumed the following day, magistrates read the Riot Act, although by all accounts, there was no disorder. The 4th Dragoon Guards were ordered to clear the ground, and in the melee a weaver was killed, and others injured. The episode led to a six-months prison sentence for the maverick Colonel Hanson of Strangeways Hall, self-styled 'friend of the weavers', who attended the event on horseback, alongside his groom, and was prosecuted for encouraging disorder.

The shadowy figure of Joseph Nadin, Deputy Constable, and his fellow constables were widely believed to have supported the prosecution of the colonel with trumped up evidence. Nadin relished his power. He became the unofficial ruler of Manchester – his authority derived from the medieval system of local government still surviving in nearly all industrial towns. Undemocratic, and self-perpetuating, the system provided Manchester with a force of four beadles for daytime duty and only forty-eight constables for the night watch. Theoretically these constables were accountable to the Boroughreeve and the Court Leet, but paradoxically, the Deputy Constable was the real working chief. Nadin, a former spinner, unlike later holders of the office who received training with London's Bow Street Runners, had no formal training whatever. What recommended him to his employers was his ruthlessness. He was over six feet tall, and a surviving portrait suggests a thick-set, fearsome-looking man.

Although the usual practice was to appoint Deputy Constables annually, Nadin had held the office continuously since October 1802. He must have given good satisfaction to his Church-and-King paymasters. He exercised his power in their interests and his own. He bullied publicans into barring Radicals from their premises, took bribes from brothel keepers, and sold off 'Tyburn tickets' (official exemptions from civic duties) for his own profit. His corruption brought him wealth, and he even made loans to magistrates. No wonder he was feared and loathed by reformers and Radicals. Elijah is bound to have known of him, and to have been amongst those whose agitation for reform attracted his attention.

Distress and bad feeling towards the authorities intensified in the last years of the war. Conditions in the towns continued to deteriorate. Organised machine breaking occurred among hosiery frame operatives in Nottinghamshire (who entered history as the Luddites) and in April 1812, there were food riots in many parts of Lancashire. Factories in Middleton, West Houghton, and Bolton were attacked. Women, desperate to feed their starving children, mobbed the Manchester potato market on Shudehill, extracting a short-lived reduction in price. A few days later, rioting broke out in Ancoats and New Cross – a stone's throw from Elijah's workplace at Houldsworth mill. A cart carrying meal was stopped, and the meal taken. The cavalry were called out. Again, the Riot Act was read. Wherever disturbances occurred, spies were amongst those taking part, attempting to identify ringleaders and provide evidence, eagerly relied on by the authorities in subsequent prosecutions.

Following a meeting, organised by John Knight at the Elephant public house in Tib Street, Nadin was responsible for arresting 38 weavers on politically based charges including conspiracy to undermine the constitution. Indeed, he employed paid spies to fabricate evidence against his victims, and worse, *agents provocateurs*, whose job was to incite violence, and then turn king's evidence. They were all acquitted, Nadin's 'evidence' being proven unsound. Meanwhile, eight people were condemned to death for rioting by a special commission sitting at Lancaster. All – including women and children – were hanged on 13 June 1812 at Lancaster Castle. According to an eye witness, a boy appeared on the scaffold looking 'so young and childish, that he appealed to his mother for help … thinking she might save him'. A contemporary chronicler, Archibald Prentice, recorded that new Home Secretary, Lord Sidmouth, gave his hearty approval to such 'wholesome severity'. It was Sidmouth, who, from his office in Whitehall, orchestrated this regime of coercion, corresponding with Nadin and local magistrates, providing them with extra powers, and urging merciless retribution as a solution to disorder.

The summer of 1812, however, saw a good harvest, and while distress remained acute, the bread shortage was attenuated, no doubt to the relief of the government as well as starving inhabitants in the towns. In November of that year, Mary Dixon died and was buried in the graveyard of St George's-in-the-Field, off Oldham Road.

On Sunday, 31 January 1813, aged 22, Elijah married Martha Dyson, two years his senior, at the church of St John, Deansgate. Elijah's occupation was given as canvasser (one who weaves, specifically, canvas or produces the thick warp from which it is made), Martha's as house keeper. Born in Huddersfield, Martha may also have been a refugee from hard times in Yorkshire. Or she and Elijah may have been introduced through connections going back to Holmfirth days. Their first son, John, was born in or about January 1814.

A general economic depression followed the final defeat of Napoleon in 1815 and nowhere did it bite more fiercely than in the districts of Manchester inhabited by working people. On 17 February 1815, Member of Parliament, Frederick Robinson, an archetypal representative of the landowning aristocracy and later to become Viscount Goderich, introduced into Parliament resolutions on the corn trade to prohibit imports of wheat when the price fell to under eighty shillings a quarter. It was a measure designed to subsidise the aristocracy and the landed gentry at the expense of the towns, dressed in the barely credible guise of protecting social order and the stability of the nation. These Corn Laws made high food prices inevitable.

The government was not to know that its folly would be compounded by a natural disaster on the other side of the world. In April that year, Mount Tambora, in modern-day Indonesia, was destroyed in a series of volcanic explosions, which in total amounted to the largest eruption event ever recorded in human history. Apart from killing an estimated 71,000 people in the area, millions of tons of ash and sulphur hung in the atmosphere, affecting harvests across Europe and America for the next two years. Crop failures and more food riots resulted. In 1816, the first year of peace in Europe for generations, farmers endured 'the year without a summer'. Of course, in those days, global weather patterns were not understood, and no-one in England could have linked an unprecedented natural disaster in the far east with dire harvests in Europe. But, together with the Corn Laws, the fall-out from Mount Tambora meant that workers in the industrial towns faced a new war – against starvation, malnutrition and disease. Social and political unrest was inevitable, and once again the government, oblivious to the coincidence and the mysteries of meteorology, was in dread of revolution.

By 1816, Elijah and Martha were living at 35, Gun Street, cheek by jowl with the mills and workshops of Ancoats, together with their firstborn, John, and a second son, baptised at the Collegiate church the previous September, whom they named Job, after Elijah's father. Job Dixon senior was shown as a ratepayer at 34, Gun Street, which – taking account of the old 'clockwise' system of house numbering – would have been next door. A combination of soaring food prices and static or falling wages bore down on the working population of Manchester. While at Gun Street, Elijah's young son John died, aged two years and five months. He was buried on 18 June 1816 at St George's church, in the same grave as Elijah's stepmother.

What could be done by powerless working people to resist distress? Reformers were well aware of the vengeance wrought on the people in 1812, and that Lord Sidmouth, though no longer Prime Minister, remained in power at the Home Office, ready to direct Nadin's men against them. If riot could not bring relief, then lawful reform of injustice by peaceful agitation offered an alternative. But the pathetic inability of Manchester's workers to change their lot was nowhere made clearer than in the unreformed electoral system. It denied representation to the burgeoning industrial towns, and the vote to its landless workers, the latter seemingly trapped in an endless cycle of poverty and disenfranchisement.

Yet in Manchester and surrounding towns, there were brave men, including Elijah Dixon, who in spite of poverty were educated and articulate, and did not accept the status quo. They were inspired and encouraged by Radical voices and writers across the country, notably William Cobbett, Francis Place, Major John Cartwright, Sir Francis Burdett and Henry 'Orator' Hunt. Discontent, distress and disillusionment with the prospects of peace distilled into the primary objective of winning the vote and changing the way people were governed. A wave of pamphlets and protest was directed at the obvious historical absurdities of parliamentary representation based on 'rotten' boroughs (voting areas which usually had no inhabitants), 'pocket' boroughs (a voting areas which was under the control of a particular family or individual), patronage and corruption. Agitation, however, did not find expression in a united movement. Cobbett and Hunt wanted root and branch reform and manhood suffrage. Cartwright, through his 'Hampden Club', wanted a widened franchise which would have included householders but excluded working men, although this did not deter the growing number of members. Its honest reforming credentials echoed the principles upon which parliament, with the help of Elijah's illustrious ancestor, had fought the Civil War against an autocratic monarchy. John Knight founded a Manchester Hampden Club, and Elijah and his friend David Ridgway were early recruits. On 15 November 1816, Hunt and his associates held a big meeting in London, at Spa Fields, at which Hunt appeared with an escort carrying the tricolour flag and a revolutionary cap on top of a pike.

On 10 February 1817, in what may have been his first serious foray into public life, Elijah made his debut as chairman of a reform meeting in Manchester, as reported in the *Chester Courant* of the following week. It is possible to infer both from Elijah's demeanour at this time, and subsequently documented statements, that from the beginning he supported universal suffrage (that is, votes for men *and* women), but was opposed to achieving political aims through violence. Indeed, the dichotomy of how to change society without revolutionary violence was at the forefront of debate among Radicals and reformers for the whole of his life. Yet it was Elijah Dixon's moderate brand of diplomacy that was to prove a key element in forging practical unity among the disparate elements in Manchester at crucial moments of the struggle.

In the meantime, as conditions in Manchester worsened, discontent intensified. In 1817, the government no doubt felt confident in its one-dimensional policy of repression when it came to dealing with unhappy, starving citizens. Coercion had ultimately preserved the social order in 1812, with the help of a good harvest. It might do so again, reasoned Home Secretary Sidmouth. In a panic reaction to the Spa Fields demonstration (an isolated event) and a stone being thrown at the Prince Regent on his way to Parliament, the government went on the offensive. Secret parliamentary committees heard evidence – likely to have been invented by spies – of a plot to seize the Bank of England and the Tower of London.

Introducing the second reading of the Habeas Corpus Suspension Bill to Parliament on the 24 February, Sidmouth sought to justify what amounted to a declaration of emergency. The Bill freed the authorities, over which Sidmouth exercised a dominating influence, to arrest at will, without formal charge. He spoke of a 'traitorous conspiracy … for the purpose of overthrowing … the established government'. Stressing the malign influence of the French revolution, Sidmouth based the need to suspend civil liberties upon his belief that 'an organised system has been established in every quarter, under the semblance of demanding parliamentary reform, but many of them… have that specious pretext in their mouths only, but revolution and rebellion in their hearts'. Manchester's feudal rulers, and their chief enforcer, Joseph Nadin, stood ready to do his bidding. Relieved of the obligation to bring suspects to trial, able to arrest whomsoever he pleased, willing to back up his caprice with the trumped-up evidence of paid spies, and eager to settle old scores, Nadin's day had come.

Elijah's experiences of events in Manchester during the wars, and particularly those of 1812, would have been fresh in his mind. As brave men and women have done, before and since, he must have weighed up a conscientious call to action against the likely consequences for his family. At the beginning of 1817, son Job was just a year old, and Martha was expecting another child. Every reformer at this time knew that he or she risked execution or transportation for life, if the authorities could make out a charge of treason or sedition.

Manchester seethed with resentment and Sidmouth's package of repression provoked an outcry on a national level. The flames of protest were fanned, in particular, by William Cobbett. In Manchester, reformers decided on direct action. A march to London was planned, to present a petition demanding repeal of repressive measures, and the right to vote. Anticipating mass arrest and confiscation of the petition, men were to set off in small groups at intervals, and each would carry a sheet bearing ten or twenty signatures, the hope being that some, at least, would get through and meet up in London. Those involved in the unhappy debacle which followed became known as 'Blanketeers', since every marching man was advised to carry a blanket for his overnight shelter.

It was inevitable that the authorities would characterise the plan as a march *on* London, with revolutionary aims. Had not Bonnie Prince Charlie marched south from Manchester intending to overthrow the Hanoverian monarchy, some seventy years earlier? Elijah was undoubtedly a signatory of the petition, but the organisers met in secret, and it was not until years later that Elijah clarified his own part in events. Hard evidence, however, meant nothing to Nadin and his crew, and in early March, in consultation with Sidmouth, they struck.

On Monday, 10 March 1817, a crowd of perhaps 25,000 – including 5,000 or so whose intention was to march to London – assembled on St Peter's Field. As the Riot Act was being read by magistrates, the meeting was broken up by troops of the King's Dragoon Guards. Two of the organisers, John Bagguley (sometimes spelt Baguley) and Samuel Drummond, were arrested on the spot. The march went off half-cocked, with some 600 marcher-petitioners who were able to get away being harried at every point by the authorities. Between Manchester and Stockport, 184 arrests were made, 163 men being taken to the New Bailey prison in Salford, and the remainder to Chester Castle. Thirty or so got as far as Leek and Ashbourne, only to be rounded up and escorted into captivity by cavalry of the Staffordshire Yeomanry. Only one man, Abel Couldwell, reputedly made it all the way to London. Given the overwhelming force used to disrupt the efforts of the Blanketeers, it is a wonder that so many men were prepared to take part, being helpless to resist arrest and inevitable imprisonment. The pathos of their situation was nowhere better illustrated than by the case of a man from Gorton imprisoned at Chester – charged with stealing his master's blanket!

It was not until 12 March that Elijah Dixon was arrested, on suspicion of 'treasonable and seditious practices'. The warrant, signed by Sidmouth, was served by a King's Messenger (either sent from London or appointed locally) alongside a representative of the magistracy – a Deputy Constable, who was almost certainly Joseph Nadin.[1] Elijah was arrested, not at his home in Gun Street, but at his workplace, at Houldsworth mill, thereby ensuring a dramatic, deterrent spectacle in front of fellow workers, and ostentatiously demonstrating the Deputy Constable's authority. Given that Nadin had been busy making arrests for the previous ten days, Elijah is unlikely to have been surprised when his turn came. He was taken to the New Bailey and put in a cell with common criminals, pending transport to London.

The *Manchester Mercury* of 18 March fairly crowed its satisfaction at the failure of the march, the intervention of the military, and the detention of those it assumed to be ringleaders, including Elijah Dixon. Its entire report was prefaced by an initial paragraph describing the destruction by fire of a spinning mill at Knott Mill, suggesting, without evidence, that the cause was arson and thereby implying that rioters were responsible. It went on, in gleeful detail, to describe the 'preposterous expedition' of the Blanketeers, and how the 'timely and efficacious interposition of our constituted authorities defeated machinations pregnant with the direst and most alarming consequences...'

However, the tone of the report became less exuberant as it continued. Of the 250 men detained in Manchester and the surrounding area, brought before magistrate W.D. Evans, forty were discharged at once, and a further eighty were only refused bail because they could not provide surety. The *Mercury* was at pains to point out that the march had been poorly supported by 'worthy, patient, and most-suffering' hand-loom weavers, implying that the trouble-makers were largely overpaid operatives from spinning mills. There had been a spinners' strike in 1810, and this group of workers was the particular bête noir of the *Mercury* and its middle-class readers. In this vein, Elijah Dixon, 'a cotton spinner' was reported to have been chairman at a meeting near St Peter's church. The meeting was addressed by speakers, including Elijah, standing on a cart – which prompted the *Mercury* to ridicule them as 'cart orators'. Another arrested man was said to have been a tailor living with his wife and six children in one room. Even among the most patriotic readers of the *Manchester Mercury* there must have been those who recognised the real cause of unrest as desperation, bred of poverty. However, the *Mercury* was right about one thing; the Knott Mill fire *was* started deliberately – by joint-owner Thomas Armstrong, who was hanged for arson the following September.[3]

Relying on his warrants, Sidmouth followed up the arrests with expedited transport of suspected ringleaders to London, there to be personally interviewed by him. Elijah was moved from the New Bailey at the dead of night and on to the Royal Mail coach. In 1817, there was a regular coach to London which left the Bridgewater Arms on High Street at 1.30am, arriving in London at 5.30am the following day, a journey of 28 hours. The likelihood is that, acting on orders from Sidmouth, ordinary passengers, if there were any at such an hour, would be kept off the coach, reserving it exclusively for Elijah and his escort. The horses were changed regularly, but there were no meal stops for passengers. Elijah was escorted by the King's Messenger, Sylvester, and a Deputy Constable, again likely to have been Nadin. For almost the whole of the journey, Elijah's hands and feet were chained, in 'double irons'.

The sympathetic – indeed kindly – Sylvester suggested the irons be removed, but he was overruled by the Deputy Constable and the irons were only taken off as the coach neared London. Sylvester may have been Lieutenant Colonel John Sylvester, a Manchester magistrate. If so there was already bad blood between him and Nadin. In 1812, presiding at the New Bailey, Sylvester had been duty bound to commit the thirty-eight weavers arrested by Nadin to Lancaster Assizes. All were acquitted when the unsatisfactory, not to say trumped-up, evidence produced by Nadin was exposed. Indeed, Sylvester and Nadin had clashed during the arrest of another Blanketeer, William Ogden. Sylvester requested that the 74-year-old Ogden be given food and shoes but was ignored by Nadin. As commanding officer of the 2nd Battalion, Manchester and Salford Volunteers, Sylvester's brother officer, commanding the 1st Battalion, had been Lieutenant Colonel Joseph Hanson, the 'weavers' friend'.

Together with Sylvester and Nadin – and possibly a special constable – Elijah was probably seated inside the coach. Outside, there were only two seats beside the coachman, so Nadin's instinct to inflict suffering was probably sublimated by officious zeal to prevent his prisoner escaping. Few sections of the route – via Stockport, Macclesfield, Ashbourne, Derby, Leicester, Northampton and St

Albans – had been macadamised; roads were rough and pot-holed, and passengers were subject to the jolting and swaying motions of the coach; uncomfortable for ordinary passengers, much more so for a prisoner manacled in double irons. Horses could be changed in two or three minutes – just time for a drink of water or a rushed answer to the call of nature. In the early hours of Friday, 14 March, Elijah arrived in London. He was not the first suspect to be taken to the capital for interrogation. On the previous Tuesday, four men, described only as 'Johnson, Ogden, Baguley and Drummond' by the *Mercury*, had preceded him from Manchester in the *Prince Coburg* mail coach, 'handcuffed, and compactly ironed to each other'.

Chapter Three

Westminster

He is a sterling nobleman
Who lives the truth he knows;
Who dreads the slavery of sin
And fears no other foes.

Edwin Waugh (1817-90), *The Man of the Time*

On the morning he arrived in London, Elijah Dixon was first confined in a cell at the Bow Street headquarters of the capital's infamous 'Runners', from where he was taken to Lord Sidmouth's office
in Whitehall, for interrogation. The *Manchester Mercury* of 18 March told
its readers that the examination conducted by Sidmouth together with Sir
Nathaniel Conant and other magistrates was 'short'. As a matter of course,
Sidmouth would have used the old ploy of promising leniency to those who
co-operated, by blaming and naming associates. Elijah steadfastly maintained
his innocence, and refused to implicate others, asserting, 'I am not guilty, and
I do not know who is'. From Sidmouth's office, he was conveyed to Tothill
Fields prison, or bridewell, a short distance from the Parliament buildings
in Westminster.

On 26 March, William Cobbett, fearing arrest and a similar fate to that being
visited on the Blanketeers, sailed from Liverpool for a lecture tour of America,
a tactic he used on other occasions..

Tothill Fields bridewell was also referred to at that time as a house of correction, there having been a prison of some sort on the site since the seventeenth
century. Those incarcerated there fell into three groups – debtors, convicted
criminals, and untried men. Convicted criminals might be put to work picking
oakum, or set on a treadmill, but as a prisoner who had not even been formally
charged, let alone convicted, Elijah was apparently spared such degradations.
At least, he never subsequently referred to them. By a strange quirk of history,
Elijah's nephew, William Hepworth Dixon, born in 1821 to brother Abner, was
to write a definitive account of conditions in Tothill Fields some thirty years
later in his *The London Prisons*, but by then, the old bridewell had been replaced
by a larger prison. Was it his uncle's experiences at Tothill Fields that inspired
the nephew's interest in criminology and prison reform?

One can imagine the anxiety felt by Elijah and others, as they waited helpless, at the pleasure of a government minister purporting to act with royal authority. These were men who had been snatched from their homes and workplaces, with no opportunity to make provision for their families. Indeed, families themselves had to carry on, often completely unsupported, with no certainty of their bread-winners ever being returned to them. Moreover, Sidmouth appears to have deliberately kept his political prisoners apart, a tactic no doubt intended to isolate and demoralise. Middleton Radical Samuel Bamford, arrested a couple of weeks after Elijah, in connection with a supposed plot at Ardwick Bridge, was housed at Cold Bath Fields house of correction, and Robert Pilkington, of Bury, arrested in April, was despatched to a gaol in Surrey. Pilkington was refused visitors, his wife being turned away at the prison gate.

Given Martha's circumstances in the spring of 1817, there was little likelihood of her travelling to London. She gave birth to a daughter Judith early in the year, possibly during Elijah's imprisonment. Judith was baptised at Manchester Collegiate church on 13 July. Little help could have come from other family members, although Elijah's brothers, twins Abner and Hezekiah, and Asa, were all living in Manchester. Abner was now married with two small children of his own. In any event, Martha and the children must have been in dread as winter drew near, with no sign of Elijah being released. At some point they were forced into the workhouse and although, in speeches and reminiscences, Elijah sometimes mentioned the fact, it is unclear as to whether it was while Elijah was held at Tothill Fields, or later.

Sidmouth's suspension of *habeas corpus*, and the injustices perpetrated as a result, however, did not go unchallenged in Parliament or even among the privileged classes. The Whigs' legal spokesman was Lord Erskine, a former Lord Chancellor. As Thomas Erskine, he had notably defended Tom Paine on a charge of seditious libel, as well as securing the acquittal of Manchester men accused of conspiracy to overthrow the constitution in 1794.[1] By and large, however, the Whigs were cowed by the unceasing frenzy of conspiracy theories, and felt obliged to give their support to coercion, albeit lukewarm.

Nevertheless, a small group of members in the House of Commons, in spite of the fact that they owed their parliamentary seats to an unreformed and corrupt system of representation, kept up the pressure on Sidmouth and the government. Foremost among these were Sir Samuel Romilly, Samuel Whitbread and Henry Grey Bennet. These men, and others, took it upon themselves to rein-in government excesses, standing up in Parliament time and again in the cause of political liberty. They were also in a position to make enquiries and to get information about the number and whereabouts of detainees. Bennet, in particular, was to play a vital role in highlighting the distress of prisoners and their families, and in exposing the scandal of paid informers.

Elijah was released from Tothill Fields, without charge, on 13 November 1817. This may have been preceded by a second interview with Sidmouth, who was anxious either to extract confessions or information from prisoners, which would have justified their further detention, or to ensure they were duly chastened by the experience. The Habeas Corpus Suspension Act was not repealed until the following February. Elijah's first thoughts would have been for the welfare of Martha and the children, whether or not they were waiting for him in the Manchester workhouse. As for his time in prison, far from being chastened by hardship, he returned to Manchester determined as ever to pursue the cause of reform.

By early the following year, the family was back at 35, Gun Street and Elijah was reinstated as an operative at Thomas Houldsworth's mill. Houldsworth, as a Tory, did not see eye to eye with Elijah on politics, and the reinstatement probably came as a surprise to Elijah himself, and others. It was assumed that Elijah was good at his job as a spinner – perhaps hard to replace after being snatched from the mill, in front of workmates.

Was it that Houldsworth's taking back of Elijah arose from personal respect for a man he knew to be educated and who had been born into privilege, like himself? Likewise, as with Hanson and Sylvester, there were in Manchester relatively privileged but honest men, whose sense of fairness was outraged by the excesses of the Church-and-Kingers, and Nadin's behaviour in particular. Elijah was by now an articulate man, unafraid to express his opinions, and although he spoke out fearlessly, there was an openness and directness about him that might have affected Houldsworth as much as it influenced others in later years.

Moreover, after the release of Elijah and the other Lancashire men, events in Parliament ensured that accounts of their sufferings received widespread publicity. Increasingly, the Habeas Corpus Suspension Act became the focus of parliamentary criticism, and Lord Liverpool's Tory government came under pressure to repeal it. The Whigs supported repeal, maintaining that while it was necessary to pass the Act there had been widespread abuses, and the perceived threat of revolution had abated. Worried there might be a rash of legal claims against its ministers and servants, the government determined upon an Act of Indemnity alongside repeal of the Suspension Act.

Reformers in parliament seized the opportunity to maximise Sidmouth's embarrassment. The means by which the world was now to learn of the Blanketeers' sufferings was the parliamentary petition, a device developed and relied upon by opponents of Charles I in the years preceding the Civil Wars. Given his legendary ancestor's role in the conflict, Elijah may have taken quiet satisfaction in this, and especially in the reports of proceedings in Parliament which appeared in the Manchester press.

The Whigs, better organised, put forward an eloquent opposition to the Indemnity Bill, and Parliament was awash with petitions. Several were presented to the House of Commons on behalf of Lancashire men by Henry Grey Bennet, Member of Parliament for Shrewsbury. There was debate as to whether the petitions were to be printed (thereby ensuring they were more widely reported), but the argument was won by Bennet's side. There was no shortage of constitutional lawyers to argue the reformers' case, and Bennet himself, who had practised as a barrister, probably assisted in drafting the petitions. Of the three he presented on 27 February 1818, Elijah's came second, sandwiched between those of Sam Bamford and Robert Pilkington.[2] On the same day in the House of Lords, Earl Grosvenor, a leading Whig, presented a petition from John Bagguley, reciting further examples of ill-treatment at the hands of Nadin's men, and followed this with Elijah's petition, neatly summarising the prayer 'which appears to be for a more just and equal representation of the people in the Common House of Parliament'.

While Bamford's petition dwelt upon the agent provocateur role of 'one Lomax, of Bank Top', and that of Pilkington on the appalling treatment of himself and his family (also forced into the workhouse), Elijah's was brief, to the point, and unrepentant. A resumé of his sufferings was followed by a prayer that the House 'will be pleased to adopt such a reform in the election of members ... as shall give each man a feeling sense that he is really represented, and enable him once more proudly to boast of our glorious constitution, in King, Lords, and Commons'. Elijah's argument was intended to show up Sidmouth's actions as a scandalous over-reaction. By appealing to men's common sense and decency, bereft of bitterness, and patriotic to boot, Elijah was applying a tactic to be repeated many times in the battles for reform that lay ahead.

The Manchester reformers, by their words and actions, and by virtue of their coercion by Sidmouth and Nadin's men, were now attracting support on a much wider front. There were 27 signatories to a petition, presented in Parliament by George Philips, a Whig member for the rotten borough of Steyning, bemoaning the treatment of prisoners and the use of paid informers.[3] Son of a Manchester mill-owner, Philips, who became known as the 'unofficial member for Manchester', described the petitioners as 'Manchester merchants'. The petition amounted to a comprehensive attack on the conduct of the police and magistracy and called for an inquiry.

The petitions did not achieve any short-term gains for the reformers. In time-honoured fashion, both Houses of Parliament resolved that they should 'lay on the table'. That is, not be actioned. But they were significant in so far as they showed up the corruption and cruelty of the police and invested the petitioners and their supporters with a degree of respectability. Less than a year before publication of the petitions, the *Manchester Mercury* had contemptuously described the Blanketeers as 'deluded', and their leaders, including Elijah, as 'oratorial members of this confederacy against the Government'. Inevitably, the status of the petitioners among reformers in Lancashire – particularly that of

Elijah and Sam Bamford – was enhanced by the publicity which followed. Both men went on to attract vitriolic criticism from their opponents over the coming years, but the attacks were never as contemptuous. These men had demonstrated that it was possible to stand up to the authorities, and once returned to Lancashire they were bound to resume leading roles in furtherance of the cause which had seen them clapped in double irons and branded as traitors.

Even so, that the Blanket march had been a debacle could not be denied, and inevitably there were recriminations. Bamford, who had flatly refused to join the Blanketeers, but had been arrested by Nadin on trumped-up evidence as a suspect in the so-called Ardwick Plot (a meeting on 28 March, that spies had claimed was to be an insurrection), blamed Liverpool man Joseph Mitchell and William Benbow, a shoemaker from Middleton, for naively accepting advice and encouragement from Cobbett and Major Cartwright in London. Likewise, many middle-class sympathisers such as Archibald Prentice thought the Blanket march had discredited the cause of parliamentary reform and 'brought much misery on many mis-led men'.

Elijah, however, who had suffered a much longer period of imprisonment than Bamford, did not seek to blame anyone. Moreover, the gratuitous vengeance wrought upon the Blanketeers by the authorities was a major cause of renewed agitation that followed; agitation which, in Manchester, led inexorably to the tragic events of 16 August 1819, on St Peter's Field.

Chapter Four

St Peter's Field

There were better harvests in 1817 and 1818, together with a revival of trade. Manchester remained distressed but was free from civil disturbance for a time. This did not, however, dim the reformers' zeal, and throughout this period they continued to hold meetings and to communicate with like-minded groups in London and the Midlands. By July 1819, Elijah appears to have quit his employment as a spinner at Houldsworth's mill. At the baptism of daughter Mary, on 25 July, he gave his occupation as 'shopkeeper'. Released from the grinding routine and long hours of mill work, family responsibility aside, it meant more time for meetings and agitation.

The reformers were quick to apply lessons learned from the Blanketeers episode. Over-reaction of the authorities had produced a backlash in public opinion, and the parliamentary petitions had invested the reformers with respectability. In particular, the shrewd wording of Elijah's petition extolling the virtues of the English constitution rebutted the easy jibe of equating reformers with foreign revolutionaries. It reflected his understanding of the evolutionary principles underpinning the English constitution, and the need to win the middle ground if it was to evolve in the right direction. While the Radicals had generally opposed the wars with France, as the cause of high taxes and bad trade, they had to recognise that they had generated genuine patriotic fervour, along with popular heroes such as Nelson and Wellington.

The Manchester Patriotic Union Society was formed in March 1819 by James Wroe, John Knight and Joseph Johnson, following a visit to Manchester by Henry Hunt in January of that year. The name of the association echoed the theme that there was nothing disloyal or unpatriotic about wanting the vote, nor in seeking relief from poverty and starvation. The Union's mouthpiece, founded twelve months earlier by the same trio, was the *Manchester Observer*, John Thacker Saxton acting as reporter and printer.

In June and July, Hunt addressed reform meetings in London, Leeds and Birmingham, and throughout the summer there was agitation across the land. In Birmingham, a meeting was held to elect an attorney to represent the city in a self-styled parliamentary convention. However, Sidmouth pre-empted this by declaring the proceedings illegal. The Manchester Radicals (as they were now increasingly labelled) played their part by organising meetings in support of a petition to parliament calling for representation.

Following correspondence with Hunt (which was intercepted by the authorities) and confident that a show of strength in Manchester would give a great boost to the cause, Johnson and the Union resolved to hold a public meeting and to invite supporters from surrounding towns. A request for a meeting was posted in the *Manchester Observer* on 31 July, giving notice of an intended meeting on 9 August.

On the same day, Manchester magistrates declared the proposed meeting illegal, and warned people not to attend. This prompted Saxton to journey to Liverpool to seek legal advice, only to be told that the ban *was* lawful. Nevertheless, another request to the Boroughreeve was made, for a meeting on Monday, 16 August, but it was ignored. The MPU posted another announcement stating that, in spite of the request being supported by 700 signatures, the Boroughreeve had declined to call a meeting but that it would go ahead in any event. Further signatures were attached to a poster displayed in the window of James Wroe's bookshop in Great Ancoats Street. The venue chosen for the meeting was again St Peter's Field, an open space close to the centre of the town.[1] The die was cast.

A bright dawn promised a hot summer's day. There was reason for optimism. When Hunt had addressed a meeting of 10,000 or so on St Peter's Field earlier in the year, the occasion had passed off peacefully, in stark contrast to the 1817 rout of the Blanketeers at the hands of the King's Dragoon Guards, and the subsequent roundup of 'suspects'.

In addition to Manchester inhabitants, men, women and children streamed towards the meeting on foot from surrounding towns and villages, wearing their Sunday clothes, and in festive mood. Many of the women, dressed in white, formed all-female contingents. Reasons for attending were multi-layered. For some it was a matter of principle and belief. Others – poor handloom weavers and their families – were more concerned about their powerlessness in the face of falling wages and unemployment. Some undoubtedly felt it was their patriotic duty to be there.

Throughout the morning, numbers swelled with the arrival of well-organised, disciplined groups, who had been drilled with the idea of preventing disorder. Bamford's large contingent from Middleton had drilled on the slopes of nearby Tandle Hill, and, indicative of the optimistic mood of the occasion, he had assured an acquaintance on the edge of the town, 'I would pledge my life for their entire peaceableness'. Crowds, estimated at 60,000, at least, filled the field and surrounding streets. The gathering was indeed entirely peaceful.

The authorities, however, had also made preparations. Magistrates had arranged for the attendance of 1,200 militia, horse artillery with two six-pounder guns, 120 cavalry, and more than 400 special constables.

It is generally accepted that Elijah Dixon was present (always to be a badge of honour on his reformer's CV) but his exact role in the tragic events of that day, and those leading up it, is uncertain. Some said he received a sabre cut at the hands of the cavalry, but he was not mentioned in the casualty lists, nor as being a member of the platform party. The event's star attraction was the charismatic Hunt, sporting a white top hat with a green brim, although Elijah's friend Johnson, as secretary of the MPU, had originally invited Major John Cartwright, who declined the invitation.

Hunt arrived about one o'clock, and with him on the platform were Johnson, Knight, Saxton, Richard Carlile and George Swift. Mary Fildes and Saxton's wife Susannah were among the five women present. Press reporters also on the hustings, included John Tyas (*London Times*), John Smith (*Liverpool Echo*) and Edward Baines Junior (*Liverpool Mercury*). The chairman of the magistrates, William Hulton, watching events from a house on the edge of the Field, initially issued warrants for the arrest of Hunt, Knight, Johnson, and James Moorhouse.

Hunt had barely begun to speak before the warrants were issued. However, it was Nadin's unnecessary request for military assistance that led directly to the deployment of a recently recruited company of the Manchester and Salford Yeomanry, whose sabres (freshly sharpened) and horses were responsible for most of the casualties. These volunteer soldiers, some already the worse for drink, were commanded by Manchester mill-owner, Captain Hugh Hornby Birley.

At about 1.40pm, Birley brought his troops round the corner from Portland Street, on to the Field, having ordered them towards the platform and into the crowd. Birley's cavalry were, in the main, recently recruited, middle-class amateurs. Initially, the crowd cheered them, before it became apparent that the horsemen (who later said they feared becoming trapped) were intent on hacking a way through, heedless of who was in the way. Nadin and his specials followed them, and Hunt and most of the platform party, plus others nearby including Sam Bamford, were taken into custody. In carrying out the arrests, however, the six-foot-one Nadin met his match. Hunt, who stood six-foot-four, was able to grab Nadin and use him as a human shield against the sabre slashes directed at him. Even so, he suffered a slight sabre cut to the hand and was repeatedly cudgelled.

Meanwhile, the field was being cleared by the militia. Estimates of those wounded vary between 600 and 700; between fifteen and eighteen were killed at the scene or died from their wounds over the ensuing days. At least 168 women were injured, four of them fatally. People desperately attempting to get out of the way were slashed by sabres or trampled by horses. Middleton men were in the thick of it. Some observers felt that women were especially targeted by the yeomanry. In the mayhem the more disciplined troops of the Cheshire Yeomanry (already on the scene) were heard appealing to their comrades in arms to 'Make way!' so that the crowd might disperse peacefully.

About ninety men and women were arrested and taken at first to the house where Hulton and the other magistrates were assembled, for interrogation.

Some were discharged almost immediately. The rest were accompanied in small groups to the New Bailey, where most were held for several days, before being either discharged, fined for minor offences, or released on bail. Ten of those arrested were remanded in custody and eventually charged with high treason, although the charges were later reduced to lesser ones, such as inciting hatred.

If, as a supporter of women's suffrage throughout his political life, Elijah had been pleased to see so many women in the demonstration, he would have been dismayed by the brutality they suffered on St Peter's Field. Elizabeth Gaunt was arrested merely because she was discovered in Hunt's carriage, but witnesses said she had been pushed into it by bystanders, for her safety. She was kept in gaol for 12 days and was almost fainting from hunger when questioned. The first fatality of the day was two-years-old William Fildes, thrown from his mother's arms when she was knocked down by one of Birley's cavalrymen in the rush to obey orders. Other victims were: Margaret Downes, of Manchester, sabred; Mary Heyes, Chorlton Row, trampled; Sarah Jones, Manchester, truncheoned; Martha Partington, Barton, crushed in a cellar.

The bungling Nadin even arrested the *London Times* reporter, John Tyas, thereby ensuring, even before Tyas was at liberty, maximum publicity for the shameful and incompetent conduct of the authorities. Other journalists from distant towns were present, and among the reformers were poets and pamphleteers aplenty, ready to give detailed and damning descriptions of the day's bloody events. It was Elijah's friend and neighbour, James Wroe, bookseller and editor of the *Manchester Observer*, who first used the term 'Peterloo'. No doubt mindful that some sabre-wielding Hussars wore their Waterloo medals, and in a masterly stroke of journalism, Wroe produced pamphlets parodying Wellington's victory at Waterloo, and defining an iconic moment in the nation's history.

Elijah's absence from the list of wounded, - drawn up not by the authorities but by sympathisers – raises the issue of whether his name might have been deliberately omitted, given his reputation, to protect him from arrest as Nadin's men got busy rounding up suspects in the aftermath. If Elijah was near the hustings, close to Hunt, as seems likely, he might have been spotted by Nadin, who in the confusion, was preoccupied with the more onerous task of arresting Hunt. He may even have been among those, such as the writer and publisher, Richard Carlile, who, being known to the authorities, were spirited away by friends to avoid arrest. Certainly, many – possibly hundreds – of wounded went into hiding for fear of arrest or dismissal from employment. They hesitated to claim parish relief or medical help at the Infirmary for the same reason. Was Elijah forced into hiding for a while? Could this have been the cause of Martha's and the children's unhappy sojourn in the Manchester workhouse?

Many years later, when as an old man Elijah enjoyed celebrity status, an anonymous newspaper correspondent writing in the *Manchester Weekly Times* of 14

September 1872 alleged that he was not present at all at Peterloo. Except in circumstances of illness – including family illness – the allegation is hard to credit. Elijah's courage and loyalty were never doubted. His close friends and allies Joseph Johnson, John Knight and James Wroe were definitely there, and Elijah Dixon would surely never have deserted nor stood aloof from them.

To say that the magistrates lost their nerve – as some historians have – is charitable in the extreme. That they intended the slaughter to be a consequence of their request to the yeomanry is unlikely, but they were certainly reckless as to the effects of their actions – more worried about losing face, particularly in the eyes of the government and Church-and-Kingers; keen to teach the protestors a lesson. Two Anglican clergymen were among the magistrates who assented to calling in the military. The supine conduct of these two gentlemen did not go unnoticed, confirming Elijah in his life-long suspicion of the Established church.

Alarmed at public opinion, the magistrates began organising a cover-up – rather in the way they had fabricated the Ardwick Plot in the wake of the Blanketeers march – by exaggeration and invention. Three days after the bloodshed, they held a meeting at the police office, adjourning to the Star Inn, to thank the constables and soldiers for their actions at St Peter's Field.[2] For months they had been sending reports to Sidmouth of an intended rising; they now set about massaging every incident of disorder to justify their position retrospectively. It is true there *was* some rioting on 16 August, especially in New Cross, close to Elijah's home, but in reaction to the massacre. Understandably, there was widespread hostility toward special constables and the military. New Cross became almost a no-go area. For more than a week, authority figures were greeted with jeers and stone-throwing. Soon, posters appeared warning that in any house from which a stone was thrown, *all* occupants would be treated as complicit.

Newspaper coverage, however, was almost entirely sympathetic to the victims, and the *Observer*, naturally, piled in. On 27 August, it carried intelligence that the day before the meeting the Manchester Infirmary had been evacuated, when all patients, including a man with a recent amputation, were sent home. Although infirmary officials denied this, it is obvious that casualties were anticipated.

Whatever the hypocrisy of the authorities, Elijah and the other Manchester reformers still at liberty must have taken solace from the palpable shift in public opinion. Archibald Prentice, a cotton merchant, who had observed events firsthand, and his friends Absalom Watkin and John Edward Taylor, also men of business, spoke out, condemning the magistrates, and got up a petition of protest which attracted 4,800 signatories. Prentice and Taylor were also responsible for despatching news reports of the carnage – including one to the *London Times* – while Tyas was still under arrest. This led the *Times* to print an excoriating leading article condemning the authorities. A sizeable part of 'the respectable classes', as Prentice referred to them, whatever their own views, 'were not disposed quietly to witness death inflicted on men whose only crime had been that they asked for universal suffrage, vote by ballot, annual parliaments, and the repeal of the corn law'.

For the rest of the year and beyond, newspapers across the nation carried reports of, and details of inquiries into, the events on St Peter's Field, as well as the trials and suffering of the victims. They were almost universally condemnatory of the Manchester authorities, both for their handling of the demonstration, and for their unconvincing attempts to justify their actions. Relief funds for victims were started in towns and cities throughout the country and – importantly – support came from upper and middle class sympathisers as well as fellow-workers.

At the same time, however, Nadin's men were on the loose, fear was in the air, and risk of arrest was attendant on any expression of opinion. Prentice showed not a little personal courage. As well as getting the facts out to the world, he was instrumental in drawing up a list of casualties, and he and Taylor raised money which led eventually to the establishment of a new weekly newspaper – the *Manchester Guardian*.

There were protest meetings in London and many other cities. Sidmouth reacted by launching another round of coercion. The government brought forward six Bills, dealing with bringing cases to trial; prohibiting military exercises; the issuing of warrants to search for arms; further restricting public meetings; conferring further powers on magistrates to seize blasphemous or seditious literature; and extending the scope of the Stamp Act to include pamphlets. Two things assisted the government – a crackpot scheme to blow up the Cabinet, which emanated in London (the Cato Street Conspiracy) and a gradual improvement in trade and the general economic situation.[3]

The tragic denouement on St Peter's Field was brought about by the clash of two diametrically opposed forces; the success of Hampden clubs and political unions in encouraging working people to seek parliamentary reform through peaceful means was confronted head-on by the stubborn, uncompromising resistance of the governing class. The outcome of such terrible and violent reaction to peaceful protest was that government at all levels conceded the moral high ground to the reformers.

The world would not be the same after Peterloo. Coercion and cruelty had been shockingly exposed. Fair-minded people of all ranks, impressed by the quiet courage of men like Elijah Dixon, began to question the status quo, and support for reform grew steadily, in Parliament, across the country, and especially in Manchester.

Chapter Five

Great Ancoats Street

Great Ancoats Street, the thoroughfare linking New Cross with Ancoats, was the main artery of life for the growing industry of north Manchester. Near it were new mills and factories providing employment for workers living in overcrowded and insanitary terraces springing up between them. It was conveniently separate from the commercial district in the centre of the city, although those who were fortunate enough to live in developing suburbs such as Ardwick, Longsight, and Whalley Range might often pass along its busy course in their carriages. Whatever the privations imposed on the population by the Corn Laws after 1815, and however devastating the depths of capricious trade cycles, industrial expansion in Manchester continued. New machinery was invented, new mills and factories opened, and the tide of humanity sucked into the city from the countryside continued unabated.

Given their background, and the influence of father Job, it is unsurprising that the entrepreneurial spirit of the Dixons was to find expression in the lives of his sons. Elijah seems to have been first to quit the mill. Within a year of Peterloo, he was listed as a ratepayer for property in Bradford Road, Ancoats, and for property at 42, Great Ancoats Street, both rented. By his own account, he was a milk dealer by 1820, and was probably selling other groceries and provisions. At any rate, the 1821 trade directory lists him as 'shopkeeper' at Great Ancoats Street. It is possible he continued to work at Houldsworth's mill, for a time, although it is difficult to imagine how the exigencies of buying milk from local farms, and supplying it to customers, could have been combined with long hours at the mill.

How were these first business ventures financed? Was Elijah able to save from his wages? Was he able to borrow? Or had the age-old proceedings in the court of Chancery finally been resolved beneficially in favour of Job Dixon and his descendants? Later in life, Elijah confided that when at last the proceedings were concluded, the resulting sum of money was disappointingly meagre, compared with Job's great expectations, but it might have been just enough for him to buy a cart or a donkey.

The story of Elijah's ass was to become legendary in later years when Elijah was feted as a successful, rags-to-riches industrialist. Told and re-told, however distorted or exaggerated, the tale was irresistible material for any speaker introducing Elijah as an honoured guest. It first gained currency in an article written in 1828 by Richard Carlile in his Radical magazine, *The Lion*. For an atheist, Carlile focussed somewhat obsessively on religious topics, but his gentle attack on Elijah's belief in universal salvation was combined with an affectionate pen-portrait and an amusing anecdote about Elijah's time as a milk-dealer.

According to Carlile, Elijah was so busy preaching and proselytising that the donkey carrying his milk cans was inclined to finish the round without him and lie down in boredom. On one such occasion, 'Down crouched the ass, and by an endeavour to be on its side, out poured the milk from the milk cans, while the master was pouring out his spiritual milk'. Another version was that on the first morning's round, with milk canisters slung over the donkey's back, Elijah went inside for a moment. While he was away, the donkey was stung by a wasp, and out came Elijah in time to see the beast rolling over and spilling the entire load of milk. The impact of this disaster – or so the story ran – was such that Elijah decided, there and then, to sell the milk round, donkey and all, and divert his energies into less risky and more profitable ventures. These stories, though told in *People I Have* Met by Joseph Johnson (c1900) *and Manchester Streets and Manchester* Men by Thomas Swindells (1906) are completely untrue. From his own accounts, Elijah's milk-selling lasted at least seven years from 1820-27.

Given a right of reply in *The Lion*, Elijah averred that the donkey was only brought in to help with milk deliveries, during a prolonged bout of ill-health. Elijah had in fact contracted typhoid, in 1820, which he described as 'nervous fever'. He contradicted Carlile's version, although, tellingly, Carlile's riposte was to say that when he had heard it told in Elijah's presence, Elijah had not demurred. According to Elijah, the donkey spilled milk on only three occasions: 'once by a slip, once by suddenly crouching down, and once in turning a corner, on a dark night'.

Elijah wove this account, somewhat tortuously, into a defence of his Christian beliefs, 'in order to shew you, how easy it is to believe a story, without knowing it to be true'. It was a detailed account of his spiritual voyage, a pilgrim's progress, prompted by a long discussion between the two men at a Radical meeting in Ashton-under-Lyne. Carlile described Elijah's faith as 'insane mysticism' but 'good natured', adding: 'Elijah Dixon separated from his religion is one of the most benevolent and kind creatures that ever carried about the milk of human kindness'. Elijah's reply suggested his enlightenment was a long time in gestation: 'during the time I had this ass, my mind was more under the influence of anti-revealed opinions.'

Whatever the truth about the ass, and whatever the differences between Elijah and Carlile, it did not shake their friendship. And Carlile the atheist, was probably right in suggesting that the story of Elijah's ass was 'a little bit of mischief' cultivated, and relished, by Elijah himself.

Although the effect of Peterloo was to stimulate the cause of reform, the 1820s remained a dangerous time for Elijah and his fellow reformers. The trials of those arrested by Nadin at Peterloo began at Lancaster in March 1820 and degenerated into farce. Serious charges of treason were dropped, replaced by lesser ones of attending an illegal meeting, and inciting hatred against the government. When the case transferred to York, Hunt was allowed to conduct his own defence and to conduct cross examination of prosecution witnesses brought against co-defendants.[1] Even so, Hunt, Sam Bamford, John Knight, and Joseph Johnson were among the five convicted of inciting hatred. Hunt got two years six months, and Bamford and Johnson, a year. An eloquent condemnation of the government by open letter from radical campaigner Sir Francis Burdett attracted a charge of criminal libel and another show trial. There were, too, trials of working men from Burnley and Stockport, charged with holding seditious meetings. John Knight, who, like Elijah, had been gaoled by Sidmouth after the Blanketeers episode, was arrested for his part in the meeting at Burnley, and eventually sentenced to two years imprisonment.

In Manchester, the authorities, keen as ever to do Sidmouth's bidding, began a new round of arrests and prosecutions for incitement and seditious literature. Not surprising then that during a parade to celebrate the coronation of George IV, the Manchester Yeomanry were booed and hissed as they passed along Great Ancoats Street. Elijah would have had a good view from an upstairs window.

The first issue of the *Manchester Guardian* was published on 5 May 1821, aimed at middle-class readership, and conservatively dedicated to the reformist cause. It had been founded by John Edward Taylor as a replacement for the troubled *Manchester Observer*, and was supported by Archibald Prentice and members of what he called the 'Little Circle' of moderates, the Brotherton and Potter families among them. Taylor and Prentice, who were next-door neighbours, had both previously written for William Cowdroy's *Gazette*. By this time James Wroe, no fan of Taylor's (he once referred to him as a 'poltroon and snaffling hypocrite') had relinquished editorship of the *Manchester Observer* to T.J. Evans. The *Observer*, stricken by writs for criminal libel and about to fold, initially wished the *Guardian* success, but weaknesses soon showed themselves.

The quality of print and reporting were not good, advertising revenue was disappointing and although it supported Corn Law Repeal and Free Trade, the *Guardian's* stance on other reform issues was decidedly lukewarm. Taylor refused to support early campaigns to reduce child labour in cotton mills and showed little interest in voting reform or in the continuing persecution of Radicals. Taylor's view that the 'mere populace' should never exercise 'a preponderating influence' summed up the position of orthodox Whigs. The ultimate betrayal, so far as the Radicals were concerned, was to come in 1831, when as a result of the testimony of a *Guardian* reporter some Radicals were imprisoned for sedition.

After three years, even the moderate Prentice withdrew his support and concentrated instead on buying the *Gazette* from Cowdroy's widow and trying to revive its flagging circulation. Through various mergers, this eventually became the *Manchester Times and Examiner*. In fact, the *Guardian* would not achieve its reputation as the respectable mouthpiece of liberalism until 1872, when Taylor's nephew, the redoubtable C.P. Scott, took over the editorship.

Meanwhile, in 1822, Elijah became a founder member of the *Northern Political Union*, dedicated to franchise reform. The bloodshed at Peterloo, together with the political trials that followed, capped by the prison sentences handed down to purported ringleaders, contributed to an atmosphere of suspicion and distrust among reformers. Although the NPU – a prototype popular front – had been formed to promote co-operation between different sections of the movement, it was liable to be the focus of disunity and sometimes violent disagreement. In these disputes, Elijah established his reputation as the voice of reason, attempting to get disparate elements – conservative reformers, Radicals, and Republicans – to sink their differences and work together.

Much of the argument centred on the role of Joseph Johnson, who had suffered separate terms of imprisonment totalling 30 months in connection with the Blanketeers and Peterloo. The purpose of a meeting held on 22 October 1822 was to agree the terms of an address to Hunt, still in Ilchester prison. 'Huntites' challenged Johnson's position as chairman. Carlile's magazine, *The Republican*, reported that the meeting was attended by more than thirty people, and that some speakers, including the poet Elijah Ridings, were shouted down for being 'Carlilites'. There were even accusations that spies were among the company.

In a classic exposition of the right of free speech and toleration, Elijah attempted to reconcile the warring factions. Dealing first with the accusation about spies, he thought suspicion might be attached to the 'source of the first cry', and appealed for unity and arguments based on principle, not personality. In answer to a rhetorical sideswipe from a Hunt supporter, demanding 'Who are you? What are you?', he said, 'I am Elijah Dixon, and I am well known by most of the persons present to have made some exertions in the cause of freedom. Mine has been chiefly *shoulder-work*. I am a *friend of freedom*'.

Although broadly supportive of the Huntite position, Elijah offered an olive branch to opponents (including dissident Cobbettites) by saying he would not have attended a meeting calling on 'Friends of Mr Hunt, to the exclusion of all others'. As the meeting became more rancorous, Elijah again appealed to speakers 'who might not see through the same optics' to refrain from personal attacks. In this vein, he went on to propose an amendment removing any reference in the address to a controversial pamphlet criticising Hunt, and apparently put out by supporters of Cobbett.

It was Elijah Dixon, 'shopkeeper', and Peter Turner Candelet, 'draper', who, in 1823, acted as sureties for their friend, Manchester bookseller David Ridgway, bound over to keep the peace for three years[2] In 1821, Ridgway had been convicted of criminal libel, in spite of efforts by his defence counsel, Henry Brougham, a future Lord Chancellor, for selling Richard Carlile's *New Year's Address to the Radicals*, and had already served a year's imprisonment. In a classic case of entrapment, Joseph Nadin's son, Thomas, a solicitor, had sent his 17-year-old clerk to Ridgway's shop on Swarbrick Street to purchase the offending pamphlet. The lad reported to Nadin that Ridgway told him he did not have a copy. Truly a chip off the old block, Nadin Junior sent his clerk back to the shop another three times before finally pulling off the sting.

Evidence presented at the trial gives an insight into the way Ridgway the 'shopkeeper' supplemented his meagre income as a fustian-cutter.[3] The shop was in reality the front parlour of a two-up-two-down terrace house; a simple kitchen lay behind the shop, with living quarters upstairs. Stock included pamphlets and books as well as 'checked linens', and, according to a notice on the front door, Ridgway also supplied tea, coffee and tobacco. His wife, Martha, also sold thread, potatoes, children's books and copies of *Mother Shipton* prophesies. The scenario was typical of the way so many Radicals – some unemployable because of blacklisting – eked out a living.

For shopkeepers, hungry mouths in the Manchester of the 1820s guaranteed demand, but not necessarily the means to turn a profit. Yet, with an apparent abundance of optimism, Elijah looked to diversify, at the same time hedging his bets against failure in any particular enterprise. Brother Abner also had other irons in the fire. When, on 12 January 1826, he appealed against his conviction at Lancaster Quarter Sessions for unlicensed hawking, he was described as a 'paper dealer'; only a few days later, when his son David was baptised at the Collegiate church, Abner gave his occupation as 'cotton spinner'.[4] In spite of hard times, however, it seems that Elijah was surefootedly succeeding in business, investing profits wisely. Alongside William Scott, described as 'milkman', he was well-off enough to stand surety for Abner in his hour of need at Lancaster.

By 1827, the Dixons may have moved to Dixon Street, New Islington. The address was stated in rates returns as *Dixon Street, Woodward Street*. It might have been that as Elijah prospered, he was able to have houses built on the end of Woodward Street, perhaps at right-angles to it, eventually acquiring a separate identity associated with its occupants. Elijah was shown first as tenant, but later as owner, of his home and two other properties in the same street. This was the beginning of Elijah's property portfolio, gradually expanding alongside other commercial ventures. The Manchester Rates Book of 1829 lists him as owner of three properties in Dixon Street, and while still renting the shop in Great Ancoats Street he remained the owner of the cellar there, probably using it for storage.

In the 1820s, there was one cause, generally supported by workers, which did not provoke the same hostility from the authorities as franchise reform. Indeed, the mill-owning aristocracy of Manchester were themselves increasingly vocal in the cause of Corn Law reform. Their self-interest in cheaper bread for workers – which would keep a lid on wage demands – was obvious, but that did not change the political reality that here was a wrong to be righted which might bring the working and middle classes together.

So it was in August 1827 that the *Manchester Courier* reported on a 'Meeting of the Working Classes' held in the Manor Court Room, Brown Street, to discuss Corn Law repeal. Elijah Dixon took the chair, thanked the meeting for the honour thus conferred upon him, and proceeded to appeal for good order, trusting that 'all hissing, and other marks of disapprobation' would be avoided, and that every speaker would be heard with candour and treated with courtesy, since the object was to 'get to the truth by hearing all sides of the question'. A burst of applause followed these remarks and when, after two or three rousing speeches in favour of repeal, punctuated by more applause and cheering, the meeting was addressed by a Mr Hopkins, who argued that repeal would make little difference to the plight of the workers, he was heard in respectful silence. The meeting, concluded the *Courier*, 'separated in a very quiet and orderly manner'. The event very much cemented Elijah's reputation as an apostle of fairness, and a natural choice for chairman when discord was in the offing.

While the majority of the rate-paying Radicals of Manchester remained voiceless and voteless as to the election of their national Parliament, and as to the pressing injustice of the Corn Laws, they were not precluded from participation in purely local bodies. Even the medieval instruments of government which bolstered the power of the Church-and-Kingers were subject to limited accountability, with provision for holding meetings. Elijah, and others, were determined to get a foot in the door. On the face of it, the reformers would have to do a lot of shoving. At the apex of this arcane structure of government was the Boroughreeve, appointed by the Court Leet, itself a creature of the Lord of the Manor. For the previous 25 years, the manorial power had been exercised by Sir Oswald Mosley, acting at his pleasure upon the advice of 'a body of gentlemen' who composed Court Leet juries.

The reformers' most obvious target was the body known as the Commissioners of Police, established in 1792, which, although largely controlled through patronage available to the Boroughreeve, had been forced by circumstance to spawn a series of committees dealing with such things as municipal premises, bridges and highways, as well as the constabulary. Given its wider role, the word 'police' in its title was more indicative of the *polis* of ancient Greece – an early manifestation of community spirit. From the summer of 1827 onwards, the Boroughreeve and his nominees were to hear a good deal of argument put forward on behalf of the wider community by Elijah and his Radical allies, notably William Whitworth, Peter Turner Candelet, and Archibald Prentice.

At a meeting on 5 September, reported in the *Manchester Courier*, Elijah seconded a motion put by Whitworth, concerning the town's gas supply. The resolution to dissolve the Commissioners' Act of Parliament Committee, which had been deputed to seek improvements in the supply, was narrowly rejected by 15 votes to 13. Whitworth argued that the committee's scheme would throw a disproportionate burden on shopkeepers, while enhancing the profits of factory owners. As for the Constabulary itself, the meeting unanimously accepted audited accounts.

By now, Joseph Nadin, scourge of the Radicals, had retired on his ill-gotten gains to live out his long life as a country gentleman in Cheadle, Cheshire, where his house was reputedly called 'Rogue's Nest'. He died in 1848, and as if to haunt his enemies, was buried in the churchyard of St James's, Manchester, a short distance from St Peter's Field and the scene of his evil deeds in Ancoats. Perhaps it was a source of regret to Elijah that his attendance at Commissioners meetings as a respectable citizen never brought him face to face with the callous adversary who had so much to answer for.

A special meeting at the Town Hall in December, was, to put it mildly, a lively affair, again reported in the *Manchester Courier*. This time, the reformers focussed on the accounts of the Police Department, suspecting that some items had been inflated to conceal bribes or illegal payments to spies. Their opponents reacted by accusing them of wrecking tactics and threatened to raise the property qualification for Commissioners. The chairman followed up by nominating the Boroughreeve, Charles Cross, as Treasurer of police funds. Prentice proposed an amendment that the Treasurer's post be filled by members of the Accounts Committee, and this was seconded by Elijah. The reformers also pressed for the vote to be taken by ballot. The meeting ended in uproar, with Commissioners leaping upon tables and the platform, the Boroughreeve and his supporters fleeing to the side of the room.

The reformers felt that the meeting had been rigged to prevent the appointment of more Commissioners, and later the same evening they acted promptly to challenge it. Within hours they had drafted, printed, and distributed a request for a special meeting for the purpose of swearing in as Police Commissioners any owner or occupier of property with an annual rent or value of thirty pounds. Elijah Dixon was the second signatory, and among the names which followed were those of Candelet, Whitworth, James Wroe, and Jeremiah Hanmer. When the meeting took place, at the end of January 1828, matters came to a head immediately, upon Whitworth opposing the usual practice of appointing the Boroughreeve to the chair. He proposed Candelet, and on losing the vote by a show of hands, the reformers, or the 'low party' as Prentice described them, demanded a scrutiny of voters' qualifications, claiming that there was a majority of regular votes against the Boroughreeve. Whitworth stood on a table, shouting 'No Boroughreeve!' and the meeting descended into chaos.

Predictably, the Boroughreeve, assisted by his legal advisors, took the matter to court. Whitworth was accused of dragging the Boroughreeve from his chair and orchestrating a deliberate attempt to disrupt the meeting. At the New Bailey, Elijah gave evidence that at the time Cross fell to the floor, Whitworth was four or five yards away. The court proceedings dissolved into pantomime, with pirouetting lawyers and contradictory witnesses, and the magistrates, clearly unconvinced by the evidence, contented themselves with binding over Whitworth to keep the peace. Arguably, Whitworth's rough-house tactics paid off. They succeeded in generating maximum exposure of the hole-in-the-corner practices of the Boroughreeve, and henceforth members of the low party, dignified by its more temperate members, such as Elijah and Prentice, were a force to be reckoned with in local politics.

Unsurprisingly, however, reactionary members of the Police Commissioners responded to this early outbreak of local democracy by attempting to raise the property qualification. They appealed to parliament, and later in 1828 the Commissioners were limited to a total of 240 elected members. Their efforts, however, failed to quell the Radicals as attention turned more and more towards franchise reform.

Chapter Six

Store Street

It would be wrong to assume that by trading as a shopkeeper, and finding time to do battle with the authorities, Elijah somehow escaped the perennial sufferings of family life in working class Manchester. Far from it. In October 1823, daughter Martha died aged 2 years and 10 months, the cause of death recorded as 'decline'. Barely six months later, daughter Eliza, aged 1 year 8 months died; cause of death, 'decline'. This term commonly appeared in the registers following slow deterioration, as opposed to sudden or acute illness. In infants, the real cause was often diarrhoea, dysentery or malnutrition. Recovery was seldom, if ever, assisted by the application of popular patent medicines containing laudanum, typically a ten per cent solution of opium in alcohol, with flavourings. One side effect was loss of appetite; a cure worse than the malady. But who could blame worried parents unable to afford doctors for doing what they were misled into thinking was best for their children?

Both Martha and Eliza were buried at Christ Church, Every Street, in Ancoats. Infant mortality was a fact of life, and it stalked the Dixons cruelly. Abner Dixon's son, also named Abner, and born in 1823, survived only a month. A year later, another son, Elijah, died, aged two months. The cause of death in each case was stated as 'inflammation of the lungs', and they too were buried at Every Street. A few months later, Asa Dixon's daughter Elizabeth, aged three, died of 'water on the brain', and in 1829 his 5-year-old son, James, died, also of nothing more specific than 'decline'. Elijah's brother Hezekiah lost a son, John, baptised (posthumously) and buried the same day.

In these tragedies the Dixons were typical victims of the great alliance of killer diseases – air and water pollution – which stalked the slums of Ancoats, New Cross, New Islington and other working class districts of Manchester. Elementary amenities such as street-cleaning, water-supply, sanitation and open spaces failed to keep pace with mass migration to the town, creating the perfect scenario for epidemics of cholera and typhoid.

High mortality rates had the predictable effect of creating pressure on churchyards for burial space. Cremation was still regarded as illegal, and local authorities had to confront the problem of where to put the bodies. It was, in today's parlance, a matter of logistics. Parish grounds and even overspill grounds, such as St Michael's lower ground, were almost full. Municipal cemeteries were decades in the future. In the meantime, beginning with the Cheetham Hill Wesleyan Cemetery in 1815, and Christ Church, Every Street in 1823, it was the Non-Conformist churches and chapels that provided the much-needed extra burial space – usually at cheaper rates than parish grounds, and regardless of the deceased's religious affiliation.

It is one thing to claw your way out of poverty by hard work and enterprise, to strive to better the lives of your wife and children, and to suffer family tragedy. It is quite another to play a leading role in politics at the same time. Only a man of extraordinary self-belief and toughness of character could achieve both, without ever deviating from the strongly held convictions which inspired him as a youth. Elijah Dixon was such a man.

There is hardly a name in the history of the Dixon family that cannot be found in the Bible, mostly in the Old Testament; Elijah, Job, Abner, Hezekiah, Asa, Oded, Isaiah, Nehemiah. Females too; Martha, Judith, Eliza, Elizabeth. Typically, the Dixons' marriages, baptisms and burials were left to the authority of the established Anglican church, but everything about Elijah's early years suggests that he was pervasively influenced by reading the Bible and the ethos of Non-Conformism in Manchester.

As well as popularising the legend of Elijah's ass, the meeting with Carlile in 1827, at Ashton-under-Lyne, prompted Elijah to give a detailed account of his religious beliefs. Few people are inclined to lay their souls bare to a hostile listener, so the two men must have got on well. They fell into discussion of their different views, and when, not long afterwards, Carlile poked gentle fun at Elijah's beliefs, in the columns of *The Lion*, Elijah responded with enthusiasm to an invitation to state his case.

In a long article in the 1 February 1828 issue, he explained his faith and something of how he found it. It was a personal statement of his belief in a God of love, and the Holy Trinity, and Elijah was at pains to point out that, contrary to the impression he had given Carlile, he was *not* a Bible Christian. 'I do not like the persons with whom you have coupled me', he stressed, although given his strong friendship with Radical Bible Christian minister, James Scholefield, and other members of that sect, this must be taken simply as a disassociation from their theology.

At first his style is matter-of-fact, salted with theological and even mystical references. Then, admitting his reasoning thus far to be 'parabolic' he changes key. His religious beliefs, he says, 'teach me to look upon all men, and women too, as my brothers and sisters, and to pray for all those among them who are in error and misery'. Respectful as ever, Elijah credits an article written by Carlile himself (in which the latter provocatively bestows upon himself the title of Anti-Christ) as having prompted a spiritual self-examination: 'I therewith took the Bible and Mirabaud's *System of Nature* [an atheistic paradigm] and went into my bed-room, kneeled me down with the books open, and prayed for that divine illumination, of which I was so much in need, and I now, thank God, have obtained my heart's desire on that point'.

In other words, Elijah's God is a personal God, and the article concludes with a personal appeal to his friend Carlile: 'I have just one soft whisper more to make to you – when you can prove to me that I should be a better natured man than the best that ever carried about him the milk of human kindness, and also that I should be happier into the bargain, by adopting your creed, then, and not until then, will I play so foolish a part as going back to your opinions - *So help me God!*'

Elijah never did go back, and less than a year later he resolved to give an extraordinary demonstration of his faith to the people of Manchester. On Sunday, 7 June 1829, after ensuring publicity for the event by placing a newspaper advertisement, Elijah attracted a huge crowd – estimated at 8,000 – for a public ceremony of baptism by immersion, reported in the *Manchester Times and Gazette* the Saturday after. The ceremony was carried out appropriately enough by a Baptist minister, Rev Robert Bradbury, close to the aqueduct over Store Street on the Ashton canal (referred to as the Peak Forest canal by the *Manchester Courier*), near open ground which accommodated the crowd. There was much merriment at Elijah's expense, and several police officers had to keep the crowd back. Even so, he received a loud cheer on emerging from the water – followed by extensive newspaper coverage. Not all of it was favourable. The *Courier* described him as 'a spouter at infidel clubs', stressing his 'notoriety' as a reformer and a member of the Police Commissioners 'under the Whitworth dynasty'.

The *Manchester Times*, however, reported more sympathetically. After the baptism, Elijah addressed a packed congregation at Great Mount Street Baptist chapel, off Lower Mosley Street, by standing on a table at the door, so his address could be heard by hundreds of people outside. His text was 'I am not ashamed of the Gospel of Christ', and his sermon was liberally punctuated with Biblical quotations, as well as an account of his spiritual journey. Elijah looked back on the erratic course of his search for truth, recalling a timid 12-year old going into empty buildings in Manchester to pray, then a happy time, beginning when he was 14 as the employee of 'a pious Methodist', followed by dark days getting into bad company and dissolute habits. It was a Road to Damascus, beset with sharp bends and awkward corners. Even after regaining his faith in 'Mr Roby's church' he lost it again, relapsing into doubt and atheism. History does not record what the curious listeners in Great Mount Street made of Elijah's reference to Mirabaud's *System of Nature*, but the *Manchester Times* records that they paid close attention, and were no doubt relieved to hear, ultimately, of his renunciation of wickedness, and his salvation through prayer and scripture. So was Mr Bradbury, who promptly informed them that Elijah would be back the following Sunday evening to deliver a discourse on the coming of

Anti-Christ – doubtless, a sermon for Elijah to hone on the friendly mill of discourse between him and his comrade in the cause of reform, Richard Carlile, atheist.

Interestingly, Elijah did not have his children baptised by full immersion. Only three weeks after his immersion in the canal, son Elijah was baptised at the Collegiate church in the conventional manner, together with Elizabeth and Ann, then aged five and three respectively. Likewise, Eliza and Martha had been baptised together in 1822, an example of the common practice of families waiting to have more than one child 'done' together. In oversights or expediences such as this Elijah is revealed as an ordinary, far from perfect, family man. While no-one could ever say that Elijah Dixon took the name of the Lord in vain, there are still strong grounds for suggesting that the public spectacle at Store Street was intended at least partly as a publicity stunt for the good of the Radical cause.

In fact, throughout his political life Elijah made friends with and allies of non-believers and idealists of all creeds. Yet he was never shy about professing his faith and bearing witness to it. Sometimes, particularly during the Chartist decade, he startled his audience with an apposite Biblical reference; on other occasions he mystified them with an obtuse prophesy of salvation for all – even for their enemies. In this distinguishing characteristic – an unshakable belief in the worth of all humankind – might be found a one-word summary of his faith – universalism. It also helps to explain why Elijah never declared formal allegiance to any particular denomination. As he emphasised to Carlile, differences of religion were to be pitied rather than condemned, and his old-fashioned faith never blinded him to new ideas.

In May 1827, Elijah chaired the first Co-operative Congress. The importance of this event is often overlooked by students of Co-operation. It was only in the early 1900s that George Jacob Holyoake, a later President of the Congress and historian of the movement, unearthed records of the 1827 Congress, thereby disturbing the conventional wisdom that the first ones were held in 1830-31.[1] Elijah sat alongside the philosophical father of co-operative idealism, Robert Owen, more humanist and socialist in his beliefs than Christian. Also present were William Pare, Rev Joseph Marriott and William Thompson of Cork. Yet, as events were to show, Elijah was greatly influenced by Owen, recognising in Owenite ideals the possibility of realising comprehensive change in society. It was a typical example of Elijah attempting to put faith into action. His was a true pioneering role, because he had already become involved in at least two shop-keeping partnerships along co-operative lines – intended to pass on price benefits to member-customers, guarantee quality of goods, and prevent the widespread evil of food adulteration, particularly prevalent in the supply of staples such as flour and sugar.

Even in the midst of the Reform Bill crisis in 1831, when Elijah was a prominent member of the Manchester Political Union, he found time for activities which typically combined idealism with practicality. In May that year, he chaired the third Co-op Congress, attended by Owen. When Owen addressed a tea-party at Salford Town Hall he elucidated, in flowery terms, on the Co-operative ideal – a system that would eventually bring about 'the millennium, that happy period when every man should sit under his own vine and his own fig tree'. In contrast, on the previous day Elijah had presided over a meeting at the Spread Eagle Inn, Salford, when forty-six delegates representing fifty-six societies applied their minds to a hard-headed business plan to form a General Union of Co-ops and to establish a warehouse in Liverpool (an idea which foretold the emergence of the Co-operative Wholesale Society). Nevertheless, the plan was for 'surplus' profits to be applied to the formation of an Owenite 'community'. This was a utopian ideal which chimed closely with Elijah's own Christian beliefs, and in particular the ideas of the Radical propagandist, Thomas Spence; an equitable redistribution of land was the key to achieving social justice.

Elijah's identification with Spenceanism was demonstrated in 1832 with the formation of a company whose object was the purchase of land on Chat Moss – a wild stretch of bog and marshland to the west of Manchester – with a view to being settled by a co-operative community. Elijah had often spoken in meetings about the possibility of alleviating poverty in towns by creating new farming communities on 'waste' land. Although he does not appear to have been the originator of this early scheme, he was probably a subscriber, and certainly a prominent advocate.

In two lectures, delivered at the Co-op schoolroom, Salford, in September 1832, Elijah spoke in favour of subscription schemes to wrest the land from those who had acquired it by 'acts of robbery and blood', and the setting up of agrarian 'colonies' consisting of two or three thousand people. Nowhere does Elijah better expose the tension between idealism and practicality. Here is the businessman, shrewd and practical, involved in organising warehouses for the nascent co-operative retail trade, speaking of doing away with money, as a pre-condition of universal happiness. According to the *Lancashire and Yorkshire Co-operator*, Elijah, quoting 'numerous passages from scripture', blamed prevailing distress on the very existence of large cities. Yet, there was hope; the company being formed consisted of 2,000 ten-pound shares for the purchase of land and 'mutual employment'.

In the second lecture, Elijah expanded upon the scheme to the extent that the *Co-operator* described it as 'the most able development of the ... proposed new system of society we ever remember to have heard'. Choosing his words carefully (these were still dangerous times when spies might be in attendance at any public meeting), Elijah preached the need for united action to get possession of the land. Not by way of violent uprising, but by superior and combined efforts to purchase the land. How to do it? If four million labourers subscribed a shilling each for five successive weeks, they could raise a million pounds, and if they kept it up for a year, they could raise ten million, enough to purchase all the land for sale in England. By this means, colonies of two to three thousand people could be set up, reducing costs by sharing machinery. It was a blue-print for collective farms.

Yet the scheme to purchase 600 acres of land, in the area south of the railway, and close to the village of Irlam, on the river Irwell, soon faltered. In July 1835, Elijah convened a meeting of members of the Royal Oak Building Society, possibly with the idea of either winding it up, or buying out other members. A link with the Chat Moss scheme is possible, though not established.

Later, in the 1840s, when Elijah was a member of the Christian Community Society, a national body formed in Coventry by Joseph Squires, there appears to have been an effort to revive the scheme. There was a meeting in Dr Scholefield's schoolroom, addressed by Captain Thomas Barlow, at which Elijah may have been present, to promote settlement on the society's land at Chat Moss - now down to '14 acres'. The *Manchester Courier* of 4 December 1841 reported that about fifteen members had subscribed a total of £200, and that the society hoped for 'greater things' and 'the accession of new members'.

In the meantime, the Reform Bill crisis deepened. In March 1832, when there were plans to withhold payment of taxes to force the government's hand on franchise reform, Elijah, liaising with Baptist minister Bradbury, gave two sermons at Walley's factory, New Islington. Collections were made after each to provide legal representation for men facing trial at Lancaster for attending 'Sunday meetings'. Elijah and the MPU began to prepare for a series of meetings and demonstrations.

Family and business reasons aside, Elijah surely paused long and hard during this period to consider the choice between the exertions of political agitation in the town and the alternative of a life in a pioneer community out on the wasteland of Chat Moss. In his forties and in his prime, he was an accomplished speaker, an authoritative chairman, and a clever tactician at rowdy public meetings. What a waste of God's gifts it might have been had he left all that behind, when there were so many wrongs to be righted in the town.

Yet, the idea of a utopian rural community remained close to Elijah's heart throughout his life, and while for the time being he was focussed on business and politics in Manchester, it would not be long before he returned to Chat Moss.

Chapter Seven

Town Hall

My countrymen! Why languish
Like outcasts of the earth,
And drown in tears of anguish
The glory of your birth?
Ye were a freeborn people,
And heroes were your race;
The dead – they are our freemen;
The living – our disgrace.

Ernest Jones (1819-69), *Chartist Poem*

Throughout the late 1820s, bad trade forced wage rates down, and there was widespread hunger and distress in industrial areas, especially Manchester. Elijah, as a shopkeeper in the early 1830s appears to have struggled to stay afloat. His partnership with Jeremiah Hanmer, in premises at 65, Oldham Street, was dissolved in April 1831, and later that year, a partnership with David McWilliams, based at Prestolee, was dissolved. McWilliams was bankrupted, but Elijah managed to stall his creditors with the same device as that used by his father Job, in Holmfirth, a legal assignment. The Manchester trade directory for 1831-32 lists Elijah in business as 'baker, flour and provisions dealer' at 47, Swan Street, and McWilliams is listed at the same address a year later.

As well as appealing to customers by distributing profits and lowering prices through bulk-buying, the co-operative model would have provided some protection against personal liability for individuals such as Elijah, still prepared to take the initiative – and the risk – by setting up shops.

By 1832 Elijah was running a shop ('store') in Oldham Street, on co-operative lines, as seen in the list of sellers in the June edition of the *Lancashire and Yorkshire Co-operator*. The same year, a co-op store was opened in Prestolee, possibly using the premises formerly occupied by Elijah and McWilliams. Given the business climate in those dark days, it is hard to imagine shopkeepers making much of a profit from unemployed workers, or those whose wages had been reduced to starvation level.

While the plan for a Chat Moss utopia had stalled, so too, the idea of co-operation as a practical means of helping working people proved to be slightly ahead of its time in the early 1830s. Bad trade and unemployment did not help. Seventeen societies were set up between 1826 and 1830, but the failure rate was high and at the end of that period there were only eleven co-op stores in Manchester and Salford. By 1832 the number had fallen to three or four.

The situation for both workers and shopkeepers was aggravated by the iniquitous truck system, by which employees were paid, wholly or partly, in vouchers ('tommy tickets') to be exchanged for goods, often inferior and over-priced, at the company store. A series of Truck Acts attempted to deal with this evil, and in 1831 the right to be paid in cash was extended to most factory workers, including cotton operatives. Other things being equal, this was bound to lead to a gradual improvement in business for honest traders, including co-operative societies.

The injustice of the Corn Laws continued to gnaw at the consciences and the pockets of Manchester men. On 25 February 1830, a huge public meeting, convened by the Boroughreeve, was held in the Town Hall to consider the 'state of the country' and widespread unemployment and poverty in north-west England. Speakers referred to the level of distress as unprecedented. In point of fact, analysis of data by economic historians has shown that real income per head in the 1830s was actually falling for the first time since 1700.

The *Manchester Courier* narrated that some 2,000 people turned up for the meeting, although they could not all be accommodated in the meeting room. 'Shopkeepers, artisans and operatives' made up the bulk of the attendees, although there were also 'merchants and manufacturers, and persons moving in the higher ranks of society'. There was little doubt, however, that the driving force of protest was supplied by the Radicals. Elijah Dixon was prominent among them, along with Richard Potter and Peter Candelet, and for the time being at least the Radicals were prepared to co-operate with moderate reformers such as Archibald Prentice, who generally aligned with the Whigs.

Paper money, high taxes and monopolies were blamed by various speakers. Prentice, however, brought the meeting back to the evils of the Corn Laws, and in this he was supported by Elijah, who illustrated the effects of starving out workers with an example which anticipated more recent migrations. The Pasha of Egypt, he told the meeting, was busy recruiting weavers from Manchester to work in Egyptian mills, at wages far above what they could earn in England. Elijah, never out of his depth, in even the most subtle economic arguments, made other contributions suggesting that a currency not backed by gold, issued by reckless wartime governments, was responsible for high taxation. This particular meeting ended with unanimously agreed resolutions being forwarded to Parliament, but Peter Candelet let it slip that it had been agreed by the requisitioners that parliamentary reform was not an object of the meeting. The Radicals were still hopeful that events in Westminster would produce fundamental reform in the electoral system. They were to be disappointed, and the alliance of moderate reformers and Radicals was to be short-lived.

Early in 1830, Whig grandee Lord John Russell had proposed the enfranchisement of Manchester, Leeds and Birmingham by re-distributing the seats of corrupt boroughs.[1] Even this was rejected by parliament. However, the death of George IV in June prompted a general election, the result of which was the return of a number of Tory members, sympathetic to limited reform. At last reform as an idea was becoming respectable, and pressure was stepped up throughout the country.

That summer, Manchester hurled its weight behind the reform cause. Nothing demonstrated the shift of opinion more than the events of 16 August 1830, when Henry Hunt visited the town on the eleventh anniversary of Peterloo. The authorities kept a low profile, and big crowds cheered Hunt and leading reformers, including Candelet, Rowland Detrosier and the Rev James Scholefield, as they processed to St Peter's Field in landaus. David McWilliams acted as a *fugelman* on one of the landaus. Like Peterloo itself it was the sort of event that participants would one day recall to their grandchildren, proudly asserting, 'I was there.'

A day of rousing speeches concluded with a dinner at Salford Town Hall, and from the report given by the *Courier* it seems that Elijah was called upon to propose a vote of thanks to Hunt. At least he made 'a very long speech' immediately after Hunt, the *Courier* commenting that it 'would not interest our readers' (!). Before the dinner, the organising committee had proposed that only non-alcoholic drinks should be consumed, anticipating perhaps the many toasts that were to be made, and mindful of the festive atmosphere which had prevailed throughout the day. There is no record of Elijah's contribution to this discussion. He was a staunch abstainer, and went on to be an advocate of temperance, but he was also a believer in tolerance and, in the end, alcohol was made available. This might have explained why, for all its lofty intent, the meeting descended into an acrimonious squabble after the contrary Prentice had objected to Hunt proposing a toast to the principles of Tom Paine, another atheist.

The fact remained that the Tory Prime Minister, the Duke of Wellington, was absolutely opposed to reform and his influence undoubtedly encouraged die-hard resistance in both houses of Parliament. Moreover, only fifteen years after Waterloo he was still hugely popular, and on 15 September 1830 he took part in ceremonies to mark the opening of the Liverpool and Manchester Railway. Some estimates put the crowds (not all of them cheering) along the length of the line as high as half a million.

The railway link to Liverpool represented a major technological leap for Manchester. It presaged a national mania for railway building, and a huge boost to the town's economy - even if the writing was on the wall for carriers like the

Rochdale Canal Company, which, 25 years earlier, had celebrated the opening of the new cut alongside Murray's mill, as the band played within earshot of Elijah's home.

There were, however, spectres at the feast. The 'Iron Duke' travelled to Manchester on one of the eight east-bound trains from Liverpool, only to witness the first fatal accident on a public railway. The duke was travelling in a special train, hauled by the locomotive *Northumbrian*, driven along one line by George Stephenson. Liverpool Member of Parliament William Huskisson, a passenger in one of the trains on the adjacent line, ignored advice not to alight, while the engines were taking on coke and water at Parkside (close to modern-day Newton-le-Willows). He walked up to the duke's special coach, but was hit by another train, hauled by Stephenson's famous *Rocket* and driven by Joseph Locke. Huskisson's left leg was badly mangled and, despite being taken to Eccles where surgeons had been sent for, died later that day. It was a tragedy in more than one sense. A few years earlier, as an enlightened Tory and President of the Board of Trade, Huskisson had attempted to introduce a sliding scale on corn duties which would have ameliorated the harsh effect of the Corn Laws on the price of bread, only to be thwarted by Wellington himself, then a minister, but soon to become Prime Minister.

In the sombre mood which followed the accident, Wellington cut short his visit to Manchester, but not before he had been booed and hissed as his train, subjected to a fusillade of stones and rotten vegetables, arrived late at Liverpool Road station. Elijah would not have approved of that sort of thing. He would, however, have had nothing but sympathy and admiration for the brave weaver of Eccles, who, dressed in rags and tatters, dragged his loom onto a lineside embankment in order to draw attention to the starvation wages of Lancashire handloom weavers. History does not record the noble duke's reaction. He was no doubt shocked and preoccupied by the horrific accident at Parkside and disposed to avert his gaze. Indeed, sensing the hostility towards him, and perhaps responding to concerns for his safety, Wellington stayed in his coach and after an hour or so was taken back to Liverpool, while the rest of the VIPs sat down to a grand dinner in Manchester.

The new railway, however, had another more favourable unintended consequence. Near the scene of the accident, the line bisected the small, scattered hamlet of Newton (for the first few months the only official stopping place), a feudal entity still represented by *two* Members of Parliament. For future travellers pausing here, the contrast with the growing town of Manchester, bereft of representation except through the Palatine county of Lancashire could not be more obvious – nor outrageous. Passengers, especially those in roofless coaches, might also have been irked by the fact that the initial requirement for steam locomotives to burn smokeless fuel such as coke (dating from rules in the Rainhill Trials of 1829) would eventually be dropped, thereby licensing the steam locomotive as a major pollutant for the next century or more.

In November 1830, Elijah was elected as a Council member of the Manchester Political Union. Intended to co-ordinate the campaign for franchise reform, the Council resolved to meet weekly at the Mechanics Institution. In the new year, Elijah was one of the speakers at a Town Hall meeting designed to put further pressure on Parliament as the reform crisis deepened.

Yet, even the Manchester reformers, hardened by persecution and inured to disappointment, proved to be over-optimistic as to the introduction and scope of franchise enlargement. In the summer of 1831, Elijah and Prentice clashed over who might be nominated as the Radical candidate in the new, putative constituency of Manchester. Elijah wrote a letter to the *Manchester Times*, edited by Prentice, which was reprinted in the *Leeds Patriot* of 16 July, nominating his hero, William Cobbett. Prentice disagreed in a good-humoured editorial. But the chance for Manchester to elect its own Member of Parliament was to be delayed for more than a year.

On 9 November 1831, the council of the Manchester Political Union agreed to tone down its demands, and passed a long-winded resolution agreeing not to oppose reform proposals, which 'though short of their own ideas of perfection' might one day 'lead the way to the peaceable adoption of measures which shall restore to the whole people their long lost rights ...'

Following wrecking amendments imposed on the third Bill by the House of Lords, in May 1832, a crescendo of agitation broke out across the country. In some towns, notably Bristol, there were riots. In Manchester, the Political Union called for non-payment of taxes, and yet another Town Hall meeting of 'highly respectable merchants, manufacturers and others' resolved to 'stop supplies' by withholding tax, and promptly despatched a delegation to London, with a petition bearing 25,000 signatures.

When, shortly afterwards, Elijah, described in the press as 'the representative of the working classes' addressed a gathering of more than 60,000, he sought to raise the threat level considerably, quoting from Lord Chatham: 'If the House of Commons is not reformed from within, it will be reformed from without, with a vengeance'. Elijah was making it clear that he – and those he represented – wanted universal suffrage, not a mere tinkering with the property qualification.

Yet the resolutions carried by the meeting did not match the rhetoric. Mandated to compromise by the MPU council, Joseph Johnson and Elijah were bound to accede to the demands of the moderates. Prentice did his best to ease their path, allowing that if stopping supplies did not oblige the Lords to back down, and all constitutional means failed, then it might be time to hold up their hands 'with something in them'. All stopped short of demanding universal suffrage, content only to deprecate the action of the House of Lords and calling, ambiguously, for 'the right of the people to have a full, fair and equal share in the representation of the country'. What most of those present did not know was that a few days before the meeting, a deputation of Radicals had attended at the home of Absalom Watkin, a leader of the moderates, to demand, as a price for their support, a commitment to universal suffrage, annual parliaments and vote by ballot.[2] Elijah Dixon and Thomas Potter (now detached from the Little Circle) were among the delegation, later referred to by Watkin in his diary as 'ill-looking, conceited fellows'. Watkin gave an assurance in terms which he confided to his diary were 'imprudent'. At the meeting, the Radicals were allowed to blow off steam, but no more. Inevitably, it was the Radicals who came to feel betrayed.

Alarmed by widespread rioting, but more worried about a run on the banks and a threat to swamp their lordships' House with new pro-reform peers, the Lords relented, but only after Wellington, amid speculation as to whether the military might take the side of the reformers, had circulated a secret memorandum, warning that further resistance would have revolutionary consequences.

Even so, their rear-guard action was successful in watering down Lord John Russell's proposals. The 'Great' Reform Act of 1832, was, in the event, the great betrayal. The right to vote remained exclusive. While it was extended to certain groups such as forty-shilling freeholders (men in possession of land worth an annual rent of at least two pounds), and those who rented property with an annual valuation of at least £10, the mass of the people remained voteless. And although the number of voters increased from 400,000 to 650,000, the vast majority of working men – and all women – were left outside the franchise. Indeed, in one very important respect, the Act was a step backwards. It specifically *disenfranchised* women, who up to that time had enjoyed the right to vote as forty-shilling free-holders. Within a short time, the Whig government, relieved that the threat of direct action had subsided, was confidently declaring the doctrine of finality; the Act, after all, was intended as constitutional perfection. In effect, the amended property qualification divided the middle class from the working class and ensured the continuance of agitation for universal suffrage in the shape of the nascent Chartist movement.

Yet the scale and scope of the first Reform Act did demonstrate that change might occur through political process, stopping short of revolution. Hundreds of rotten and pocket boroughs were abolished, and 130 new seats were created in England and Wales. Two of these were in Manchester. That appeased the middle classes, but for Elijah Dixon and his friends the struggle for reform remained unfinished business.

Chapter Eight

Camp Field

The Factory-Fiend in a grim hush waits
Till all are in, and he grins
As he shuts the door on the fair, fair world
Without, and Hell begins!

Gerald Massey (1828-1907), *Lady Laura*

Not even die-hard reactionaries, well-represented in the England of 1832, could have expected the Reform Act of that year to put an end to popular agitation. Elijah and the Manchester Radicals had already shown what might be achieved through a limited, property-based franchise as it applied to the unincorporated structures of local government. In the years that followed, they re-doubled their efforts to make the authorities accountable, and to challenge the power of the Manchester Church-and-Kingers.

Following the passing of the Act, the election for Manchester's first two Members of Parliament was eagerly anticipated by all parties. Local Whig candidate, Mark Philips, son of a prosperous merchant, was supported by a conservative faction of the town's moneyed class, with whom the Radicals had formed their uneasy alliance during the passage of the Bill. The Radical candidate was Elijah's mentor, William Cobbett, and supporters ran a lively campaign against Philips. Elijah was prominent in the Radicals' organised heckling at Philips's public meetings. They were incensed by Philips's refusal to support the effort of Tory Member of Parliament, Michael Sadler, to regulate hours and conditions in the factories, and Elijah clearly relished the role of spokesman. What distinguished the Radical caucus – Elijah, James Scholefield and James Wroe in particular – as men of principle, was that in spite of the fact that they personally qualified to vote by way of property ownership, they continued the reform campaign on behalf of working men who could never hope to qualify under the minimal provisions of the 1832 Act.[1]

At a meeting in front of the King's Arms, Great Ancoats Street, on 19 July 1832, Elijah tied Philips in knots in an argument over taxation. Time and again he denounced high levels of taxation, designed to reduce the national debt, for the disproportionate burden it imposed on the working man. How could this 'tax on labour' be justified? Philips struggled to give an answer to the question of why the debt had to be paid down. The *Manchester Courier* of 21 July reported a heckler's voice shouting, 'Why can't you rub it out with a dish-clout?' It was as pithy as the interjection when Philips expressed his qualified opposition to the slave trade, 'Do away with slavery at home. Never mind the West Indies!' Both Elijah and Edward Nightingale were adept at heckling, and there is a good chance that on both occasions the voice from the crowd belonged to one or other of them. The *Courier*, describing the uproar during Philips's 'catechising', reported that the meeting ended when he and his friends 'very prudently retired into the *King's Arms*'. Whereupon, the Radicals took over the meeting and made their own speeches. Not for the first time, Elijah, the 'cart-orator', had made his mark in the streets of Ancoats.

Elijah was indeed busy that day. Later on, he attended a Vestry meeting at the Town Hall, in his capacity as a leypayer. The meeting had to be adjourned to a bigger room, which the *Courier* reported was 'soon filled, chiefly by the working classes'. Elijah and James Wroe went to work with a vengeance. Seconding Wroe's motion to deprive the beadles of their process-serving fees, Elijah made a long, and, according to the *Courier*, 'violent' speech, although the details went unreported. It was the precursor to a co-ordinated attack on the customary remuneration of beadles and constables, in which Edward Nightingale, Elijah's future business partner, led the charge. The salary of the Deputy Constable, Stephen Lavender (who succeeded Nadin, and whose daughter had married Nadin's son Thomas) attracted much criticism and once again, Archibald Prentice stepped forward to propose a conciliatory amendment. The accounts were duly passed, but not before Elijah and friends had had a field day exposing the petty corruption, to say nothing of nepotism, presided over by the Boroughreeve.

At a Vestry meeting in September 1832 at the Collegiate church, Wroe and Nightingale, supported by Elijah, attempted to shed light on the appointment of 'surveyors' of highways, and their remuneration from rates levied on the parish. They proposed, as members of the 'Leypayers Association', their own list of surveyors to replace the incumbents, and again blatant corruption was alleged. Money was being spent, on Store Street, for example, to enhance the development value of land. Wroe accused the 'esquire' surveyors of allocating funds so as to 'improve and beautify the roads to their country houses and their town houses'. Elijah, referring to summonses being issued to enforce collection of rates, said that magistrates were being used as the instruments of 'tyrannical despotism', and on this occasion Prentice's efforts to find a compromise were swept aside by an overwhelming majority vote in favour of the Radicals' nominations. Some of the proceedings were rendered inaudible by the sound of an organ being played in the body of the church, and Prentice, never afraid to offend, was accused of having 'ratted' on the Radical cause. It was another example of the alliance between Radicals and middle-class reformers falling apart in the bitter aftermath of the Reform Act.

Elijah was at home in the rough and tumble of public meetings, but he was just as astute when it came to legalistic arguments arising from the widening of the franchise under the 1832 Act. There was an ambiguity in its provisions dealing with payment of Poor Law rates, so that more than 1,800 ratepayers challenged their exclusion from the list of voters. The Radicals suspected there was a plot to exclude eligible voters for non-payment of rates, and during a hearing at the Town Hall on 8 November reported in the next edition of the *Manchester Courier*, appearing alongside several barristers, Elijah put this to the Poor Rates Overseer, George Lings. James Wroe suggested that the rates had been artificially inflated to ensure non-payment and consequential loss of voting rights. The Overseer denied collusion and at the end of the day, the vast majority of appeals, nearly 1,400, were dismissed. If their appeals had been allowed, most of these putative votes would have gone to Cobbett. At a meeting two weeks later in Chorlton-on-Medlock, called to support Charles Poulett Thomson, the absentee Whig candidate, Elijah, Wroe and others were there to orchestrate opposition. Elijah scathingly referred to Thomson's spokesman, the Member of Parliament for Preston, John Wood, as 'the volunteer advocate'. In the event, Cobbett came bottom of the poll with 1,305 votes, and Philips (2,923) and Thomson (2,069) were elected well ahead of their Tory rivals.

The results exacerbated the sense of betrayal felt towards the Whigs, and increasingly the Manchester Radicals, including Elijah, came to feel that the middle-class mantra of Corn Law repeal was a wholly insufficient answer to the town's problems. Chronic and pervasive poverty in the slums, together with appalling conditions in mills and factories, demanded action, and the Radicals looked for allies wherever they heard the voice of conscience and reform. Complacent mill owners such as Philips were an obvious target, and it fell to privileged, but often highly-principled, Tory Members of Parliament to prick the nation's conscience by exposing the cruelty of life in the mills, focussing in particular on child labour.

No-one knew more on the subject than Elijah Dixon, and not surprisingly he threw his weight behind the efforts of Tory Michael Sadler to curb the exploitation of children. Sadler, an enigmatic politician, who had opposed early franchise reform, hoped to build on existing regulations, rarely enforced and easily evaded by employers. His Ten Hour Bill had the objective of banning the employment of children under nine, and limiting the hours of under-eighteens to ten a day. Opponents, using delaying tactics, contrived the setting up of a Select Committee, and while this meant the Bill was lost when Parliament was prorogued during the Reform Bill crisis, it ensured that the issues were widely debated when the Committee's report was published in the next session. In turn, its supporters in Manchester deployed the, by now, well-worn procedure of requisitioning the Boroughreeve to call a public meeting of electors, with the intention of petitioning parliament in support of Sadler's bill.

Alongside Richard Oastler and other speakers, Elijah addressed what the *Manchester Times* described as 'an immense meeting of the manufacturers, merchants, clergy and other inhabitants', held in the Manchester Exchange on 14 February 1833. There was unanimous support for the petition's agreed terms, and because Mark Philips was a known opponent of the Bill, it was decided to by-pass him by entrusting the Boroughreeve and the Senior Constable with the duty of delivering it to any Member of Parliament known to support it. *The Times* stressed that the assembly comprised 'Tories, Whigs and Radicals'.

Yet life was not all rough-house meetings and oratory for the Manchester Radicals. The relative independence that many, like Elijah, achieved through business ventures and shop-keeping did more than get them out of the mind-numbing drudgery that was the lot of so many operatives in the mills. It also meant that they were well placed to circulate information and ideas, and to propagandise for good causes. In this way, and in spite of setbacks in the late 1820s, Radicals helped bring about a revival in the Co-operative movement. By the early 1830s, the *Lancashire and Yorkshire Co-operator* was being sold by Elijah from his co-op store in Oldham Street, as well as from the co-op stores of McWilliams in Swan Street and William Willis at Half Street, Hanging Ditch.

Similarly, these Radical free-thinkers, whatever privations they suffered for their beliefs – and many suffered greatly – were not afraid to look outwards at injustices beyond the confines of Manchester, particularly in the direction of wrongs which had a direct impact on the lives of many of the town's citizens. Nowhere in England were the intractable problems of Ireland better understood than in the Lancashire towns of Liverpool and Manchester. Both had growing populations of Irish refugees from rural poverty. By the 1830s, there were at least 20,000 Irishmen living in Manchester, eager to right the wrongs, as they saw it, inflicted on the mainly Catholic population by the London government. Terrified of revolution in Ireland, the Whigs resolved on measures of brutal coercion in what amounted to a declaration of martial law.

The Manchester Radicals joined forces with the Irish to protest, and Elijah Dixon and Peter Candelet were among the proposers of resolutions passed at a large meeting on Camp Field, on 4 March 1833, addressed by Irish leaders. It was a sign of things to come, in so far as the 'Irish Question', as it became known, was to plague British governments throughout the century and beyond. Elijah was to have his problems with Irish activists in Manchester, especially during the Anti-Corn Law campaigns, but he appears to have been an early English convert to the cause of Irish independence. The *Waterford Mail* in its 29 March edition, reported on Elijah speaking in sardonic vein at an 1833 St Patrick's Day rally in Manchester. Acknowledging the concerns of English workers having their wages undercut by Irish immigrants, he stressed the real root of the problem was universal poverty for which landlords were to blame. Playing up his Yorkshire origins – and dialect – he hit upon a theme directly referable to his belief in Christian brotherhood; some might say the Irish could be left to 'eat taters and salt ... and red herrings', but if (here, allowance must be made for an Irish reporter's attempt to record Yorkshire dialect) 'our 'arts were sa 'ard as to let un die at the door, our noses are too saftish to do such a thing.'

Chapter Nine

Stevenson Square

Away from family responsibilities, and the demands of business, the 1830s was a time when Elijah threw himself into political activity. The battle to wrest control of the town from its traditional rulers was paralleled, as in the case of Manchester's involvement in the Irish question, by causes and crises which reflected a nation-wide challenge to privilege, and the established order.

The case of the Tolpuddle Martyrs became the greatest cause celebre in the early history of trade unionism, and in spite of their remoteness from rural Dorset, Manchester Radicals played a big role. Nothing illustrated the ruthlessness of the old order in defence of its privileges and its determination to keep the peasants in their place so much as the ill-advised prosecution of six agricultural labourers attempting to resist wage cuts. They had made the fatal error of administering oaths of loyalty, and the Act of Parliament relied upon by the prosecution – supported by Whig Home Secretary Lord Melbourne – was a response to naval mutinies at Spithead and the Nore in 1797. Following the convictions, and the sentence of transportation, protest meetings against the sentences erupted all over the country. Especially in the north.

In Manchester and other towns, after repeal of the Combination Acts in 1824-5, workers were better led and better organised; trade unions and friendly societies had become a fact of life. Prominent among their leaders was Manchester Irishman, John Doherty, who, in 1831, had founded a local branch of the National Association for the Protection of Labour. Manchester rallied to the support of the Dorset farm labourers.

In the meantime, on 25 September 1833 the Dixons suffered a poignant bereavement with the death of their youngest daughter Martha, from scarlet fever, aged 15 months. She had been named Martha, in spite of that being the name of an earlier child who had died ten years previously. Fate now dealt a cruel blow to the hope that this Martha would perpetuate the memory of her sister and mother as she grew. Her baptism at the Collegiate church only six weeks before her death suggests that the Dixons were prepared for the worst, as parents at the time were perhaps right to do. Little Martha, like her namesake and sister Eliza, was buried in Dr James Scholefield's chapel ground.

A protest meeting on behalf of the Tolpuddle men took place at the Every Street chapel, known as the Round Chapel, of Dr Scholefield, in Ancoats, on 7 April 1834. The building survived until 1986, and given its history and architectural distinction, it is a pity it was lost. Nothing has been built on the site, and the forlornness of its brick remnants set in green open space is sharpened by the uprighted gravestone recording the lives and deaths of Scholefield, his 'amiable wife', Charlotte, and five of the seven children, who pre-deceased them. The tragedy of infant mortality was not all that Elijah and Scholefield had in common. They were born the same year, Scholefield at Huddersfield, seven miles from Holmfirth, and his Bible Christian ministry was consonant with Elijah's own deep reverence for the Bible. Like Elijah, Scholefield was arrested for his outspokenness, and – perhaps according to the same religious articles of faith – his political activity embraced parochial issues and those of national and international concern.

According to the *Manchester Courier*, about 1,500 people attended the meeting in the chapel yard, including delegates from London and Edinburgh. The protesters were not only outraged by the harshness of the sentences, but also alarmed at the precedent the government had set by using the Oaths Act. The meeting heard that two men from Nantwich had been arrested under the same Act. Doherty made an impassioned speech in support of a motion to petition Parliament for remission of the sentences. Ever the pragmatist, Elijah seconded a motion dealing with oath-swearing. He suggested trade unions would be better to drop the practice altogether, leaving it to the likes of the King, 'to make a tom-fool of himself, taking an oath as a free-mason ...' He also took a sideswipe at the operation of the jury system in which labourers could not hope to be tried by their peers, and at the presiding judge, Baron Williams, who had 'preached up popular rights' as an advocate.

Even a national petition bearing 800,000 signatures was not enough to prevent George and James Loveless and their fellow labourers from being transported. But the protest campaign did not go away, and in 1836, all six were pardoned, through the offices of new Home Secretary, Lord John Russell. It took another three years, however, before they all arrived safely back in England from Australia.

The Whig government's crass handling of the Tolpuddle Martyrs, together with their response to other issues, dismayed the Radicals, who found it more difficult by the day to stomach their posturing as 'reformers'. The Reform Act itself had released a head of steam, but in respect of the great issues of factory conditions and poverty, and the need for further franchise extension, Whig governments of the 1830s seemed merely to prevaricate for fear of upsetting vested interests. Typical of their property-based outlook, they took pains to address the issue of compensation for slave owners when they abolished slavery in the colonies. It was disingenuous of Nightingale to suggest that the treatment of mill operatives was a form of 'white slavery' but the phrase was often repeated to discredit the out-of-touch Whigs.

No single issue illustrated the ambivalence of the Whigs, and the reasons for them being increasingly despised by Elijah, Wroe, and other Manchester

Radicals, more than their so-called reform of the Poor Law. True, reform – genuine reform – was needed, for it was obvious that existing law for poor relief, dating back to the Elizabethan Poor Law of 1601, was no longer fit for purpose. It took no account of the increase in, and re-distribution of, population brought about by the industrial revolution. Moreover, because of the increase in distress and destitution in the towns, the system of levying poor rates was becoming a growing burden on rate-payers – including the leypayers of Manchester – and it was this factor above all others which shaped the attitude of Whig politicians.

Their response became a blueprint for future evasive and insecure governments faced with difficult issues; the appointment of a Royal Commission. This was headed by Edwin Chadwick, born in Longsight, Manchester.[1] Chadwick, an apostle of the new school of political economy, personified the official mind in its most ruthless and impersonal form. The Commission's report formed the basis of the new law, which as well as being controversial, turned out to be impractical. Elijah and the Radicals used every avenue open to them to protest. By supporting opposition in Parliament, increasingly led by Tories, they began to acquire the description of Radical-Tories, and this confirmed their breach with middle-class Whiggery. During the parliamentary election of 1835, they took every opportunity to embarrass the incumbent Whig candidates, and from year to year, they hammered away at the issue at local level.

While Parliament was debating the terms of the Bill to amend poor law relief, a Vestry meeting, on 2 July 1834, signed off the year's accounts in a rare show of unity and good will. But this was not until Elijah, Wroe, Candelet and Prentice had taken the opportunity to complain, on behalf of Dissenters, at the amount of money applied to meet incidental expenditure of the Collegiate church – including altar wine – and to question its legality. Prentice, in typically obdurate mood, and contrary to the spirit of the meeting, proposed a motion to deprive the workhouse chaplain of his salary, but Elijah, reflecting on the fact that the churchwardens were about to lose their role as guardians of the poor, opposed him, supporting the original motion, proposed by the Boroughreeve, to approve the accounts. Rather than pursue querulous amendments, it was better that they should 'part as friends'. If the Whigs thought this outbreak of amity signalled quiescence, they were soon to be proved wrong. Elijah and the Radicals were merely keeping their powder dry, watching what was happening in parliament.

By the end of August, the Bill had still not been passed, and so it became necessary for the churchwardens to levy another year's rates. Two thousand people descended on the Collegiate church intending to take part in a Vestry meeting, during which it became obvious – as it must surely have been all along to Elijah, Wroe and Candelet – that the rate would have to be put to leypayers for approval, by way of poll. In the meantime, the meeting, after hearing speeches from Dissenters, including Elijah, and also churchmen, voted by way of an overwhelming show of hands, to refuse the rate. Polling was carried out over a seven-day period, at the end of which the Radicals were able to celebrate a tremendous victory; in a poll of 12,916, there was a majority of 1,122 against setting the rate. Votes registered on the last day of polling were decisive. At a Vestry meeting held two days before the polls closed, at which the interim returns were made available, the new fault lines in Manchester politics were neatly illustrated by speeches from Wroe and Elijah. Wroe heaped scorn on Whig-supporting, dissenting members of the middle classes who had chosen to abstain, calling them 'cowardly hypocrites', while Elijah praised the 'perfect fairness' with which the contest had been conducted by the 'Church party', extending his tribute to churchwardens and clergy.

The fall of the Whig ministry in the autumn prompted a general election, and in the meetings which took place in Manchester during the campaign to return Philips and Thomson, the terms of the Poor Law Amendment Act came under bitter attack from the Radicals. Justifiably so, for the Act resulting from the report of the Royal Commission consisted of a hotch-potch of high-sounding phrases, based on the flawed pseudo-scientific Utilitarian principles expounded by Jeremy Bentham, and the cynical but largely unspoken object of reducing the burden of poor relief on middle-class ratepayers. Its most controversial provisions, dressed up in theological justification, were intended to put the workhouse at the centre of the system. It abolished 'outdoor relief' (financial or other assistance which allowed recipients to stay in their own homes) in most cases and placed the administration of relief under a newly created Poor Law Commission and local Boards of Guardians. It was the conscious intention of the Act to make workhouses more punitive, more of a gaol than a shelter. No wonder its opponents took up the cry 'No bastilles!'.

The Act was also an early example of the perils of delegated legislation, in which the Commissioners were given wide powers, with little provision for parliamentary scrutiny. They were, in effect, given the impossible task of balancing provision for the needy, with the perceived need of deterring claimants. Putting into effect the Royal Commission's recommendation that workhouses ought to 'deter the indolent and vicious' by 'work, confinement and discipline', the Act guaranteed harsh conditions, including the separation of husbands from wives and children.

At a meeting held on 27 November, in the Manor Courtroom – adjourned to Stevenson Square as numbers swelled – the Radicals got stuck into what was seen as further proof, if proof were needed, of the Whigs' indifference to social justice. Impassioned protests were delivered by a series of speakers whose names read like a who's-who of Manchester Radicals, preparing the ground for their hero, Cobbett. John Fielden, now Radical member of Parliament for Oldham, led the way, responding to a self-serving speech from Philips by attacking the Whigs' sanctioning of the 'workhouse dungeon'. He reminded his audience that the Whigs had broken the promise made by Lord John Russell to introduce voting by ballot, and that they had refused to pass the Ten Hours Bill.

Following up comments from Fielden that the country could fare no worse under a Tory government headed by the Duke of Wellington, Elijah launched into another bitter attack on the Whigs. The people had been humbugged long enough. He cared neither for the Whigs nor the Tories, but at least the Duke of Wellington said what he meant and acted in a 'soldier-like way'. Elijah no doubt recalled the help he and the other Blanketeers had received from Henry Bennet in 1817-8, and, more recently, he would have been mindful that the parliamentary movement for factory reform was being driven by Tories such as Sadler and Oastler. The latter had also come out strongly against the Poor Law Amendment Act. Elijah's speech was punctuated by outbursts of cheering, but when he ventured to say he was prepared to vote for 'a decent Tory ... rather than any of your turn-coat Whigs', the cheers were mingled with hisses.

Elijah dismissed the hisses, and his speech and others that followed, marked the end of the uneasy alliance between Radicals and Whigs in Manchester. James Wroe described the Whigs as a parcel of 'truckling fellows' and reminded the crowd that during their ministry, 300 men had been transported for speaking their minds; a speech in similar vein followed from John Doherty. Once again, the Radicals had succeeded in disrupting, and then taking over, a meeting called by their opponents. Resolutions condemning the Melbourne government were carried by a show of hands, and the occasion was rounded off by a rousing speech from William Cobbett. The Whigs could win elections in the town – as they went on to win this one – relying on middle-class, property-qualified voters, but the fundamentally undemocratic nature of their position was glaringly exposed by events in Stevenson Square.

It was, however, as everyone acknowledged, no solution to the Radicals' predicament to join up with the Tories. The absence of a proper democratic franchise hobbled them at every turn. But now the massive wave of opposition being generated against the new Poor Law, in Manchester and other northern towns, was providing the numbers for a mass movement to secure the vote for working people. Over the next few years, feelings of frustration manifested at meetings such as this led inexorably to the formation of political organisations outwith the staid and cosy representation of privilege in Parliament. Although the People's Charter was not published until 1838, it was foreshadowed by the Radicals' continuing battles against complacency, and the sense of injustice expressed by William Cobbett, Elijah Dixon and others in Stevenson Square on 27 November 1834.

Chapter Ten

The Manor Court Room

The election in Manchester, which did not take place until April 1835, allowed plenty of time for the Radicals to campaign on working men's issues; factory reform and the Poor Law Amendment Act. It also guaranteed deepening divisions between them and the Whigs. Even a cursory reading of the speeches made by Philips and Thomson during this period chimes with the criticisms made of them by Elijah and others, to the effect that they were but party placemen, representing their privileged constituency of middle class voters, always re-active, and never pro-active when it came to big issues. Indeed, Thomson, with his aristocratic background, became a minister in the Whig government which succeeded Wellington's short ministry. This required him to re-submit himself to the electors of Manchester and, despite his unpopularity, he was returned with a comfortable majority.

Nevertheless, the Radicals, even though their voting constituency was excluded, continued to attend election meetings with the intention of embarrassing the main party candidates, Whig and Tory alike. Thomson was especially reviled, and his appearance at any public meeting was guaranteed to provoke a storm of booing, as when he spoke from the hustings on 7 January 1835, as reported in the *Manchester Courier* of 10 January. Likewise, Philips faced a barrage of crisply worded questions from James Wroe, covering abolition of the franchise property qualification, the Ten Hours Bill, disestablishment of the church, the increase in the size of the army, and the malt tax. Wroe was accused by part of the crowd of speech-making, but Philips's answers – an army of vacuous phrases marching across Manchester in search of an idea – were weak and evasive. When Elijah's turn came, he concentrated on the Tory candidate, Benjamin Braidley.

He led with a direct invitation to Braidley to oppose 'the abominable Poor Law Bill' and followed up with supplementary questions combining directness and forensic politeness. This extracted an unambiguous commitment from Braidley to oppose the cruel 'bastardy clause'. Subsequent questions were put by Elijah on inequalities in the remuneration of clergymen, the malt tax, property-based voting, child labour, patronage, and the hated Sturges-Bourne legislation of 1818-9. The latter had introduced a plural voting system, based on rateable value, allowing up to six votes for wealthy landowners, and making a formal distinction between deserving and undeserving poor, with the power to decide reserved for the clergy.

The questions amounted to a concise statement of Radical concerns and were diplomatically answered by Braidley. Although Elijah succeeded in his task of airing issues relevant to the unenfranchised poor, the answers elicited were also likely to have had the effect of switching support away from the Whigs towards the Tories. Elijah may well have respected Braidley as a 'decent Tory', but needless to say, the Radical candidate, Sir Charles Wolseley, was given an easy ride and lots of cheers.

Opposition to the new Poor Law, together with support for Sadler's Ten Hours Bill now became the central planks of the Radical platform. Because of the great number of provisions delegated to Poor Law local Guardians – and thereby to the ratepayers responsible for their appointment – it proved relatively easy to obstruct its implementation. This was another example of just how out of touch the Whigs were. Elijah and George Condy denounced the Act at a public meeting on 18 February in the Manor Court Room, calling for its repeal. Elijah also used the meeting as an opportunity to attack the burden of taxation borne by the working classes to support interest payments on the national debt. The meeting was, however, sparsely attended, according to the *Courier* of 21 February.

Not so a meeting, a few weeks later, in support of Sadler's Bill, which was now being promoted by another Tory, Lord Ashley, in the wake of Sadler's defeat at the hands of the Leeds electorate. It had, in effect, been defeated by Lord Althorp's wrecking amendment, further evidence of Whig duplicity. Richard Oastler, the Tory, received a warm welcome from the Radicals. Elijah's contribution was to suggest that ten hours was too long for a child to work, anyway. He suggested an Eight-Hours Bill, and for good measure lamented that English workers were obliged to work longer than slaves in the West Indies.

As with earlier comments made by Nightingale, comparing the lot of slaves in the Caribbean with that of mill operatives, these remarks by Elijah would have provoked an outcry from modern day audiences. Was not slavery arising from racial persecution so debasing of the human condition as to hardly warrant discussion in the same breath as conditions in Manchester? Was it not making light of a vastly greater social evil? In truth, the Radicals were offended by slavery as much as anybody. They supported the fight against it, but there was only so much they could do. By attempting to relieve the suffering of down-trodden masses in English towns they saw themselves as fighting their own battle against slavery, albeit in a different theatre of war. Moreover, the Whigs proposed to pay slave-owners £20 million in compensation raised from general taxation; that is, taxes levied in some cases on men being paid starvation wages.

In March, Elijah preached the sermon at a memorial service for Henry Hunt, who had died on 15 February. 1,000 people processed from the Major Cartwright public house in Ancoats, to the site of Peterloo, and thence to Stevenson Square, where two thousand people heard Elijah speak to the text 'Honour all men', from the First Epistle of Peter, chapter 2, verse 17. As was its policy (or so it claimed), the *Courier* did not report the words of the sermon in its coverage on 7 March, but had it done so the core of Elijah's Christian faith would have shone through the tributes. Hunt, said Elijah, had followed the example of Christ, suffering in a righteous cause which was part of God's plan. Many Radicals, including Hunt himself, had little to say for religion, and it was a measure of the esteem in which Elijah was held by the 'brotherhood' of Manchester reformers that he had been invited to eulogise Hunt on their behalf.

When Thomson became President of the Board of Trade following the election, the law required him to submit to re-election. The Radicals knew he would win, but they kept up the pressure. At the formal election meeting on 27 April 1835, James Wroe, Condy and Elijah turned up well prepared. Wroe, in fact, had no fewer than forty questions ready, and, incredibly, the Radicals were able to insist on their legal right to put them to the candidates. Once again, the Tories nominated Braidley. Wroe ploughed through his list of questions, and again, the main target of the Radicals' 'catechising' interrogation was the hapless Thomson.

When Wroe had finished, the *Courier* reported, 'Mr Elijah Dixon then took up the catechism'. As with Wroe, his questions were expertly prepared and concisely put. Elijah – again in forensic mode – focussed on an obvious piece of chicanery, in which Thomson was personally implicated, whereby the Whigs had deliberately selected out of date property tables to determine the register of voters. Thomson was forced to admit that 'mistakes' had been made. It was a rumbustious election which prompted the Whigs to launch a dirty-tricks campaign. They published placards falsely claiming that the Radicals had resolved to support Thomson, and Elijah was obliged to make a formal rebuttal. Worse, before the calumny could be scotched, Elijah was attacked on the Town Hall steps by what the *Courier* described as 'a mob of Irishmen' and had to be rescued by police officers.

Elijah, by now, was more of a businessman than a workman; more middle class than working class. Yet he remained fixed and firm in his commitment to social justice. In the tumultuous years of popular agitation that lay ahead, he never wavered from his rock-solid faith in the brotherhood of man. As a matter of course, his life spoke in terms which honoured all men.

And, in the 1830s, Elijah had a lot on his plate; he was in his prime. Despite the ravages of infant mortality, by 1833 he and Martha had six surviving children, ranging from their newly born and last child Martha to their 18-year-old son Job. In business he was constantly diversifying, following up one idea, then another, sensibly moving out of less profitable lines, ready to seize on new ideas with a view to turning a profit. At the beginning of the decade, he was selling cardboard pill-boxes as well as groceries, and by degrees the focus of his enterprise shifted from shop-keeping to manufacturing.

As a shopkeeper, Elijah knew what people wanted. With a combination of shrewdness, business acumen, and powers of observation, he had the knack of anticipating the needs of a poor but growing urban population. Perennial ill-health of factory workers and their families, unable to pay doctors, created an infinite demand for cures and tonics for common ailments. By the end of the decade, in addition to pill-boxes, Elijah was involved in making wooden syringes (of the ear-clearing kind) and diachylon, an early form of sticking plaster. Wherever possible, he involved family members and fellow Radicals.

Elijah's partnership with friend and fellow Radical David Ridgway, probably formed in late 1833, was crucial. It was his first long-lasting partnership, focussed on selling sundry items to the rapidly-growing chymist (as then spelt) and druggist market, and, increasingly, in manufacturing them. Elijah applied his innate ability in chemistry to refine the process of plaster spreading, producing a better quality adhesive dressing. Also – and probably as a sideline at first – he began to make matches.

Match-making involved some similarities with plaster spreading.[1] The key, as Elijah was quick to grasp, was ensuring the right proportions of ingredients to produce mixtures that were effective, simple, and cheap. Soon, the whole Dixon family was involved in one way or another. Elijah was a natural talent-spotter; if a friend or family member came up with a good idea, he knew how to exploit it.

When, on 22 April 1838, Elijah's son Job married Matilda Marsh at the Collegiate church, his occupation was given as 'pill-box maker', and his place of residence as Newton Heath. Job's move to Newton, a couple of miles to the north of Ancoats, and still largely rural in character, presaged the most important move of all for his father's nascent business empire.

Chapter Eleven

Collyhurst Bridge

In the aftermath of the Reform Act, Elijah and the Radicals settled down to a determined guerrilla campaign against their betrayers, the Whigs, and nothing symbolised Whig complacency so much as the new Poor Law. The Radicals were determined to undermine its harshness, and if possible to prevent the new rules being introduced in Manchester.

This they partly achieved through their domination of leypayers' meetings. At such a meeting in the Collegiate church on 9 June 1835, attended by the Boroughreeve, Elijah, Wroe and Candelet turned up to ask about plans to enlarge the Manchester workhouse, still administered by the churchwardens. The plan to erect a sick-bay was approved in a show of what the *Manchester Courier* of 13 June described as 'perfect unanimity'. In a statement clearly calculated to contradict the principles of the new Act, the Boroughreeve hoped they were all in agreement with the desirability of making the poor 'as comfortable as possible' in the workhouse, and the meeting concluded without a murmur of dissent.

Elijah rarely spoke of his own family's stay in the Manchester workhouse. Martha had been forced to take refuge there when her husband was unable to work – during his detention by Sidmouth in 1817, or possibly as a result of illness or in the aftermath of Peterloo. For all the family – Martha may have given birth to daughter Judith in the workhouse - it must have been a harrowing experience, and yet the meeting on 9 June 1835, with its talk of making its residents comfortable, suggests that it was managed humanely, at least compared to what was intended under the Poor Law Amendment Act of 1834. Built in 1792, to house up to 400 'paupers of all ages', a contemporary observer described it as 'spacious and elegant'. Its rules, made by Churchwardens and enforced by an Overseer, were read out loud to inmates every month, and included provision for corporal punishment and confinement in stocks. Children were to be instructed 'in the arts of winding, warping and weaving'. Conditions were undoubtedly harsh, but by the standards of the time they might have been considered relatively benign.

Here, at local level, the campaign to obstruct the new Act was a perfect example of Radicals and Tories working together against Whiggery. Proposals to ensure that husbands and wives were not separated, and for the separation of 'lunatics', were discussed in a spirit of wishing to improve conditions, rather

than to make them harsher. The Overseer gave assurances that bodies of paupers would not be handed over to the medical profession for 'dissection' in cases
where other inmates or relatives raised objection. The new, so-called science of
'political economy', so much favoured by the Whigs, was being thwarted by a
united demonstration of common humanity, for which Elijah and the Radicals
were entitled to take credit. They would not allow the Manchester workhouse,
at least, to become a 'new bastille'.

Alongside Elijah's gradual move into manufacturing, an intriguing notice in
the *Manchester Courier* on 11 July 1835 suggests that he was wisely investing
profits, as usual, in land and property. The notice, appearing over Elijah's name
as the convenor of the meeting, invited 'all persons who have been members of
the Royal Oak Building Society' to make any outstanding claims on it. In what
was obviously intended to be a winding-up meeting, at the Soho Foundry in
Great Ancoats Street, Elijah probably intended to buy out the shares of disappointed investors in the hope and expectation of them increasing in value.
Radical politician, yes. Anti-capitalist, no. The shares may have been secured on
plots of land at Chat Moss – a faltering scheme which Elijah still nursed hopes
of rescuing.

In November 1835, Elijah's father, Job Dixon, died at Dixon Street, New
Islington, aged 73. He was buried in the graveyard of Scholefield's chapel in
Every Street, at great distance in time and place from his native Holmfirth.
His occupation was described as 'labourer'. Perhaps the slings and arrows of
the misfortunes he suffered after ruination as a clothier were compensated for
by the achievements of his sons in Manchester. He must have worried a great
deal for them over the years, but it appears that they, Elijah in particular, were
dedicated to caring for him in old age. He is invisible in the Rates Books for
Manchester after 1818, and quite apart from his name not appearing by virtue
of Elijah being head of household, there may have been sound and sensible reasons for keeping a low profile. The legal assignment in Huddersfield, although
it relieved him from the immediate pressure of creditors, did not absolve him
from liability. Far better that everything – especially growing business assets –
should be in the name of his son. Even so, there is nothing to say that Job might
not have been an influential business adviser in the background of Elijah's
ascent from rags to riches.

The sheer persistence of the Manchester Radicals had its effect in almost
every aspect of local administration. By diligent attendance at Vestry meetings
they mounted a campaign to rein-in old abuses and corruption in expenditure
on highway repairs. Meetings were held twice a year to approve accounts, and
no detail was too small for James Wroe and Elijah to question. On 30 March
1836, Wroe wanted to know the cost of flagging and paving land purchased
by the improvement committee, and Elijah followed up with questions about
the delay in, and expense of, repairing Collyhurst Bridge. 'Enormous jobbing'

had been involved in its erection, said Elijah, and it appeared that the burden of repairs was falling unfairly on the town. So too, at a meeting of leypayers in July, Elijah and Wroe attended to query Constabulary accounts, although, as in the case of Highways, they did not dissent from approving them. But even in low-key yet painstaking committee work, Elijah and Wroe could combine to get a dig in at the hated Whigs. In a Highways meeting, Wroe complained that they had given compensation to shopkeepers and publicans who had votes, while the poor got no benefit whatever, adding: 'the streets the poor have to go through are up to the knees in mud, while the others are well paved'.

Elijah had always supported the Irish cause, and the majority of Irishmen in Manchester supported the democratic causes espoused by the Radicals. But, following the attack on the Town Hall steps, Elijah's outspokenness once again attracted the hostility of Irish opinion in Manchester.

The trouble arose at an open-air meeting in Stevenson Square, on 20 June 1836, organised by supporters of the charismatic Irish leader, Daniel O'Connell. Specifically, the meeting was intended to encourage the Irish population of Manchester to subscribe to the Catholic Association, by way of the Catholic Rent.[1] The Association was a body founded and controlled by O'Connell, which had raised huge sums to sustain his campaign for Catholic emancipation, from penny-a-month subscriptions. The success of the campaign removed legal impediments to Catholics holding public office, and established O'Connell as a national hero. It did not, however, address the parallel issues of independence, electoral reform, tenants' rights, and – most urgent of all – the scandalous situation in which poor Catholic peasants were further impoverished by the imposition of tithes to support the established Anglican church. Naturally enough, O'Connell sought support from the Irish diaspora, particularly in Manchester's Little Ireland – overcrowded slums on the banks of the River Medlock – and it was, therefore, an issue on which Elijah felt entitled to have his say.

In fact, Elijah was more passionately opposed to the Irish tithe – to all tithes – than was O'Connell, and he was angered by O'Connell's apparent watering down of the demand for complete abolition. Following a backstairs deal with the Whigs, known as the Lichfield House Compact, O'Connell, hoping to obtain further concessions, was showing a willingness to consider appropriation of the tithes to other bodies. Elijah was already het-up about O'Connell's failure to support universal suffrage, his quiescence over stamp duties on newspapers, and his lukewarm support for the Ten Hours Bill. Accordingly, and courageously, he arrived in Stevenson Square ready to appeal to a crowd of 1,500 angry Irishmen to desert their hero.

In the event, Elijah was denied the opportunity to speak, after a show of hands called for by the chairman, John Brindle, an Irish attorney. From his own account, published shortly afterwards in the *Manchester Courier*, Elijah was embarrassed by the procedural wrangling, but without the intervention of the ubiquitous Archibald Prentice, he may have suffered a worse fate. Prentice, sensing the angry mood of the meeting, stepped in to re-state the question put by Brindle, because he feared it had not been heard, and Elijah was dismissed in a chorus of 'horrid yells, curses and threats'. There is no doubt that Elijah was incensed by his treatment, and it prompted him to make an angry, no-holds-barred declaration of his views, which the *Courier* published in full on 25 June. There were no soft whispers in Elijah's attack on O'Connell; he fairly bellowed it.

In his anger, Elijah failed to acknowledge that Prentice had probably saved him from being roughed up; had he gone on to address the crowd in the terms of his press statement he most certainly would have been. In calmer mood, he might have contented himself with a scathing debunking of O'Connell's unwise alliance with the Whigs, but not on this occasion. O'Connell was 'either wrong-headed or dishonest, or both'. He was not the 'immaculate patriot' he was made out to be. Moreover, the behaviour of the 'O'Connellites' (a large proportion of the meeting) was 'cowardly and un-English' and they were ene-mies of free speech. For good measure, he described them, 'both rich and poor', as 'misguided' and 'the most tyrannical and overbearing portion of the British community'. Prentice had surely acted in good faith to protect his old sparring partner in reform from the consequences of his plain-speaking.

However, Elijah was right to be angry with O'Connell's manoeuvrings on behalf of Ireland, at the expense of the English poor. He heaped scorn on O'Connell's support for a tame Factory Act, designed to scupper Sadler's Bill, introduced in parliament by Poulett-Thomson. With reference to O'Connell's fudging stance on tithes, he was 'Ireland's greatest enemy in the House of Commons'. Understandably, Elijah attacked O'Connell for supporting the Poor Law Amendment Act in England, while opposing similar legislation in Ireland. There was a strong suspicion that one way or another, O'Connell had been bribed. Once again, Elijah was re-stating his core belief in brotherhood. He reiterated his 'profound respects for the rights of all men'. Yet Elijah insisted he was proud to be 'an Englishman who would not allow his mouth to be stopped'. Whatever the threat – double irons, imprisonment without trial, mob violence – Elijah Dixon was never afraid to speak his mind. Moreover, Elijah's poor opinion of O'Connell was shared by the latter's illustrious fellow countryman, and future Chartist leader, Feargus O'Connor.

Chapter Twelve

Corn Exchange

Elijah and friends took every opportunity to contribute to Manchester's local democracy, such as it was in the late 1830s. Every piece of law-making by the Whig government in London was suspect, and the Radicals feared each initiative as an attempt to out-manoeuvre them. On the face of it, the Municipal Corporations Act of 1835 was an attempt to rationalise outdated local government by replacing the Boroughreeve, Vestry committees and Police Commissioners. It was consistent with the Utilitarian philosophy to which the Whigs paid lip-service, and as with the Poor Law, its advocates spoke in terms of 'improvement.'

Progressive opinion was, however, divided on the issue of whether Manchester should be incorporated. Abel Heywood and Prentice were in favour, but the old guard, including Elijah and Wroe, were sceptical, and feared it might set back the success they had already achieved in holding local officials to account.

From a modern perspective, the resistance to Incorporation must seem short-sighted, but it has to be seen in the light of contemporary conditions; the unrelieved poverty of working people, the further assault on them by the new Poor Law, and the determination of the ruling class to deny them the vote. Elijah's school of Radicalism could not accept that the Whigs were acting in good faith.

While pressure to incorporate mounted, Elijah and friends were busy holding existing bodies to account. Nobody could say that these Radicals were profligate with public money. Their own experience of authority had taught them to be wary of its abuses. The seeds of socialism may well have been sown in the mass movement for franchise reform which grew out of the turbulent 1830s and 40s, but Elijah himself never saw big government as the means of achieving social justice. Rather, he stood for accountable government, and while nobody could accuse him of shying away from big issues, he had a flair for nipping wasteful expenditure in the bud, by careful scrutiny of the accounts. For obvious reasons the Radicals were particularly vigilant when it came to the police.

So it was in July 1836, at a leypayers meeting, that certain items in the Constables' Accounts took Elijah's eye. He objected to an item of expenditure for compensating a householder whose property had been attacked when officers sought refuge there, pursued by a mob on St Patrick's Day. It was setting a bad precedent. In an equally querulous and slightly petulant mood, Elijah queried an item of £8 for police expenses at Manchester racecourse. Why should he, having religious objections to race meetings, have to pay towards them? After the Clerk had explained the good work done by officers in catching thieves and pickpockets, Elijah failed even to find a seconder for a motion opposing the expense. Then, in a flash of inspiration, he came up with a solution; he changed his motion to a suggestion that the racecourse stewards should be requested to foot the bill. It was carried unanimously, thus laying down a blueprint followed to this day for meeting the costs of policing large sporting events.

There was a much livelier meeting concerning policing in February the following year. It had been requisitioned, apparently in the usual manner, through the Boroughreeve and Constables of Manchester, with the intention of furthering a plan to consolidate the Day and Night Police and to amalgamate surrounding township constabularies such as Chorlton-on-Medlock and Newton. Again, a seemingly sensible improvement. But the Radicals smelled a rat.

First up was Edward Nightingale, who wanted to know why the requisitionists had not followed the usual practice of meeting to determine the agenda. Prentice and Elijah followed up by demanding that resolutions prepared by the requisitionists be read out straight away. Prentice wanted to import the provision in the Municipal Corporations Act which gave the vote to ratepayers at large, as compared with the £16 assessment which the Whigs had imposed a decade earlier. Elijah, apparently speaking on behalf of Newton, caused uproar by suggesting that 'the poor farmers' there could manage well enough without night watchmen, and insisted that Incorporation was irrelevant. The episode suggests that Elijah and Martha may have already moved to Oldham Road, Newton Heath by 1837, while Elijah still owned, or was renting, houses in Dixon Street, New Islington.

Nightingale best expressed the suspicion pervading the meeting. Was a consolidated police force going to be used to enforce the new Poor Law by investigating households, spying and snooping? Poor James Wroe, to whom this scenario had obviously never occurred, was put on the spot by the line taken by Nightingale and Elijah and had to explain why he had taken part in preparations for the meeting. It ended in a mesh of procedural points, with an amendment to Prentice's 'household suffrage' motion, proposed by Nightingale and seconded by Elijah, being carried overwhelmingly, and Prentice's motion being likewise defeated. The resolutions prepared by the requisitionists were not even put. Once again, the Radicals had demonstrated their hatred of the Whigs, their hostility to the new Poor Law, and their ability to disrupt proceedings in purposeful defiance.

The politics of police control was a hotbed of intrigue and alliances, in which Elijah was well versed, and the *Times* reported on deals being done to agree electoral lists. Given their stance on Incorporation it was hardly surprising that Elijah and Nightingale objected strongly to outlying townships, especially Newton Heath, being absorbed into a consolidated force. On Elijah's initiative, a

Tory-Radical list was drawn up in collusion with 'one of the most hot-headed of the Tories', George Peel. By this means, the alliance against the Whigs secured control of police District Number 1 (New Cross) and the 'more aristocratic' District Number 9 (St Ann's).

How Elijah would have missed such shenanigans had he turned his back on the town and gone off to till the soil and a life of quiet contemplation at Chat Moss! But conditions in the towns remained grim. Above the accounts of Incorporation and the Police Commissioners on the front page of the *Times* of 27 October, there was a briefer item which portended ill for the mass of Manchester's poor working people, the operatives, as the press liked to describe them, and their families. It read: 'THE PRICE OF WHEAT, not withstanding a large supply, was increased from 4s to 5s a quarter at yesterday's Wakefield market. There is very little doubt that, before Christmas, we shall have, in the present circumstances of the country, a famine price. When the mischief is done it will be too late to look for the remedy'.

In this context, the Radicals' preoccupation with the new Poor Law was inevitable, especially for Elijah, with memories of his wife and children's stay in the Manchester workhouse. As with the senseless slaughter at Peterloo, the Act was condemned by wide sections of the public, beyond the Radical caucus, but it was Elijah and comrades who led the campaign against it, with a series of meetings and denunciations.

At such a meeting on 1 March 1837, held in the new Corn Exchange, Hanging Ditch, shortly after its opening, Elijah laid into Home Secretary, Lord John Russell. As 'Finality Jack', the Whig minister who had pronounced the 1832 Act to be a final measure, he was a fitting target. It was a case of 'follow that', for Elijah's contribution was preceded by a passionate address from George Condy, who suggested that the government could only impose the new law on Lancashire 'with the aid of 50,000 troops'. Elijah stilled the wild cheering which Condy generated, and got the attention of his audience, by referring at once to the experience of his wife and children in the workhouse. Even as a guest of the king, in prison, he had 'been better provided for than inmates of the workhouse would be under the new law'. He focussed his attack on provisions requiring husbands and wives to be separated, and spoke contemptuously of Russell, 'the little lord', a disparagement, Elijah insisted, not of his lordship's small physical stature, but of his 'exceedingly little mind'. Would Manchester be willing to submit to such an Act? The answer came in a mighty shout from the audience, 'No, no! We'll die first!'

Reflecting his knowledge of the writings of Tom Paine and John Locke, Elijah accused the Whigs of breaking their constitutional contract with the people, which justified their privileges only when they accepted their responsibility to the poor. Wroe and Nightingale completed a comprehensive demolition of the Act, and Elijah followed by attacking the clause which imported the property qualifications introduced by the Sturges-Bourne Act, allowing the wealthy up to six votes in elections for Poor Law Guardians. It was a typical piece of Elijah mischief, preparing the ground, because soon afterwards, just as the meeting was closing, he seconded a resolution in favour of universal suffrage. Condy opposed it as being beyond the remit of the meeting, being supported by well-meaning Archibald Prentice, who once again braved the wrath of the meeting, only to be booed off. The resolution was carried unanimously.

Elijah, mindful of the behind-the-scenes manoeuvrings which preceded the February meeting convened to amalgamate the police, reserved plenty of ire for the local establishment which shared Russell's indifference to the poor. At a Vestry meeting in April for the election of Surveyor of Highways, and still concerned that too much money was being spent on roads in more affluent areas, Elijah complained about locals with too much power.

The effect of the Anti-Poor Law campaign was to re-invigorate agitation for franchise reform, and as Elijah and his Radical confederates had demonstrated at the meeting in the Corn Exchange, they would not let it be pushed aside. Along with persecution of trade unions, the Poor Law Act served as a reminder that power remained in the hands of the elite – an alliance of landed gentry and industrialists – determined to keep the poor in their place, and indifferent to their needs.

Through all this, Elijah was working away at expanding the manufacturing side of his business, still in partnership with David Ridgway, and focussing in particular on match-making. Years later, a fellow Radical and teetotaller recollected meeting Elijah in temperance bars when both men were 'on the road' as salesmen. Joseph Johnson (a younger man, not to be confused with his namesake in the Northern Political Union) remembered Elijah 'in his glory... surrounded by half a dozen commercial travellers, after a hard day's work... Bible in hand, expounding his favourite doctrine of Universalism'. According to Johnson in his *People I Have Met* written around 1900, Elijah relished such 'friendly' encounters, confounding 'objectors' with scriptural references. Cart orator, electioneer, fireside debater – you would be hard put to say that Elijah did not like an audience.

Chapter Thirteen

Carpenters Hall

And like the baseless fabric of this vision,
The cloud-capped towers, the gorgeous palaces,
The solemn temples, the great globe itself –
Yea, all which it inherit – shall dissolve.

Lines from *The Tempest*, quoted by Edward Nightingale
against Cobden's case for Incorporation

The Age of Reform, beginning at the end of the Napoleonic wars, proceeded at a snail's pace. Between 1815 and 1884 there were only two grudging enlargements of the franchise, and while from the 1850s onwards there was a general growth in prosperity, the 1830s and 40s were characterised by despair and poverty.

In the towns, especially Manchester and Liverpool, with their growing populations of Irish refugees fleeing rural poverty, life was made worse by overcrowding, and hastily built slums. According to the census of 1831, Manchester's population, estimated at 41,000 in 1774, had risen to more than 270,000 and conditions in working-class areas such as New Cross and Ancoats were almost certainly worse than when the Dixons arrived at the beginning of the century.

Even Benjamin Love, writing in 1839 in his *Manchester As It Is*, and inclined to see the town through rose-tinted glasses, was obliged to accept evidence of the Manchester Statistical Society to the effect that in 1831, more than 10,000 dwellings in working-class areas were 'uncomfortable', with at least 4,000 cellar dwellings, and an equal number of single room households. James Kay-Shuttleworth, however, a pioneering social scientist, on whom Friedrich Engels was later to rely to support his polemical revelations of squalor in working-class Manchester, painted a vivid picture of as many as sixteen people crammed into a single cellar, with back-to-back houses round courtyards used as pig-sties.[1] No wonder there had been an outbreak of cholera in 1832.

On top of all this, in 1838, the country was moving into a depressive trade cycle (which did not improve until 1842). In the same year, the repressive new Poor Law was implemented in Salford. Renewed agitation for franchise reform gained momentum.

Feargus O'Connor was already well-known to Elijah and comrades for his part in agitation against the new Poor Law, but it may have been at a meeting in the Palace Inn, Market Street, on 5 February 1838 to co-ordinate regional petitions against the Act, that Elijah first witnessed the legendary orator in full spate. A gathering of delegates during the day was followed by a public meeting in the Carpenters Hall, to which the press was invited. O'Connor was on good form – and so was Elijah.

No-one other than God Almighty, Elijah told the packed audience, had a right to impose starvation. Defending trade unions in Glasgow against (unfounded) accusations of 'assassination and murder', Elijah demanded, ' Are there no kings, no queens, no priests, that do it? No rich men that do it?' Confident that on the theme of murdering monarchs he held the audience in thrall, Elijah permitted himself an oddly extraneous sermon. 'When the great day of judgment comes, I pray to God that I may be their judge.' This indulgence, unsurprisingly, provoked laughter. Elijah, unfazed, solemnly exhorted the audience, 'Don't laugh. If the Almighty Being who gave me birth and organised my body and mind, speak the word of truth, I shall be their judge.'

The report of the meeting which appeared in the *Liverpool Mercury* was redolent of the caustic disdain with which the Manchester press had reported on the Blanketeers some twenty years before. O'Connor, Oastler and firebrand Methodist minister Joseph Rayner Stephens, the principal speakers, were described as a 'mad trio of agitators' out to delude the thousand or so people, 'the very off-scouring of the factories', who turned out to hear them. Elijah himself was dismissed as 'a person named Dixon'.

In their speeches at Carpenters Hall and the Palace Inn, O'Connor and Stephens modelled the template of strategy for the nascent Chartist movement. They talked of violent resistance, of the inevitability of 'physical force', without advocating it in specific terms. Typically, O'Connor fired up his audience with ambiguous oratory. The Poor Law Bill could have been defeated by 'two or three hundred thousand' knocking at the door of the House of Commons, adding, 'Physical force will come, as soon as the cup of suffering is overflowing...'

Stephens went a step further by localising the threat. 'Every Englishman becomes not an assassin, but a constitutional resistant ... even to the death, against every man who dares withhold from him the bread of which he and his household stand in need. I do not want the shops of Manchester to be entered; I do not want the mills to be burnt down; I do not want one set of the inhabitants of Manchester to be arrayed against another, but I say that if gentlemen will not take warning, they must be ready for the fight; I tell them that the whole of Manchester will not be worth twelve months' purchase if they suffer the... rules and regulations of the Poor Law Commissioners in this town.'

Businessman and shopkeeper, Elijah might have shuffled his feet a little nervously during Stephens' tirade. In contrast, sandwiched between the speeches of O'Connor and Stephens, Elijah chose his words more carefully. By inviting the judgement of the Almighty upon the murderous Whigs, he even stole some of Stephens' religious thunder. Moreover, as well as referring to the atrocity of Peterloo, he had the astuteness to illustrate his theme by reference to current events in far away Canada, where the British were putting down unrest by naval actions with licensed 'midnight assassins'.[2] There was, in fact, nothing in the *Mercury's* report to justify the averment that Elijah's speech was characterised by 'violent expressions' and that he, too, was mad. The description of his voice as 'one continued scream' would have been difficult to believe by those who were familiar with his usual measured delivery, as the man from the *Mercury* assuredly was not.

The meeting, and the reactions to it, manifested a sea-change in the nature of protest that was coalescing into the nascent Chartist movement. Given the obduracy of the Whigs, increasing unemployment and worsening distress in the towns and countryside alike, a mass movement of protest was developing across the country and, step by step, the first working men's party in the world was emerging. Because there was no give in the system, no means of achieving change democratically, it was inevitable that the sections of society represented by the *Mercury* – whom Engels was already calling the 'bourgeoisie' – were once again in fear of violent revolution. Yet what else could the Radicals do, other than to bring about a French-style revolution, which would make their rulers listen? If they could not win by argument, or through the ballot box, they were bound at least to make their enemies frightened.

In the meantime, the Whigs' presence in Manchester had been reinforced by a conspicuous rising star. Like Elijah, Richard Cobden was an in-comer, and indeed both men hailed from independent country stock fallen on hard times. Picture the scene, then, on 9 February 1838 when, probably for the first time, the two men came face to face. Again, the Whigs were intent on driving through their modernising agenda, and on this occasion the subject was the proposed Incorporation by way of municipal charter, and a root and branch reform of the old medieval structures.

Cobden was their champion, and at a meeting requisitioned by the Whigs in Manchester Town Hall, he was accorded a thunderous welcome. Reading through the closely-argued case for reform of the old feudal institutions, in a speech lasting an hour and half, it is hard to take issue with it. It *was* ridiculous that at the top of the ancient pyramid consisting of Court Leet and Boroughreeve, sat Sir Oswald Mosley, Lord of the Manor, now living miles from the town, enjoying the country air at Rolleston Hall, Staffordshire. Sir Oswald himself had made it clear that he wished to be rid of his hereditary responsibilities. It was equally absurd that the police and highways of a growing industrial town were administered by ad-hoc committees of commissioners and the Vestry; and that voting qualifications were anomalous and undemocratic.

But for the Radicals, on this occasion represented by Elijah, Nightingale and Wroe, the fact that an incorporated Manchester might bring into existence a more efficient system of government, while remaining fundamentally undemocratic, was an unacceptable diversionary tactic, bound to undermine their case. Cobden was concerned at the growing co-operation between the Radicals and Tories, and, aware of the Radicals' presence, went out of his way to provoke them. Only the 'vilest of the vile, hired by the stupid and ignorant Tories' could oppose the case for incorporation, he said. Reasonably enough, given this assault on the Radicals' good faith, Elijah sought to raise a point of order, but, according to the *Manchester Times*, he and the others were 'borne down by overpowering applause'. When Cobden contemptuously dismissed Radical concerns about the Tolpuddle Martyrs and the new Poor Law as 'ravings', diverting attention from the subject in hand, Elijah interposed with exquisite timing, 'Same as *yow* do!' he shouted so that everyone heard it.

Burly, strong-lunged Elijah Dixon, sitting near the front, was not a man to be silenced by force or guile. Cobden, clearly stung, affected not to know who Elijah was, but the remark, and other telling contributions from Wroe and Nightingale made the point that it was Cobden and the Whigs, not they, who were diverting attention away from the most serious issues of the day. Wit and wisdom were not, however, one-way traffic. Nightingale got carried away in a long, flowery speech, and when he began quoting from *The Tempest*, a wag told him, 'Sit down, Shakespeare!' Even Elijah must have joined in the merriment. And in the years ahead, when arguments raged as to repeal of the Corn Laws, Cobden got to know Elijah and comrades very well indeed. No wonder he once described all three members of this Radical triumvirate as 'low blackguards'! This was an era of hard-edged politics. Later, allegations were made that Radical disruption of Anti-Corn Law League (ACLL) meetings was financed by Tory gold. O'Connor and Nightingale, in particular, were accused of involvement, but not Elijah.

In May 1838 – six months after Queen Victoria's accession – a parliamentary Bill was published containing six points: a vote for every man over 21; secret ballots; abolition of property qualification; payment of MPs; constituencies equal in size; and annually elected parliaments. These 'Six Points' became shorthand for the 'People's Charter'. Its supporters were led by the charismatic Feargus O'Connor, and the document was drafted under the auspices of William Lovett's London Working Men's Association. The effect was to galvanise Radicals throughout the land and to prompt the growth of 'Chartism' as a mass movement which was to dominate the political agenda of Britain for the next decade. Throughout this period, the Radicals of Manchester formed the nucleus of Chartist agitation in the north.

As for Stephens, hell-bent on martyrdom, Elijah must have realised that the true purpose of his rhetoric was to stir up the authorities to act against him, and that his seemingly wild talk about resistance to the death was couched in vocabulary deliberately chosen to gain maximum publicity. Sure enough, in December 1838, Stephens was arrested on a warrant served by Bow Street Runners and charged with using violent and inflammatory language at a meeting in Leigh.

Had the facts which featured in the case arisen twenty years earlier, Stephens would have been charged with treason, and given the events in Newport only two months previously, where charges of treason were brought against Chartist ringleaders, Stephens was fortunate. He was equally fortunate in having the support of Manchester's Radical leaders, who ensured he was represented by counsel when he appeared before magistrates at the New Bailey on 28 December. Elijah and Nightingale were among those in court to give moral support, and they were joined by Richard Oastler. The case was adjourned and Stephens was granted bail, subject to the court being satisfied by sureties offered by Abel Williamson and William Willis.

Later the same day, Elijah and Nightingale were among the speakers at a hastily convened meeting of the Manchester Political Union in the Carpenters Hall. Nightingale and Elijah drummed up support for Stephens. The inherent tension in the Chartist camp, between those who foresaw violence as inevitable and were disposed to sabre-rattling, and those who eschewed even a threat of violence, came to the fore. Reginald Richardson's resolution calling for action in support of Stephens was met by an appeal to insert the world 'lawful', but the meeting was in no mood to trim. A subscription fund was opened, and the meeting ended with three times three cheers for Stephens. Yet, while the Manchester Radicals were looking to protect one of their own, they were also looking forward to participating in protest at a national level. The MPU was already selecting its delegates for the first Chartist national convention to be held in London, early in 1839.

In due course, the government's Corporation Commissioners sat at Manchester Town Hall to hear objections to incorporation and Elijah attended as one of the representatives of Newton. He may even have been involved, as a Tory-Radical, in the petition got up by the Tories against Incorporation. They obtained nearly 32,000 signatures, as opposed to only 12,000 in favour. That made no difference to the main recommendation of the Commissioners, and in October 1838, Manchester received its Charter of Incorporation. Chorlton-on-Medlock and Hulme voted to join the new borough. However, the Anti-Incorporators of Newton must have argued their case well, because the township remained outside the borough for the rest of Elijah's life, and beyond.

More than thirty years later, however, in a series of articles on the history of the town, an anonymous contributor to the *Manchester Evening News* in the edition of 12 December 1871 suggested that Elijah, Wroe and Nightingale had used dubious methods to achieve their aim. They had 'procured' canvassers to obtain signatures to an anti-Incorporation petition, amongst whom were two

Irishmen, Finney and Lonegran, 'whose doings ultimately brought the party whom they served into great disgrace, and form perhaps one of the most curious chapters in the whole municipal annals of Manchester'.

Although he was at home in the rough and tumble of Manchester politics in the 1830s and 40s, it is hard to believe that Elijah would have countenanced the employment of heavies to achieve political ends. Nightingale, however, might well have. Which begs the question; would Elijah have been prepared to look the other way, while Nightingale did the dirty work? Given the dearth of specific allegations to back up the anonymous charge, both men are entitled to a 'not guilty' verdict in the court of history. Whatever means were employed, Elijah and Nightingale fought a spectacularly successful rear-guard action against Incorporation on behalf of the township of Newton.

As so often with the imperious Whigs, their drive for efficiency was hobbled by circumstance, and a natural inclination on the part of opponents to cling to old institutions. They probably had no alternative but to roll out their reforms – as in the case of the Poor Law and Borough Incorporation – through commissions and locally appointed bodies, thereby giving opponents every opportunity for sabotage, and prompting Elijah and friends to join forces with the Tories, notably in defence of the Police Commissioners. Ironically, on 27 October 1838, the day the *Manchester Times* reported on the formal reception of the Charter of Incorporation at the Town Hall (with Prentice a prominent celebrant) it carried a juxtaposed report explaining the continuing role of Police Commissioners.

The first elections to the incorporated town council were held in December, those for New Cross Ward being conducted in a shop at 27, Great Ancoats Street. Elijah acted as checking clerk for the Radicals. Unlike the Tories, who boycotted the polls, the Radicals fielded candidates under the banner of the Manchester Political Union and fought a doomed campaign on Chartist principles. Wroe was among the defeated candidates and following the elections, a public dinner in the Abercrombie tavern was addressed by Elijah, as well as Wroe, Nightingale, Scholefield and Richardson. There were calls for ratepayers' suffrage and the election of municipal officers. The diners drank a toast to 'working men who so nobly struggle in the defence of local freedom'.

Chapter Fourteen

Walker's Croft

There's a grim one-horse hearse in a jolly round trot;
To the churchyard a pauper is going, I wot;
The road it is rough, and the hearse has no springs,
And hark to the dirge that the sad driver sings:
Rattle his bones over the stones;
He's only a pauper, whom nobody owns!

Thomas Noel (1799-1861), *The Pauper's Drive*

The arrest of Stephens had followed the first great Chartist demonstration at Kersal Moor, on 24 September 1838. The venue was still used as a racecourse, and a carnival atmosphere prevailed. Estimates of those attending varied between 30,000 and 300,000, but whatever the figure, it was a memorable event and a prelude to the National Convention in London early the following year.

The primary purpose of the convention was to facilitate the presentation of a Petition to Parliament, signed by 1.3 million people, but when the House of Commons voted not to hear the petitioners, the Chartists began to lose patience. Elijah, Nightingale and Wroe spoke at a supporting rally held in Manchester on 4 March 1839, dubbed by the *Leeds Times* as a meeting of 'Ultra-Radicals'. Nightingale in particular engaged in rhetoric intended to alarm, with references to 'physical' harassment of government which barely fell short of incitement to revolution. Feargus O'Connor was expected but bowed out through illness. Many Chartists saw the convention as an alternative parliament, and further support was expressed for Stephens.

However, although Chartism became the great crusade of the 1840s, it did not subsume other great causes. Radicals and trade unionists continued their campaigns against the new Poor Law and remained on constant alert as to the effects on the poor of changes in local government. In common with others, Elijah sensed that the middle classes were holding back on the Charter, using the scale of protest as an excuse to distance themselves.

This growing division manifested itself in the Radicals' changing position on the Corn Laws. Elijah and Nightingale, apparently in collusion with local Tories, determined on a campaign to disrupt Anti-Corn Law meetings, signalling an era of rough-house politics in Manchester, centre of the Anti-Corn Law League. They reviled the repealers' leader, Richard Cobden, now 'ennobled' as an alderman of the new town council. At a meeting in the Corn Exchange on the day after the Chartist rally, Radicals attended in force. Under the direction of Nightingale (still smarting from his 'Shakespeare' put-down at Cobden's pro-Incorporation meeting) they achieved total disruption. A week previously, the Radicals had forced an adjournment by 'disorderly interruption of the proceedings'. They had the numbers to replace the chairman with one of their own, a favourite Nightingale device. With one Pat Murphy in the chair, amid great cheering, they then carried a resolution supporting Chartist delegates to the National Convention. Once again, Archibald Prentice was on the side opposing Elijah, as were other stalwarts of the League with whom he had shared reform platforms; Absalom Watkin and James Hampson.

Henceforth, the ACLL campaign tried to keep Chartists out by making their meetings all-ticket, but clashes continued right up to repeal in 1846. On one occasion, in 1841, Chartists disrupted an open-air meeting in Stevenson Square by hoisting banners proclaiming 'Down with the Whigs' and 'No New Poor Law'. Sticks were produced on both sides, and some of the Chartists, disputing tactics with their comrades and clashing with the Operatives' Association, were chased out of the square and up Lever Street towards New Cross.

Given the eventual success of the Anti-Corn Law League, and its wide support among the Manchester Irish through the Operatives Anti-Corn Law Association, the Radicals' position seems difficult to understand. They genuinely believed, however, that repealers wished to draw off support from franchise reform by defusing the issue. In addition, they argued that bread made cheaper by imports might in turn prompt employers to reduce wages. Or, as Elijah and others believed, that repeal would not itself bring cheaper bread, but might, if English farmers were not supported, lead to higher grain prices. In the event, repeal did not bring immediate relief to the starving poor and came too late to prevent the catastrophe of mass starvation in Ireland during the potato famine.

Elijah and Nightingale, fast becoming a regular double act, weighed in once more at the annual Vestry meeting on 2 April 1839, reported in the *Manchester Courier* four days later. The ostensible business of the meeting was to elect Churchwardens, Sidesmen, and Surveyors of Highways, but Nightingale wanted to know what would be done – or not done – to thwart the new Poor Law. He invited those elected to 'resist, by every legal means, every clause which is not peremptory on them by law'. Elijah was out to attack what he obviously considered to be petty corruption in Newton, where tithes and poor rate levies appeared to show 'a determination that all public money should go through the hands of the Lancashire family' (the Lancashires, Philip, Samuel and James, were well-to-do stone merchants, builders and land agents in the

Newton area). Elijah put forward new nominations for Churchwarden and Sidesmen in Newton, after delivering a gentle reminder to the local clergy that it was time they took their civic duties more seriously. In fact, Newton had long had a different poor rate system from other Manchester townships, with a plot of church land set aside for tenant farming, the rental from which off-set the poor rate. When the land was sold off for building, the rental value increased, and not surprisingly, the Newton Overseers did not want to see their applecart upset by Incorporation. In the event, Elijah's nominations were unanimously accepted. It was another example of his attention to detail, his mastery of procedure, and the thoroughness with which he always prepared for meetings.

By the end of the 1830s, Manchester was in the grip of railway mania. The work of surveying and building lines to connect with Birmingham, London and Leeds was well in hand. Passengers could already travel to and from Liverpool and Bolton far quicker than by coach or canal, and a single locomotive could move the same quantity of goods as two or three hundred horses. There were proposals for more lines in all directions, and Elijah, the matchstick entrepreneur, stood to gain as much as the cotton kings from expanding markets. Railways would change the landscape of the town forever. For many, the great infrastructure of embankments, cuttings and viaducts, which survives to this day, defines the Victorian era. Demolition of existing buildings on a huge scale was inevitable, and although Acts of Parliament provided compensation for property owners, the poor, as usual, had simply to get out of the way. Elijah, at least, spoke up for them.

The Manchester and Leeds Railway Company naturally wanted to bring their line, still under construction in early 1839, as close as possible to the centre of the town. They were building a permanent way to a terminus at Oldham Road, but even before its opening in July, they had applied for an extension, as had the Liverpool and Manchester Railway at Castlefield, and the Bolton Railway, opened the previous year from Salford, the idea being for the three lines to meet at a mid-point. The advantages were obvious. Unfortunately, the Manchester Workhouse and the adjacent Collegiate church new burial ground at Walker's Croft were in the way. St Michael's new burial ground also was about a quarter of a mile to the east.

The ensuing controversy might easily have been avoided had the Company not been dead set on locating the new station at Hunt's Bank, to the east of the River Irwell, just within the Manchester boundary near its confluence with the River Irk. Had it been sited on the west bank it would still have traversed the cemetery, but much less intrusively. Which begs the question: was the Company's determination informed by backstairs political machinations aimed at keeping the station out of Salford, or was it taken purely on the grounds of there being more land available for platforms on the Manchester side? There were already plans for a new workhouse, but what would happen to the bodies at Walker's Croft?

At a leypayers' meeting in February 1839, probably prompted by Elijah, the churchwardens had resolved to send a deputation to London to oppose the Bill authorising the line. At a report-back meeting in May, in response to Archibald Prentice's belabouring the expense of sending the delegation, Elijah declared an interest: 'I have a brother buried there, and I cannot divest myself of those feelings of humanity which characterise civilised and savage men alike. That alone was the consideration which influenced me; the cost is nothing, the principle is at stake'.[1]

The brother referred to could only have been Isaiah, two years younger than Elijah; his death was all the more likely to have affected him, because it occurred so soon after the family arrived in Manchester. In fact, on 3 December 1801, Isaiah would have been buried at the *old* Collegiate church ground, not at Walker's Croft, which only opened in 1815. Did Elijah deliberately mislead the meeting for dramatic effect? Or did the inconvenient truth only dawn on him later, when statistics (including the opening date) were being discussed? Then he would have looked daft, retracting the solemn contribution which had established his *locus standi*. Harmless poetic licence in a good cause? More likely that Elijah's memory of events was hazy; it was over 37 years ago and in any case the old and new burial grounds were less than a quarter of a mile apart.[2]

The respectful silence prompted by Elijah's personal revelation can be imagined, but it was soon followed by the report of the Senior Churchwarden, George Clarke, on his delegation's trip to London to give evidence before the Parliamentary Committee. At first, leypayers may have begun to wonder what all the fuss was about. But soon they had every reason to be alarmed.

The Company had told the committee that it had no intention of disinterring any bodies at Walker's Croft, in that it planned only to 'go over the surface'; this after its representatives at an earlier meeting had stayed silent when anxiety was expressed about the possible disinterment of five or six thousand bodies. There were, in fact, at least 33,000 bodies at Walker's Croft by 1839, the majority buried at public expense – many no doubt, from the workhouse – known popularly but never officially as 'paupers graves', although there were family graves as well. Moreover, the company had deliberately misled the Committee so as to disarm objectors. Now they were making it up as they went along, giving differing widths for the strip of land that would be required, but admitting that the building of the line might affect land covering at least 5,700 bodies. Clarke was no fool, and he put it fair and square to the meeting that they would have no means of knowing how the Company would deal with the bodies once they had possession of the land and had 'put up their walls'. How could ground, hollowed by graves, support the weight of trains going 'over the surface'? And what about burials in future, in the remainder of the cemetery, amid the clamour of excavation and building work? And what about inmates at the workhouse, cheek by jowl with the building works, and later the railway? Suspicions were further aroused by the reading out of oleaginous and eva-sive letters from the company's solicitor, and the stage was set for resolutions renewing opposition to its Bill.

Elijah seconded the motion put by a Mr Statham, and both proposer and seconder sprinkled their speeches with Old Testament quotations and hell-fire damnation of the company's officers. Elijah attacked the promoters as 'base, unprincipled, money-loving men' willing to trample on the poor, to 'buy and sell them, living or dead'. Again, referring to the burial of his brother, Elijah chal-lenged the railway 'speculators' to envisage similar desecrations in Westminster Abbey. Nor would the well-off Unitarians or Quakers in Manchester permit the bones of their dead to be defiled by a railway running over them. In a speech, clearly unrehearsed, Elijah's anger was palpable, his words intoned with all the *hwyl* of a Welsh preacher, condemning the company's contemptuous attitude towards 'a parcel of paupers'. It was a clear case of one law for the rich, another for the poor. 'Be they who they might, let the men who attempt to trample upon these sacred remains beware of the consequences', capped with Biblical author-ity. Quoting from Genesis, Elijah insisted that the words of Jacob the Patriarch, 'When you go up out of this land, take my bones with you', were good authority for showing respect to the 'image of the Deity'.

James Wroe, supported by Elijah, launched a bitter attack on 'moneyism' and the greed of Company directors who showed respect for neither the liv-ing nor the dead. Would the directors and shareholders of the Company want to be disturbed, like the inmates of the Workhouse, by the passing of car-riages and the hissing and spluttering of locomotives? Wroe touched on the nub of the issue; the Company had tricked the town by refusing to meet its representatives in Manchester, insisting on dealing with concerns before a Parliamentary Committee in London, where the local delegation was master-fully outmanoeuvred.

Elijah and Wroe elicited both cheers and laughter by their merciless attack on the Company, but they knew that in the end, the line would go ahead. In fact, apologists for the railway were well represented, and even Statham acknowl-edged that it would benefit the town. No-one opposed progress, but it had to be executed properly and respectfully. In the event, the Company's assurances were generally accepted by all present – rather like the Pied Piper accepting the promise of payment from the burghers of Hamelin – on trust, in good faith, and with no means of enforcement. Elijah was right to say that the churchwardens had set a bad precedent by allowing part of the old church burial ground to be cut away some years before. The duplicity of the promoters ensured that it was too late to divert the course of the line, and the hollowness of their assurances was to be graphically exposed later.

Few people travelling by train to or from Manchester's Victoria station today have any knowledge of the bones under the tracks, or those that ended up in embankments or in the ground below the viaducts over the river Irk. Some, though, are aware of observations on Manchester life in the 1840s recorded in the classic work of Friedrich Engels, collaborator of Karl Marx. In his *The Condition of the Working Class in England*, written in 1845, Engels drew heavily on his first-hand knowledge of Manchester, recording facts – possibly in this case coming across the controversy in the *Manchester Courier* – on which both he and Marx later predicated the demise of capitalism and the birth of communism. Engels' post-script to the Walker's Croft debate confirmed Elijah's worst fears, and belied the complacency which allowed well-meaning, middle-class businessmen, such as Prentice, to be duped:-

'In Manchester, the pauper burial-ground lies opposite the Old Town, along the Irk … a rough, desolate place. About two years ago a railroad was carried through it. If it had been a respectable cemetery, how the bourgeoisie and the clergy would have shrieked over the desecration! But it was a pauper burial-ground, the resting place of the outcast and the superfluous, so no one concerned himself about the matter. It was not even thought worthwhile to convey the partially decayed bodies to the other side of the cemetery; they were heaped up just as it happened, and piles were driven into newly-made graves, so that the water oozed out of the swampy ground, pregnant with putrefying matter, and filled the neighbourhood with the most revolting and injurious gases. The disgusting brutality which accompanied this work I cannot describe in further detail'.

Later, in 1848, the Company purchased the whole cemetery site for just under £10,000. The church authorities promised to use the money to open a new burial ground, but never did, and in the 1850s the workhouse site was also purchased for further station enlargement. In the 1880s, Manchester Exchange station was built on the west side of the Irwell, actually in Salford, despite its name. As recently as 2013, during work on new roof supports for the Metrolink platforms at Victoria station, body fragments were found on land directly above the old burial ground.

Accordingly, and although many historians and economists argue that the paradigm theories of Marx and Engels were mistaken, we have Engels to thank for proving Elijah Dixon right. Except in one thing; even Elijah accepted the assurance of the Manchester and Leeds Railway Company that it did not intend to 'take up the dead', but only to 'rattle their carriages over them'. Perhaps, on a day when the navvies were busy doing their dirty work at Walker's Croft, the inquisitive Engels was bold enough to look over the wall, whereas Elijah never did. In spite of his love of literature and politics, it is unlikely that a copy of Engels' work ever fell into Elijah's hands – and anyway, it was not translated from German into English until after his death.

Elijah, in the meantime, developed and diversified his business, in a manner which reflected what today would be described as the acceptable face of capitalism. Profits from shop-keeping and dealing wholesale in provisions were ploughed back into new, more challenging enterprises. He began to recruit employees from beyond his immediate family (although members of the Dixon family were always involved) and so far as is known he was enlightened and benign, even, according to one anecdote, encouraging street sellers of matches by advancing them one shilling and a supply of matches. Competitive, yes. But never ruthless. Nor are there press reports of industrial disputes or strikes, or feuds or rivalries of the kind which led to some owners becoming objects of hate. Elijah's business partners were nearly always fellow Radicals, and neither he nor they would have contemplated desecrating a burial ground for profit.

Chapter Fifteen

St Ann's Square

While railway promoters earned contempt for their indifference to the poor, their achievements naturally assisted Elijah the entrepreneur to market his products – notably matches and medical items – as well as facilitating the supply of raw materials. He would therefore have welcomed the opening of the Manchester and Leeds Railway, from Oldham Road station as far as Littleborough, on 3 July 1839, still hopeful that the company would honour its pledge not to desecrate the graves at Walker's Croft.

The second half of 1839 saw repeated appearances by Elijah and Nightingale together at public meetings, defending the Radical cause, and – equally, if not more fervently – taking the fight to the Whigs.

A general meeting of Manchester leypayers in August, reported as ever by the *Manchester Courier*, brought the ambiguities of Incorporation into sharp focus. Thomas Potter, the Borough's first Mayor, who had sided with the reformers on many a platform, had declared the meeting to be illegal, and Elijah and Nightingale, joined by George Clarke, were incensed at the Corporation's attempt to levy the churchwardens for an expansion of the police force. Once again, the rough edges of Whig legislation provided hand-holds for its opponents. Parish officials were unconvinced that it was their legal duty to hand over funds already raised for relief of the poor to the new Corporation. Clarke and J.B. Wanklyn, Overseer of the Poor, put up a comprehensive case against meeting the levy.

The Radicals lined up their big guns to support the legal arguments. Powerful speeches were made by James Wroe and James Dyer, before Elijah and Nightingale were given the job of calling into question the proposed increase in police, or 'bluebottles', as Elijah delighted in calling them. Here again, it could be said that the Radicals were short-sighted in that they did not understand the need for modern policing methods in a rapidly growing town. However, and with good reason, their opposition was based on an apprehension that the new police force would become as politicised as in the days under Nadin and Lavender. Elijah concluded with a warning as to the 'impolicy of teaching policemen to use arms'. In the light of violent events in the decade of Chartism which followed (and, indeed, in much more recent times) the warning was prophetic, and neatly stated the need for the civil power not to be suborned by its servants. Once guns had been fired, said Elijah, the knowledge was very likely to be used 'to an evil purpose'. Nightingale echoed the warning by referring to a recent meeting at Every Street Chapel at which the police had intervened.

Manchester's second by-election, in the autumn of 1839, was again prompted by another step up the ladder for Poulett-Thomson, when the Whigs made him Governor-General of Canada. It was, no doubt, a fitting destiny for Thomson to take charge of implementing a colonial policy based on gun-boat diplomacy, of which Elijah wholeheartedly disapproved. When and wherever the Radicals met to discuss their strategy, it produced a result which underlined the reality of the Radical-Tory alliance. The compact over lists of candidates for Police Commissioners was now to be echoed in a parliamentary election.

The hustings erected in St Ann's Square on 4 September, for the nomination of candidates, were the scene of extraordinary events. It first appeared that Whig candidate, Robert Hyde Greg, owner of Quarry Bank Mill, Styal, was to be opposed by a Tory, Sir George Murray, *and* a Radical, Colonel Thomas Perronet Thompson. Greg was abroad, hardly respectful of the electorate and which fact gave rise to a subsequent call for his election to be voided. Among his supporters on the hustings were Cobden, Potter and Prentice.

From the beginning, however, there was obvious good will between the supporters of Murray and Thompson, among the latter being Elijah, Nightingale, Scholefield, Condy, Wroe and William Willis. Among Murray's supporters was Clarke, who had assisted Elijah in the Walker's Croft episode, Wanklyn, and Hugh Hornby Birley, a former Boroughreeve, now in his sixties, who twenty years previously had led the infamous charge of the Manchester and Salford Yeomanry at Peterloo.

Elijah, Nightingale, Scholefield and Wroe proceeded to ask Murray questions, in response to which, according to the *Morning Chronicle*, Murray's replies were to 'their entire satisfaction', although the *Liverpool Mail* thought that they were not quite to the satisfaction of Nightingale. Murray was evidently a genial man, and also having served in the army, there was much back-slapping between him and Thompson, the 'Chartist Colonel', as gallant brother officers. Condy gave a brilliant speech in support of Thompson, and when he challenged Cobden to say whether he could spin a cop of cotton, Elijah took his cue, interjecting, 'He cannot spin but he can *turn*.' The jibe created much amusement amongst the crowd.

Following the usual procedure on an inconclusive show of hands, the Boroughreeve announced that polling would begin the following day, but when the poll opened there was only *one* candidate opposing Greg – the Tory nominee, Sir George Murray. The Radicals, in an effort to dislodge the Whigs, had agreed not to nominate Thompson, and announced their support for Murray.

This early example of tactical voting nearly paid off. Out of a total of more than 6,000 votes, Greg scraped home by a majority of 140. The manoeuvrings, likely to have been orchestrated by Elijah and Nightingale as the Radical party's fixers, were far more than an expression of petulant resentment against the Whigs. In making common cause with liberal-minded Tories such as Sadler, Oastler, Braidley and Murray, the Radicals portended the re-alignment of English politics which was to occur in the next twenty years or so. Indeed, it was already afoot. When the tumult had settled, Elijah himself was to become, at local level, just as much a grand old man of the new Liberal party as was its leader, William Ewart Gladstone.

Even allowing for political pragmatism, Elijah's presence on the same platform as Hugh Hornby Birley, promoted from Captain to Major after Peterloo, must have been a hard pill to swallow. Might there, however, have been a feeling of Christian forgiveness in Elijah's heart, towards a man whose defence was that he was only obeying orders? And surely it was not he who issued the order heard by panic-stricken members of the crowd, as the yeomanry bore down on them, 'Have at their banners!'

If the Radicals were pleased with their performance in almost breaching the Whig monopoly of parliamentary representation, they suffered an unexpected setback in November, at the first contested election for 'councilmen' of the new Corporation. Wroe and Scholefield, who had been returned as Police Commissioners in the Tory-Radical list for Number 1 District, were defeated by Prentice and a fellow 'reformer' when they stood as candidates for the new ward of New Cross - very much, until his move to Newton, Elijah's home patch.

Letters printed in Prentice's own paper, the *Manchester Times* – an early form of election address – suggest a degree of over-confidence, and perhaps bad tactics, on the part of Elijah and Nightingale. Although they continued to apply their well-tried strategy of attending opponents' meetings to hijack the limelight by asking awkward questions and making long speeches, Nightingale went too far. He accused one of his nay-sayers of being a 'liar and a jackdaw'. A compelling argument against the Radicals was that a relaxation of the property qualification had increased the electorate from 300 to 800, and when the results were in it was obvious that Prentice and his running mate, John Swindells, had got most of the new votes.

Here was an early demonstration of another theme in the changing political landscape; it could not be assumed that newly-enfranchised voters would show gratitude by voting for suffragists who had helped them win the vote. Many, by virtue of deference or social pretension, were attracted by the respectability of the Whigs, and, indeed, by their conservative reform agenda, especially Corn Law repeal. Later, in more prosperous times, when the reform mantle had fallen on the new Liberal party, Elijah lived to witness the growth of working class Tories, whose emotions were more easily stirred – and whose votes were more easily won – not by the plight of the poor, or those to whom the vote was still denied, but by the derring-do of imperialism and colonial wars.

Many theories have been advanced for what most see as the failure of the Chartist movement, although this has to be seen in the light of the ultimate achievement of its objectives. For a start – and nowhere was this more the case than in Manchester – the determination of the Chartists to disrupt meetings of the Anti-Corn Law League was probably counter-productive. When the Corn Laws were eventually repealed in 1846, Manchester basked in a glow of righteousness and a gush of civic pride. Within a few years there was a statue to Cobden and an iconic building – the Free Trade Hall – to act as perpetual reminders of victory. Although Elijah, Nightingale and all the other stalwart veterans of the Northern Political Union were prepared to suffer – and had suffered – imprisonment for their beliefs, their tactic of disrupting ACLL meetings put them in a bad light. Once again, the press began to adopt a censorious, disdainful attitude, describing their entirely lawful, indeed cunning, interventions as 'disturbances' or 'antics'.

Nevertheless, Elijah and Nightingale knew their job, and were good at it. They were also brave. They made a typical appearance in tandem at a well-attended repeal meeting in the Town Hall on 19 December 1839. Anticipating trouble, a police constable was elected to the chair, and the organisers were ready for Nightingale when he attempted to make a speech early on. He was stopped in his tracks and obliged to give way to the anodyne Mark Philips. Later in the meeting, as so often, Elijah tried a different tack, deploying a bit of joshing with Cobden, whom the *Canterbury Times* described as a friend. After a tirade from Cobden, slamming profiteering landowners, Elijah wanted to know, 'What tempted you to leave the fields of your native Sussex, and come here to turn calico-printer?' It was a gentle dig, intended to break Cobden's stride, and like as not succeeded, although Cobden did not answer the question.

Press reports of the meeting mention only one other intervention by the anti-repealers in an effort to turn them from the business in hand. It came from Hugh Hornby Birley, who responded to what amounted to a chairman's interdict to keep discussion tightly focused on the Corn Laws. In an act of conspicuous bravery, Birley respectfully asked whether it might be difficult to separate this question from 'others of a political nature'. There were boos and hisses, and shouts of 'Peterloo!' He then sat down. Was this gesture in support of his old foes intended as a small act of atonement?

In October 1839, Manchester businesses had benefited from the opening of the Manchester and Salford Junction Canal, which linked the Rochdale Canal with the Manchester, Bolton and Bury Canal via the River Irwell. Although it subsequently became known as Manchester's 'forgotten' canal, as it was largely tunnelled over, it demonstrated that canals were still regarded as important, even into the railway age (indeed, the Bolton Railway, opened in May 1838 from Salford, was owned by the canal company). It was to be the last stretch of canal to be built in the area, however. Less than two years later, Manchester at last

got its through rail route to the north and east via Leeds, with the comple-
tion of the Summit tunnel under the Pennines, at that time the world's longest
railway tunnel. By then, the brutal truth of the company's actions at Walker's
Croft may have been out, leaving critics of the Manchester and Leeds Railway
Company to reflect that only the rich could hope to divert the unstoppable
march of progress.

Chapter Sixteen

Newport

I disapprove of what you say,
but I will defend to the death your right to say it.

Evelyn Beatrice Hall (1868-1956), biographer of Voltaire
(to whom the line is often misattributed)

As the movement to repeal the Corn Laws gained momentum, the Chartists changed tactics. By degrees they trimmed their case against repeal while continuing the ingenious strategy of turning up at meetings as an organised body to use the proceedings for their own purposes, stopping short of outright opposition.

Elijah's seems to have been the last Radical voice to be heard in wholehearted opposition to the repealers. Apart from the support received from the Tories in Vestry politics, and even, perhaps, feeling an obligation towards Hugh Hornby Birley, Elijah remained convinced that repeal and free market *laissez-faire* economics would expose the workers to greater privations. At any rate, a meeting of 19 December 1839 saw Wroe and Scholefield moving and seconding the resolution in favour of repeal, leaving Elijah to denounce it as a plot to 'gain the advantage in the mere exporting of cloth for grain, merely to benefit the manufacturer'. Birley was also present, but in spite of the apparent friendliness shown to him by those on the platform, there was little forgiveness for Peterloo among the audience. Some reports said he was hissed and heckled – an experience to which by then he was surely inured.

The tactics of the Radicals, who could nearly always command a majority at public meetings, was to append amendments about the Poor Law, taxation, and franchise reform to narrowly worded resolutions concerning the Corn Laws. The fact that Richard Cobden and other 'moderates' were now pushing for free-trade across the board, thereby encompassing abolition of the malt tax, was bound to have an effect on Wroe and Nightingale. Both had spoken against the malt tax, as an unjust levy on the working man's pint of beer, and Nightingale was a landlord. Pro-temperance Elijah could hardly be expected to follow suit!

Elijah was also fighting another, doomed, rear-guard action to maintain the residual power of the churchwardens and sidesmen in the face of encroachment from the new Corporation of Manchester. Cobden himself led the attack at the annual Vestry meeting in April 1840, hoping to dislodge the Tory-Radicals with his own list of Whig-moderates. Two-thousand people turned up at the Collegiate church, and from the beginning there was bitter argument between Cobden and George Clarke.

Once again, Elijah, Wroe and Scholefield represented the Radicals, and Elijah used the occasion to air his views in favour of universal suffrage by extolling the virtues of the parish system whereby men *and women* had customarily played a part in nominating lists of candidates. In effect, Cobden and the Whigs were making a concerted effort to end Tory-Radical control of the Vestry, and Elijah ridiculed their love of secrecy. The Vestry meeting was all that remained of popular liberty, he asserted. Not for the first time, Elijah's description of the Whigs as a privileged cabal had Cobden on the back foot. 'It won't do, Mr Cobden!'

One issue was the Whigs' determination to levy a precept on the poor rate to finance the new borough-wide police force. 'It will make the poor-rate bigger, thou thickhead!' Elijah told an unfortunate man at the meeting who had some difficulty understanding how the precept would work. On these occasions, very much on his own midden, Elijah could always be relied on to get a laugh.

But the Whig assault on the Vestry had the serious aim of pre-empting any further opposition to the Charter of Incorporation. The Churchwardens had already begun a legal challenge to the Charter, and again, from a modern perspective, it is hard to resist the Whigs' (already calling themselves Liberals) argument that this was a vexatious and pointless attempt to stem the march of progress. Even so, both Tories and Radicals were determined to die hard. Elijah's sardonic contribution was followed by Wroe, who made an impressive denunciation of the Whigs' 'petty despotism' and concluded with an invective against their support for the new Poor Law. At close of polling, there was a narrow majority for the Tory list.

Away from the parish pump, there was a steady improvement in organisation of co-operation which Radical and reforming movements could muster at national level. The railways helped, and so did the introduction of the uniform Penny Post, which together improved the level of communication between disparate groups. As conditions in the towns and countryside worsened, Elijah's participation in the rumbustious politics of the 1840s saw him involved in all the great issues of the day. It was a decade of meetings and demonstrations, strikes and lock-outs, and for those at the bottom of the pile, especially in Ireland, brutalised by the Potato Famine, misery, degradation and starvation. Little wonder that the authorities grew more fearful of revolution, much in the way they had reacted to distress after the Napoleonic wars, when Elijah and the Blanketeers had begun to mobilise public opinion.

An outbreak of disorder in South Wales hardened opinion on both sides of the class divide. Manchester Radicals flocked to the colours of John Frost and other Chartists sentenced to death for their part in the Newport Rising of

1839. It was, of course, no such thing, and when the facts of the episode came out, Elijah and friends in Manchester would have recognised similarities with their own protests as Blanketeers and at Peterloo more than twenty years previously. A show of strength – a crowd of three thousand people – had induced the authorities to call in the military, who opened fire; some twenty or so Chartists were killed but the blame was laid squarely on the ringleaders.

Frost, Zephaniah Williams and William Jones had been found guilty of high treason and sentenced to be hanged, drawn and quartered – thankfully the last occasion on which this sentence was handed down in England and Wales. At a meeting at the Olympic theatre, in January 1840, Elijah, together with Nightingale, Scholefield, Richardson, and Wroe, made speeches prudently disassociating themselves from the 'physical force' element of Chartism.[1] It was a fact that firearms had been discharged, and other weapons used, by demonstrators intent on freeing arrested leaders. Nightingale proposed, and Elijah seconded, a motion calling on Queen Victoria to exercise her prerogative of mercy. Elijah spoke to, and moved, a similar resolution at another meeting in Stevenson Square.

There was a national outcry; petitions for a free pardon were rejected, but eventually the Prime Minister, Lord Melbourne, announced that death sentences would be commuted to transportation for life. The episode damaged Chartism in more ways than one. It allowed the Whigs to drive a wedge between suffragists and large parts of the bourgeois class who feared that armed rebellion really might break out. It also underlined the simple, stark fact that no matter how a great a show of strength might be put on, the government had the guns, the troops and the law on its side, and would always be able to suppress dissent by coercion.

In some things, however, Elijah stood alongside the Whigs. Cobden, and most of the self-styled reformers, had supported the petition for clemency – including Members of Parliament Mark Philips and Robert Hyde Greg. And when bookseller Abel Heywood was prosecuted, Elijah took the side of his occasional sparring partner Archibald Prentice. Heywood was in trouble for selling copies of a pamphlet urging Bible burning, but Elijah lived out his Universalist Christian beliefs in the cause of free speech. Indeed, it must have been an irresistible opportunity to publicise those beliefs. At a meeting at the Hall of Science in support of Heywood, he saw the hand of the established clergy behind the prosecution and contended ('at some length' according to the *Birmingham Journal*) that it was not in accordance with the spirit of the Gospel. Elijah had a profound belief in religious toleration, but then – as now – it was not shared by everyone.

So, too, did the relentless campaign against the new Poor Law attract support beyond the Radical caucus. In calling a public meeting to oppose the government's continuation of the Poor Law Commissioners, Elijah's name appears in a long list indicating growing cross-party support, alongside that of his younger brother Hezekiah, by now firmly established as a bookseller and stationer. The names of Hezekiah and Heywood also appeared alongside that of Elijah as subscribers to an anthology, *The Poetical Works of Elijah Ridings*, published by William Willis in 1840, another example of Radical solidarity.

In the meantime, the Radicals refused to let the spotlight settle on Cobden's meetings, without illuminating the Chartist cause. Things got very rough indeed. At an ACLL meeting in March 1841, in the Town Hall, the Radicals turned out in force. Elijah, Nightingale, Scholefield and Richardson attempted disruption from the start, with the usual tactic of trying to elect their own chairman. Spotting that the Mayor, William Neild, was absent, seemingly late, Elijah and Nightingale gave a masterclass in tactics. Elijah proposed Scholefield as chairman, promptly seconded by Nightingale. They had no time for Thomas Potter (now Sir Thomas) assuming the right to deputise for the Mayor. That was a red rag to the bull as far as the anti-Incorporators were concerned. Amid growing pandemonium, Scholefield stepped onto the platform and then attempted to conduct the meeting by calling on Cobden as first speaker. In the end, the meeting got underway, with Neild, having now turned up, refusing to budge from his mayoral chair, but with Scholefield, sitting below him, as de facto chairman.

When at last permitted to proceed, Cobden gave a long speech, a closely argued tour de force of the economic case for repeal and free trade, referring at one point, in respectful terms, to the counter-arguments put forward by 'Mr Dixon' to the effect that the Corn Laws made little difference to the plight of underpaid workers. Elijah, diplomatically restraining himself from arguing in favour of import duties, spoke briefly on a favourite theme; the misery of the poor could best be relieved by levying a 'tax on accumulated property' in the hands of the 'middle and higher orders'.

This was hardly calculated to appease Cobden and his followers, who Engels described as 'the liberal corn law repealing bourgeoisie ... for whom nothing exists in this world, except for the sake of money'.[2] Unsurprisingly, within a few minutes, the hall was in uproar. When Neild attempted a come-back as chairman, by putting Cobden's motion before the meeting, Scholefield intercepted him by calling for a vote on the amendment, and then declaring the amendment carried. As the Chartists climbed out of their seats to invade the press table, the reporters fled, and so did a large proportion of Cobden's bourgeois supporters.

At the next big ACLL meeting in the Town Hall, in May, the 'Cobling Whigs' were better prepared, and ready for Chartist disruption. Men, handy with their fists, were recruited by Edward Watkin, a future railway magnate, mainly from Irish members of the Manchester Operatives' Anti-Corn Law Association – a body set up to recruit working-class converts to the cause, and successful in attracting Chartist supporters. In cahoots with the police, the organisers ensured opponents were kept out of the building. Those who did get in, among them Elijah and Scholefield (now apparently persuaded by Elijah's case against repeal) were roughly handled by the Irish lambs. When Scholefield proposed, and Elijah seconded, an amendment putting the case that repeal would do little to relieve distress, they found themselves in a beleaguered minority. Mayor Neild, firmly ensconced in the chair, still smarting from the assault on his dignity earlier in the year, was primed to resist any encroachment on his authority. With his encouragement, Elijah and Scholefield were shouted down, and when their amendment was put – and lost – those voting in favour were set upon. According to the *Northern Star,* it took Elijah a full five minutes to reach the platform, all the while being kicked and punched.

Cobden made another long speech, laying the current unemployment in Manchester firmly at the door of the Corn Laws, by promoting retaliatory tariffs against Manchester-made goods. Inviting members of all parties to join him, he again mentioned Elijah by name, hoping he would be their standard-bearer. There can be no doubt that Cobden's appeal to men of good will to sink their differences behind the repeal banner was sincerely meant, but that does not alter the fact that once they had achieved their objective, the repealers abandoned the Chartists – exactly as Engels, and Elijah, had predicted.

Chapter Seventeen

Clerkenwell

But waved the wind on Blackstone-height
A standard of the broad sunlight,
And sung that morn with trumpet might,
A sounding song of liberty!

Ernest Jones (1819-69), verse recalling a Chartist Camp meeting

By the time he was 50, Elijah's centre of operations had shifted to the area of Manchester now known as Newton Heath. Although retaining ownership of properties in New Cross, Ancoats and New Islington (with separate voting rights attached to each) Elijah was proud to describe himself as an inhabitant of Newton when he spoke at the annual Vestry meeting in 1839. And it was in order to preserve the accountable institutions of the ancient township of Newton that Elijah had fought to keep it from being incorporated into Manchester.

Only three miles from New Cross, Newton was still largely rural, and forty years previously, it would have been the last patch of farmland traversed by the refugee Dixon family as they neared the town. Farms and farmers thereabouts were also likely to have been known to Elijah, the milkman. The uncultivated heathland separating Newton from Manchester was an apocryphal haunt of highwaymen, and as recently as 1798 a gallows had been erected for a crowd to witness the last public hanging on the heath when George Russell was executed there on 15 September.[1] Now the heath was giving way to buildings of all kinds as the town expanded southwards. Paradoxically it was about this time that the village became known as Newton *Heath*.

Son Job seems to have led the exodus from Ancoats, described as a resident of Newton Heath in the record of his marriage to Matilda Marsh at the Collegiate church, in April 1838. In the census return of 1841 they were shown at Oldham Road, Newton Heath, along with daughter Martha. Next door was the home of three of Elijah's four surviving daughters – Judith, in her twenties, and sisters Elizabeth and Ann, in their teens. Both Judith and Job were described as 'pill-box makers' (later Judith was to describe herself as '*fancy* box-maker'). Brother Hezekiah, often listed as stationer or producer of account books, was an obvious supplier of stationery – receipt books, invoices, order forms and the like. Elijah was a stickler for paper work, reputed never to have destroyed a single business document.

Elijah stated that together with wife Martha, and second eldest daughter, Mary, he was still resident at 5, Dixon Street, Ancoats, on the census night of 7 June, but it was the rates book for August the same year that indicated the landmark development. A 'house and works' at Oldham Road, Newton, next door to Job's house, were shown as rented by 'Elijah Dixon and Son'. Josiah and Betty Wood were the owners of the works, formerly used for making glue, and a bleach works before that.[2] It and possibly the nearby cottages were known as The Cloughs, once belonging to the Collegiate church, and the home of a John Cloughe in 1636. By November 1843, five houses in Oldham Road were occupied by the firm, three of them in Job's name and one described as 'house and garden' for Elijah. They were also renting a house and stable on Mitchell Street, close to the Rochdale canal wharf. The tithe map for 1844 showed Job as the occupier of another plot of land west of Dean Lane, where four shops were later built.

The crucial moment in Elijah's business career came in 1841 with a partnership agreement, between himself, son Job, now in his mid-twenties, and Edward Nightingale, long-time comrade in Radical politics.[3] The agreement stated that the partners were to engage 'in the trade of plaister spreaders, Congreve match makers, Pill box and syringe manufacturers and general dealers'. In so far as it marked a commitment to mass production, it was a landmark event. By then Elijah and David Ridgway had been making druggists' supplies for at least seven years, so it is reasonable to assume they were already making a comfortable living at it, with profit to finance Elijah's and Job's £400 up-front investment in the firm. Accordingly, Elijah and Job were given credit – as against Nightingale – for that sum , expended on 'the engine, machines, stock in trade, tools and fixtures' they had already bought. All partners' personal expenses were limited to the princely sum of £4 per month – quite a contrast with expense account profligacy in the modern era. His personal motto, and advice to others, was said to have been 'Live on sixpence a day, and earn it'.

Up to this point, production of pill-boxes and plasters, also involving Elijah's family (especially Job and Judith), appears to have been carried on as a cottage industry at 5, Dixon Street and 3, Baker Street (Ridgway's address), nominally under the Dixon-Ridgway partnership. And even in 1841, Elijah was still listed as shopkeeper, baker and flour dealer at Dixon Street. These smaller, established businesses may well have been run by family members, including Martha, Elijah's brothers and children, and quite possibly Ridgway's relatives too.

With the formation of Dixon, Son and Co, Elijah knew he was on to something. Three days prior to the partnership agreement on 8 June, the dissolution of the partnership between Elijah and Ridgway was announced in the press, but there is no reason to suppose that the severance was acrimonious. In 1841, it would have been an understatement to say that the market for pills – and there-fore pill-boxes – was buoyant. Trade directories show that there were, by then, over ninety chemist and druggist shops just around the Manchester centre and they all needed everyday supplies. Even the Chartist connection helped; there were Chartists Pills 'guaranteed to avert much of the illness affecting the work-ing classes' – and to raise money for the cause. Elijah and Ridgway must have had a fair share of the market for their sticking-plasters, and there was clearly a ripe demand for boxes and containers for every conceivable variety of pills and potions that did not need bottling.

Not surprising therefore, after dissolution of the partnership with Elijah, Ridgway immediately set up as 'druggists sundries supplier' in another success-ful partnership which brought in his son-in-law, William Steele, and Samuel Mather. The new arrangements must have been preceded by detailed discus-sions between Elijah and Ridgway. For whatever reason, they had each decided to go their own way, though both set up in close proximity, on Oldham Road, Newton Heath, as contemporary trade directories show. At any rate, both firms carried on producing matches, pill-boxes, plasters, and syringes, although with Elijah listed in the rates book as owner of a house and works, his was likely to be a larger operation than that carried on by Ridgway, listed as owner of house and shop. Perhaps Ridgway was more cautious, less willing to take on the risks of production on an industrial scale. Likewise, it was Elijah who later diversified as a timber merchant, installing saw-mills, importing timber, and selling it on.

As if to reaffirm their friendship, on 29 January 1843, Elijah's daugh-ter Elizabeth married David Ridgway's son, Thomas, at St John's church in Manchester, witnessed by William Steele and Judith Dixon. For both Thomas and David, occupation was written as 'pill box maker', and for Elijah, father of the bride, it simply says 'same'. However, the marriage was to last less than six months; Thomas died of consumption on 13 July, aged only 22.

Flints and tinder-boxes of one form or another had been relied on for centu-ries. The idea of mass producing matches for daily use was, like as not, suggested to Elijah by his interest in all things scientific, and particularly chemistry. There were parallel developments in Germany, but the firm of Dixon, Son & Co, of Newton Heath, was the real ground-breaker in producing affordable matches for everyday use. Until the introduction of handy automatic forms of ignition, such as cigarette lighters, the box of matches was to become an indispensable commonplace, a feature of everyday life, and a necessity in every home. Within ten years, the product which was at the centre of the new firm's ambitions, the universally popular Congreve Match, was a market leader.

The inclusion of Nightingale, eighteen years Elijah's junior, as a partner in the new enterprise, was a masterstroke. Business partnerships were, and are, notorious for discord, disillusionment and ultimately dissolution. In contrast, Elijah and Nightingale, despite the age difference, trusted each other implicitly.

They had fought many a fray together, especially in the early years of Chartism, with Nightingale leading the attack, and Elijah following up his gambits, pressing home resolutions and disrupting opponents. Yet, they were very different in background and temperament. Not for nothing was Nightingale once known as the Dictator of New Cross. As landlord of the Sir Ralph Abercrombie tap room, he was street-wise, and had a reputation for protecting himself and comrades when violence threatened. Elijah, an ardent adherent to the Temperance movement, and deeply religious, moved in different circles and radiated bonhomie. In addition, he was naturally entrepreneurial, inventive and scientifically-minded. In their different ways, however, both men were tough, shrewd and clear-thinking, and it is a measure of Elijah's respect for the younger man that Nightingale remained a partner for the rest of his life.

The meteoric success of Dixon, Son & Co is both astonishing and ironic, given Elijah's continuing involvement in Chartism, and the generally depressed state of the economy. However, at a crucial period in the early progress of the firm, trade picked up, from 1843 onwards, and in so far as investment in timber, chemicals and machinery was needed, buoyant demand created favourable conditions for growth.

Nonetheless, Elijah continued to be active in Manchester politics. Inadequate poor relief was as urgent an issue as ever, and the conduct of the Whigs at the meeting in Stevenson Square still rankled with the Radicals. Elijah was among speakers at a protest meeting in Newton Heath, called to keep up the pressure. In February 1844, Elijah spoke at a Chartist meeting in Preston, still arguing that repeal of the Corn Laws would result in further wage cuts, and the *Northern Star* of 10 February reported that a show of hands demonstrated overwhelming support for him. The fact remained, however, that in his all-out opposition to repeal, Elijah was becoming increasingly isolated from the mainstream of Chartist opinion.

Elijah's difference of opinion on the Corn Laws together with increasing demands of business may help to explain his low profile during the wave of Chartist meetings and demonstrations in the 1840s. He may have attended, but appears not to have spoken at, the demonstration in Manchester on 27 September 1841 to celebrate O'Connor's release from York castle. It was a great, festive occasion, with O'Connor ostentatiously wearing a suit made of fustian, hard-wearing working man's garb, famously made in Manchester, soon to become the definitive Chartist fashion or indeed, a uniform of class confrontation. Nor was there mention of Elijah in press reports covering meetings during O'Connor's visit to Manchester in 1842, when O'Connor, who shared Elijah's antipathy to Corn Law repeal, laid the foundation stone of a memorial to Henry Hunt in the grounds of Every Street Chapel.

The rejection of the second Chartist petition in 1842 was followed by riots in Manchester, and a wave of strikes, notably in the Stalybridge and Stockport areas. These events, however, were more a direct response to unemployment, wage cuts and hunger, than an expression of political frustration. So too, were the Plug Riots, a milestone in the development of trade unionism in which striking workers removed lead boiler plugs to prevent factory engines being started up. For a time, the rawness of these confrontations eclipsed the demand for franchise reform.

While Manchester grew with astonishing rapidity, the progress of reform was characterised by surges and setbacks. The sudden death of James Wroe in August 1844 was surely felt keenly by Elijah. As with Nightingale, it must sometimes have seemed that these few doughty warriors in the Radical cause, a band of brothers if ever there was one, had taken on the world together. Outnumbered and overwhelmed by force on so many occasions, yet still able to argue their case, they remained fiercely loyal to each other. When it emerged that Wroe's widow and children had been left in financial distress, a relief subscription was organised by Peter Candelet, and the premises of Dixon, Son and Company was listed in the *Manchester Courier* of 24 August as among the collection points for donations.

Indeed, more fortunate than most of his Radical and Chartist allies, Elijah helped establish a network of mutual support for prisoners' dependants, much of this carried out through a Chartists victims fund based at George Redfern's Temperance hotel in George Street.[4] The Manchester Relief Fund Committee paid out four shillings a week to 'victims of tyranny', a provision, which had it existed thirty years earlier, might have saved Martha and children from the workhouse.

There was absolutely no question of Elijah pleading the demands of business as a reason to desert the cause, and his presence at the denouement of Chartism, which came with the fiasco of the third petition, in 1848, is a measure of the man. On 3 April, a week before a great gathering at Kennington Common, Elijah chaired an open-air meeting in London, at Clerkenwell Green. Given that Manchester was now connected to the capital by rail, Elijah most likely travelled by train. No record survives of his thoughts and feelings as he journeyed through the Midlands – probably as a passenger on the recently formed London and North Western Railway. As the train steamed south of Rugby at fifty miles an hour or more, from time to time running alongside or crossing old turnpikes and waterways, he may have recollected the same features – villages, grand houses, and boats on the Grand Union canal – seen in the cold dawn of a March morning in 1817, as the mail coach rattled along towards London. His journey to the capital as a representative of the Manchester Chartists must have been a lot more comfortable than as a Blanketeer prisoner of the odious Nadin, wrists and ankles chafing on double irons.

At Clerkenwell, there was another reminder of the Blanketeers, as the Chartists addressed their audience from a waggon provided by a sympathetic carter. Elijah had the job of reconciling two opposing lists for election as delegates to the National Convention, and of introducing Ernest Jones, the main speaker. According to a report in the (extremely hostile) *Morning Chronicle*, Elijah was known by – or introduced to – his audience as The Manchester Man. He was, said the *Chronicle,* ill at ease, 'grave as a mute at a funeral'. It turned out that he needed all his experience as chairman to keep order, apparently grimacing during the embarrassing speech of a precocious youth, full of 'juvenile bombast' trying to imitate Daniel O'Connell. There was also something of an O'Connor cult in the air. So as not to offend his hosts, and no doubt conscious of his role as ambassador for the North, Elijah acceded to a request to wear a pair of green spectacles in imitation of O'Connor's trademark gimmick. Elijah would not have approved of making a pantomime of such serious issues. Near the end of the meeting, after the singing of the *Marseillaise* and *Rule Britannia*, and notwithstanding undignified green spectacles, Elijah was called upon to deal with a sudden and unexpected challenge to his authority. A young and ambitious poet, James Elmslie Duncan, leapt on to the platform to advertise sales of his new edition of Chartist poetry, only to be stopped in his tracks by Elijah ruling that he was out of order.

The presence of Ernest Jones, may, however, have compensated for the vexations of youthful enthusiasm. Jones, an inspirational figure – and a far better poet than Duncan – was a rising star of the movement, as surely as O'Connor's star was in decline. Jones and Elijah probably met a couple of years earlier at an open-air Chartist 'Camp meeting' near Blackstone Edge, on the borders of Lancashire and Yorkshire's West Riding. Elijah was among the speakers from towns on both sides of the Pennines. Jones, standing atop a moorland boulder alongside O'Connor, gave a memorable address to at least 25,000 people. Speeches covered not only the Six Points but also ownership and possession of land, a mix of idealism and practicality which helped inspire the formation of the Halifax Building Society a few years later. Jones himself was deeply affected by his first meeting with Elijah and other northern leaders. And, as on the moors of Blackstone Edge, government spies were amongst the crowd at Clerkenwell. They would have heard Jones's ambivalent encouragement to behave 'peaceably', but if not allowed to proceed, to 'scatter the policemen before you like chaff before the wind'.

Again, terrified by events on the continent, and fearing civil disorder at home, the government of Lord John Russell prepared a show of overwhelming strength. In February, King Louis Philippe of France, faced with barricades and insurrection, had abdicated, before fleeing to England. And while a working class uprising was fermenting in Paris, English commander-in-chief Sir Charles Napier drilled his troops in public and put artillery in position. There were rowdy meetings in Manchester, where the authorities also struggled to contain growing Irish nationalism. Yet, for all the bluster heard on Kennington

Common on 10 April – and by now Elijah had heard more than most – there were 100,000 special constables on duty, backed by the army, to expose the ambiguous rhetoric of physical force as a hollow threat. In the end, the Chartists were not allowed to cross the Thames, and the petition was sent tamely over to Parliament in hansom cabs.

Jones was to become the last great leader of Chartism, the man who kept its ideals alive following the death of O'Connor. After Kennington Common, the authorities watched him carefully, and it was in Manchester that they arrested him for an allegedly seditious speech made days earlier in London. In all probability, Elijah was among the disappointed audience in the Oddfellows Hall, waiting to hear Jones speak, when news of his arrest was announced, on 6 June 1848. Jones served two years imprisonment in solitary confinement, and afterwards spent the final years of his life in Manchester. As a friend of Marx and Engels, he merged the ideals of Chartism with those of nascent socialism. Elijah's life was moving in an entirely different direction, yet in their idealistic support for co-operation and land schemes, they had as much in common with each other as they had with O'Connor.

It was Jones who was the driving force at a Chartist Convention in March 1851, which, in opposition to the failing O'Connor, confirmed a broad socialist programme for radical change; *The Charter and Something More*. The document added further points to the original Six, including state control of land, separation of church and state, universal education, development of co-operation, and democratisation of the armed forces. Elijah would not have demurred from a single one.

Chapter Eighteen

Newton Heath

It is a quirk of history that some episodes in Elijah's story came down to the world through an act of nepotistic journalism. The life of Elijah's nephew, William Hepworth Dixon, son of Abner, is almost as intriguing as that of his uncle. Born into poverty in Ancoats, in 1821, where his father lived and worked as a spinner, he appears to have been sent away from home to benefit from a private tutor, Michael Beswick, a relative living in Over Darwen near Blackburn. This begs the question, was this by act of charity, or was it paid for out of funds provided when the mysterious Dixon inheritance claim was settled? At any rate, early in his distinguished career as journalist and man of letters, still in his twenties, he wrote an entertaining article, one of a series, in the *Daily News*, published on 19 September 1850, under the heading *Mornings at the Mills*. By way of double coincidence, at the time William was researching his well-known book on London's prisons, published the same year, Ernest Jones was a prisoner at Tothill Fields – the gaol where Elijah was lodged as a 'guest of the King'.

In *Mornings at the Mills*, allowing for a fair degree of poetic licence, William reviewed his uncle's amazing business achievements in the context of changing times in Newton Heath. It was an area he remembered in romantic, chocolate-box images, where an ancient mansion lay 'buried behind the trees of a pretty orchard, and a variety of trailing plants – the pea, the woodbine, the garden rose, the honeysuckle, and odiferous shrubs…' However, and notwithstanding an undeclared family bias, the article also provides impressive insights into the rise of Dixon, Son & Company to a position of industrial pre-eminence.

According to WHD – Dixon's pen-name – the mansion described, formerly occupied by 'high dignitaries' of the church in medieval times, stood in the middle of the heath and had been converted into premises for Dixon, Son & Co's match-making business. The reasons for the success of Dixon's 'Lucifer or Congreve match' are described at length. They were safer than lighted spills, and infinitely more convenient for lighting fires, lamps and candles, than the tinder-box. They replaced 'the clink, clink, clink of the flint and steel, the smell of burnt brimstone, and having to convert your mouth into a blowpipe of the nasty tinder.' WHD goes on, ' On every side of you – in almost every incident of social and domestic life – the lucifer match plays its part'.

What a winner! For the firm and the people. 'It is these small things, not less than in great events and national works, that the full force and character of

modern civilisation are made apparent', William elaborated, expounding that
no longer were the wonders of science monopolised by the rich, but were now
available 'for the convenience of the masses'. William's style perfectly expressed
the hubris of mid-Victorian England; its limitless possibilities brought about
by railways, steam-powered factories, and colonial expansion; its reputation as
workshop of the world. As for Elijah, the self-taught chemist, whose genius had
created this particular wonder of the world, readers of the *Daily News* were
introduced to a man whose public image was very different from that of the
'ill-looking, conceited fellow' encountered by Absalom Watkin, or the 'cart orator' clapped in irons to the delight of the *Manchester Mercury*.

The entrepreneurial Elijah had not just struck lucky. True, he was not
the inventor of the friction match; that was laid claim to by John Walker of
Stockton-on-Tees. Neither was he the first to engage in mass-production, in
that the Germans were first. It was, rather, the combination of a scientific mind,
business nous and a network of contacts which propelled Elijah to riches. The
Dixon match established a reputation for safety and reliability. Its chemical
composition was not as explosive as Walker's early product. The secret was in
a precise mix of phosphorous and sulphur, fixed with gum arabic. Not enough
sulphur and the phosphorous ignited too quickly for the splint to catch light;
too much, and they would not light at all.

There was, however, an element of good luck. Competitors in Germany
– still a patchwork of independent and landlocked principalities – did
not have the same access to markets, either external or internal. Although
Germany was moving towards unification and a nationwide customs union,
its economy was still hamstrung by internal tariffs. This contrasted with the
free-trade philosophy which boosted British exports after the repeal of the
Corn Laws. Elijah thereby benefited from a change in government policy
that he had always opposed, and, though there may be other factors in the
matrix, there seems little doubt that the condition of the workers improved
steadily after 1846. By 1850, the price of flour was half that in 1840, and
cheaper bread meant more spending on items other than food; more consumer demand.

One factor which boosted demand for the products of Dixon, Son & Co, not
alluded to by Elijah's articulate nephew, was the increase in smoking. By the
1830s, cigar smoking had become fashionable among the wealthy, as snuff-tak-
ing declined, and in 1847 hand-rolled cigarettes went on sale in London. The
real boost, however, was to come with the Crimean war, when British soldiers
learned the habit from their Turkish allies and brought it back home.

As for William's visit to the mill, and assuming he would have been known by
– or made himself known to – his uncle, it was, perhaps, the canny Nightingale,
anxious to guard trade secrets, who made sure their visitor was not 'in the trade'
before admitting him.

By the 1850s the match-making and timber business at Newton Heath had reached a breath-taking scale, directly employing 300 workers in its large, no doubt noisy, steam-powered mill and adjacent buildings. Hundreds more families depended on Dixon, Son & Co, as work was sent out to local women and children to be done in their homes – much in the way that Job, the Holmfirth clothier, had put out wool to be woven in the cottages of the Yorkshire Pennines.

Average output, according to William, had reached 43 million matches a week, and the imagination of *Daily News* readers was further taxed by calculations to show there were 72 matches for every man, woman and child in the country, and that if laid out end-to-end they would more than circle the globe. A steady stream of carts, going to and from the factory and railways sidings and canal wharves, brought in raw materials and took out the finished product. Representatives of the firm – Abner Dixon by now among them – travelled throughout the land and abroad to secure markets and supplies, including pine trees from Norway and Canada.

They say nothing succeeds like success, and the progress of Dixon, Son & Co well illustrates the point. When the government resolved to showcase the best and most innovative of Britain's industry to the world in the Crystal Palace at the *Great Exhibition* of 1851, for which William Hepworth Dixon was appointed as one of the deputy commissioners, Dixon, Son & Co were prize-winning exhibitors.[1] For this honour they owed thanks, in part at least, to William for his laudatory article in the *Daily News*.

Central to the Dixon's exhibit was a safer match technology using amorphous phosphorous (the discovery of an Austrian chemist, Anton Schrötter) although it was probably some years away from commercial production. In March 1853, in the journal of the *Society of Arts*, readers learned in response to enquiries, that the firm was aware of the benefits of amorphous (red) phosphorous in eliminating the risk of 'phossy jaw'.[2] The cause of this had been traced to the inhalation of white phosphorus fumes and was a form of necrosis affecting bone tissue, especially of the jaw-bone. It often led to horrendous disfigurement and, if the affected bone was not removed, ultimate death from the failure of other organs. However, a couple of weeks after the first reply, readers were informed that Dixons had now overcome their technical difficulties, and that new, safer matches would be on sale later in the year. This was in stark contrast with competitors – some of them well-known firms – who continued to use white phosphorous for another thirty years or more; it was finally banned by law in 1906. Elijah was quite capable of doing the right thing without being made to.

Large scale importation of timber led to diversification beyond the fabulously successful line in matches. By the 1850s, Dixons were promoting themselves as timber merchants, with an eye especially on the growing building trade and so, indirectly, aiding the expansion of Newton Heath as a suburb. Their sawmills, originally set up to make matchwood, were adapted to produce sawn and planed timber by the yardage, which, according to a *Manchester Times* advertisement, was offered 'at prices equal to any house in the trade'.

When the historic Failsworth Pole, dating from 1793, was blown down by a gale in 1850, it might well have been a cause for celebration in the Radical camp. It had been erected, on a site used for maypoles since time immemorial, by Church-and-Kingers in an outburst of patriotic and anti-revolutionary zeal, and, to emphasise the point, an effigy of Tom Paine was burnt alongside it. Perhaps aware of the unfortunate provenance of the damaged Pole, Elijah moved fast. It was soon replaced by a new Pole made of sturdy timber supplied by Dixon, Son & Co. Some accounts claim the timber was taken from a ship's mast, not inconsistent with the omnipresent Dixon, Son & Co having procured it. The new Pole, bereft of any nationalistic or anti–democratic connotation, and consisting of 255 cubic feet of timber weighing five tons, was rooted ten feet into the ground (embedded in compacted stone), and stood 79ft 6ins above it, topped by a seven-foot brass weather-vane.

It should not be forgotten that this was still very much the age of the druggist, the line of business which provided the demand for some of Elijah's earliest enterprises. Populations, stricken by disease and ailments of all kinds, unable to afford doctors' fees, had to doctor themselves as best they could. Remedies based on old wives' tales from the countryside were being replaced by chemical concoctions, many of them of dubious efficacy, and some nothing but quackery. Advertisements carried on a single page of the *Manchester Times* for 4 January 1851 tell their own story: Respirators to cure Weakness of the Throat and Lungs; The Gout cured for a Shilling by Henry's Magic Pills; Mrs Johnson's American Soothing Syrup for Children Cutting Their Teeth; Manson's Enamel to prevent Tooth Ache; Ford's Pectoral Balsam of Horehound for Coughs, Influenza, Asthma, and All Respiratory Organs; Consumption Curable with Bufton's Cod Liver Oil; Preventative Lotion to address Manhood and the Cause of Its Premature Decline With Plain Directions For Its Perfect Restoration. And so on, more or less ad infinitum, thereby generating an infinite demand for pill-boxes. In Victorian England, an unhealthy urban population inevitably created a healthy demand for any product claiming to be a cure for common ailments.

The old line in pill-boxes expanded into fancy (trinket) boxes and packing-cases, as well as – of course – matchboxes. One of the new processes promoted by the firm was 'scale-board cutting'. Existing machinery, installed for match splint production, produced a veneer of thin timber when logs were turned against a long sharp blade.[3] The veneer would then be chopped crossways into strips, from which boxes could be made instead of card, or it would then be further cut to make the match-splints. By taking the veneer off before chopping down, it could be sold as scale-board, which was commonly used at the time for book-binding, picture-backing, or for hat-boxes. By utilising existing machinery and raw material it was an ingenious way of diversifying at little extra cost.

Now the mass markets created by the new railway system were generating demand for consumer items once beyond the reach of all but the wealthy, and Dixon, Son & Co could not have been more perfectly poised to take advantage of these new conditions. It was some time, however, before the infrastructure of Newton Heath was adequate to cope with the demands of mass-production. The Lancashire and Yorkshire Railway opened a station at Clayton Bridge in 1846, but it was a heavy haul for carters to bring materials such as timber into Newton Heath, up the notoriously steep Berry Brow from sidings in the Medlock valley. Likewise, Dixons were already market leaders by the time the LYR got round to investing in a station and sidings for Newton Heath, and they remained major users of the Rochdale canal well into the 1850s.

There were, of course, commercial dangers attendant on large-scale manufacture and distribution and one of them was 'long fraud', a form of dishonesty from which its modern manifestation – internet fraud – is directly descended. So it was that in April 1852 Dixons fell victim to Samuel Barber, whom the *Nottinghamshire Guardian* of 13 May described as a 'notorious swindler'. Barber, with the help of an accomplice, ordered consignments of matches to be delivered to him in Derby, which he had no intention of paying for. The matches were transported by canal, and when Barber was arrested, Elijah was obliged to attend court to give evidence in a prosecution for obtaining goods by false pretences. Bizarrely – and probably arising from a witness subpoena – it was midnight when Elijah learned that he was required in court at 11am the following morning, in Derby. He made it, somehow or other.

Barber was apprehended through the instrument of the Nottingham Trade Protection Society, and Elijah was no doubt grateful for their intervention. Later in life, relieved of the burden of day-to-day management, Elijah, ever a joiner of good causes, gave up his time to be president of a similar organisation closer to home - the Manchester and Northern Counties Wholesale Building Trades' Protection Association. When in February 1852, Elijah's birth town of Holmfirth was devastated by a great flood, Dixon, Son and Company were among those who promptly petitioned the mayor of Manchester to get involved in a national relief fund.

Success in business, however, did not detach Elijah from politics or idealism, any more than poverty, imprisonment, and bereavement had dimmed his passion for reform. As with other men of principle, who fared well in business, Elijah saw wealth not as a gateway to privilege, but as a means of putting ideals into practice. It also brought the opportunity to help others, including Radical colleagues who faced business failure. During the 1850s, echoing the procedure which had saved his father from bankruptcy – and by which he had extricated himself from difficulties as a flour dealer in 1831 – Elijah got himself appointed

as trustee in assignment for James Ridings and Robert Wilson. Given that trustees were entitled to derive reasonable remuneration for collecting debts owed by
assignors, this was another example of Elijah's dexterous entrepreneurship, and
anticipated a similar role assumed by son Elijah a decade later.

Elijah had seen how the noble objectives of the Christian land scheme had
enthralled congregations at Every Street Chapel in the 1830s, and how putting
those ideas into practice had been thwarted by hard times and the need for
action on more immediate issues. Now, like his mentor in co-operation, Robert
Owen, he had the breathing space to consider schemes which might still bring
about organic change in society. At the start of his seventh decade, Elijah Dixon,
cart orator and capitalist, was eyeing pastures new.

Before the fall: Hey End, Holmfirth in 2015. The Dixons' hill–side home looked down on the town, reflecting their superior status as clothiers.

Downhill: the Dixons' move to Hey Gap portended Job's ruin. Their cottage was just high enough to catch chimney smoke rising from the town.

Typical housing on Gun Street, Manchester, early 1800s. Many immigrants to the town had to make do with cellar-dwellings.

Post-haste to London at dead of night: Elijah and fellow Blanketeers, hands and feet bound in chains, had a rough ride.

MANCHESTER PUBLIC MEETING

THE public are respectfully informed, that a MEETING will be held here on MONDAY 9th AUGUST, 1819, on the area near ST. PETER'S CHURCH, to take into consideration the most speedy and effectual mode of obtaining Radical Reform in the Commons' House of Parliament; being fully convinced, that nothing less can remove the intolerable evils under which the People of this Country have so long, and still do, groan:— and also to consider the propriety of the "Unrepresented Inhabitants of Manchester" electing a Person to represent them in Parliament: and the adopting of Major Cartwright's Bill.

H.HUNT, Esq., *in the chair.*

Major Cartwright, Sir Charles Wolseley, Mr. Charles Pearson, Mr. Wooler, and Godfrey Higgins, Esq., have been solicited and are expected to attend.

(SIGNED):-

William Ogden, 26, Wood-street; James Broadshaw, 32, Newton-street; Wm. Drinkwater, 29, Loom-street; Thomas Bond, 7, John-street; James Lang, Spinning-street; James Rhodes, 46, Henry-street; Edward Roberts, 2, Ancoats-street; Timothy Booth, 1, Little Pitt-street; Thomas Plant, 18, Oak-street; James Weir, 11, Gun-street; Nath. Massey, 2, School-street;

CHAIR to be taken at 12 o'clock.

Manchester, July 23, 1819.

* The Boroughreeve, Magistrates, and Constables are requested to attend.

On the same day, after the meeting, there will be a Public Dinner, at the *Union School Rooms, George Leigh Street.*— Dinner on the table at 5 o'clock.

Tickets, 10s 6d each, including all expences, may be had at Mr.Wroe's Bookseller, Market Street.

Facsimile of the first August 1819 handbill requesting a meeting at St Peter's Field – the phrase 'electing a person to represent them in Parliament' was deemed unlawful by the magistrates.

Impression of shops on Great Ancoats Street, mid-nineteenth century. Elijah's first shop was second from the right, on the corner of Jersey Street.

Typical Liverpool train waiting to leave Manchester, about 1832 (from photo taken at Museum of Science and Industry, Liverpool Road, 2005).

Elijah's first shop in Great Ancoats Street; originally numbered 42, and now coincidentally the home of youth charity 42nd Street. Shown here in 2017, it is presently numbered 87. The renovated Coates School of 1821 is behind it, on Jersey Street.

Belgrave Road (formerly Dixon Street) New Moston, where it gives on to Elijah's "Twelve Yards Road".

Dixon Family Tree

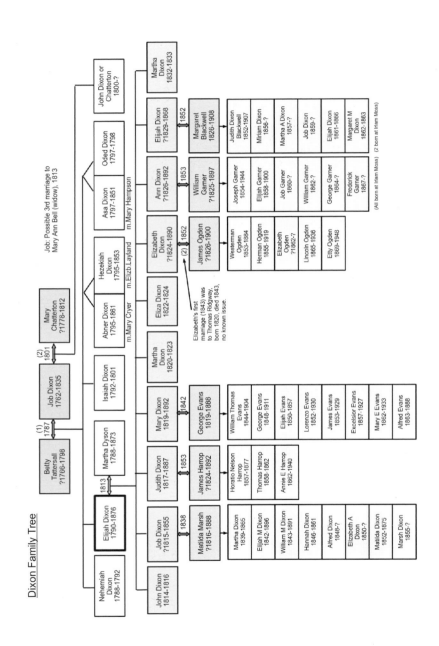

Dixon family tree, from Elijah's parents down to his grandchildren.

Chapter Nineteen

Chat Moss

That nothing walks with aimless feet,
That not one life shall be destroy'd
Or cast as rubbish to the void,
When God hath made the pile complete.

Alfred, Lord Tennyson (1809-92), *In Memoriam*

The flat, boggy stretch of land known as Chat Moss, extending westward from Manchester across the Lancashire plain, presented a famous challenge to George Stephenson, renowned engineer of the Liverpool and Manchester Railway. For centuries, the unproductive and hostile environment of the Moss had kept man at bay. It had a sinister reputation for unwary explorers and animals disappearing into the mucilaginous depths of its layer of peat, and from time to time vast, storm-saturated chunks split off into bordering rivers, hazarding navigation and causing floods. However, perhaps encouraged by Stephenson's success in 1830, land-hungry idealists made renewed attempts to bring this inhospitable terrain into cultivation.

Elijah had been an original subscriber to the Christian Community scheme which purchased 14 acres situated a mile or so south of the railway, in the late 1830s and early '40s. Distracted by Manchester's furious political fights, he did not at first play an active role, but by 1848 he had become the owner of land and built a farmhouse on the Moss, just north of the village of Irlam, near the confluence of the River Mersey and its tributary, the Irwell.

According to George Jacob Holyoake, chronicler of the Co-operative movement, earlier attempts to cultivate the Moss involved a scheme encompassing 600 acres of 'waste land', its black, spongy soil absorbing those who toiled on it up their knees, and requiring horses to wear wooden pattens.[1] 'England had not a drearier spot in which to begin a new world ... It was literally a Slough of Despond'. The reference to John Bunyan's allegorical bog in *Pilgrim's Progress* points up the ideological inspiration behind this and other land schemes supported by Radicals such as Elijah. In these they were ahead of the Chartist Land Plan, advocated and organised by Feargus O'Connor, after the rejection of the second National Petition in 1842. That is not to say, however, that O'Connor's scheme did not influence Elijah's renewed interest in going back to the land.

There may also have been a touch of shrewdness – an eye for the main chance – on Elijah's part, in recognising that if Stephenson could tame the moss in the north, it might be possible to do something similar with its southerly reaches near Irlam.

In point of fact, the famous device of floating the railway over brushwood, with which Stephenson is usually credited, was suggested by his contractor, John Dixon (no relation), who may himself have got the idea from efforts made to reclaim the Moss by Robert Stannard, in 1816.[2] Stannard, observing the difficulties experienced by the earlier venture of William Roscoe, realised that the key to successful reclamation lay in the construction of horse-drawn tramways. By building an eighteen-inch gauge tramway from the Mersey to enable marl (a mixture of clay with chalk or lime) to be brought in and dumped on the moss, he was able to stabilise it enough to bear the weight of people and horses.

Not only did Stannard go on to lay the contractor's railway for Stephenson's line, but at the same time his idea was followed by Edward Baines (senior), who was responsible for building a more substantial tramway to the east of Stannard's. By the time Elijah purchased and settled land on Irlam Moss, nearly all of it situated between the two tramways had benefited from the reclamation work of Stannard and Baines. There was, moreover, another factor which assisted reclamation of the Moss. It was realised that by adding manure, waste and night-soil to the marl the land could be made highly fertile. Here then, not ten miles from the half-starved, landless populations of insanitary slums in New Cross, Ancoats and Angel Meadow, was a unique opportunity to kill two birds with one stone.

It is easy to see so-called utopian land schemes as a retreat from the reality of industrialisation, the realm of cranky dreamers, but given Elijah's involvement at Chat Moss contemporaneously with his own industrial success story, that view makes no sense. In mid-nineteenth century England, many industrial workers were still artisans – hand-loom weavers for example – rather than operatives or factory employees. Many of those, encouraged especially by Cobbett, hoped that the tide of industry might one day ebb. The most important Radical influence on Elijah in this respect was Thomas Spence, a Bible-based Christian, born in 1750, who appears to have taken the idea of Jubilee, in Leviticus 25, as a scriptural basis for a redistribution of land in accordance with egalitarian principles. Even Elijah's atheist friend Richard Carlile was influenced by Spence, and many of the Co-operative associations inspired by Robert Owen had ultimate plans to settle members on land - either as communities or as independent smallholders.

One clear, unarguable fact underlay the reality of power in nineteenth century England – it was the monopoly of land ownership by the aristocracy which underpinned their political monopoly. To Elijah, therefore, time-served veteran of rough and tumble Manchester politics over 35 years, and now a man of means, the acquisition of land was a way forward, perfectly consistent with his Radical ideals. Doubtless, also, in spite of soggy soil, Chat Moss, with its big skies, fresh air, and the absence of mill chimneys, offered an enticing prospect of relief from the noisy realities of life in Ancoats and Newton Heath.

Relief or release? For the time being, Elijah kept on his house at Newton Heath, perhaps employing local people to work the land, or as servants at Hephzibah Farm, while relaxing there at weekends.[3] Or, he and Martha may have spent most of their time on the Moss, leaving the match works and the timber yard in the capable hands of son Job and old friend Edward Nightingale. The name of the farm, which survives to this day, has an obvious association with the Dixons, as that of the Biblical wife of Hezekiah, namesake of Elijah's younger brother, twin of Abner.

For whatever reason, Elijah chose to provide his Chat Moss address to the census-takers of 1851, also listing wife Martha, brother Asa, and visitor William Thomas Evans, son of daughter Mary and her husband George Evans. However much business was booming in Newton Heath – or perhaps *because* it was boom-ing – it seems that Elijah intended Hephzibah Farm to be his primary address. Other information suggests that, at least between 1848 and 1852, Hephzibah was home for Elijah and Martha. Elijah's painstaking census return, for exam-ple, exhibits a concentration rather beyond his usual thoroughness. Into the small space allowed for occupation, Elijah managed to cram in the following; 'Firm of Dixon, Son and Co, Timber Merchant, Congreve Match and Pill-box Manufacturer, employing 350 to 400 hands at Newton Heath, Lancashire' (this, somewhat surprisingly, was painstakingly copied into the census book by the enumerator). A case of if you've got it, flaunt it ? Perhaps. But in 1851, Elijah was also likely to be contemplating another clash with authority. On principle, he had no intention of paying the tithe (a rateable levy due to the parish church) and he was probably in the habit of letting everyone know that a man of no lit-tle substance had come among them. Perhaps he hoped to provoke a test case, with resultant publicity to the discredit of the church. If so, he was not to be disappointed.

Elijah may also have co-operated with his friend James Scholefield at this time, following suggestions from him and others, to relieve chronic unemploy-ment, and pressure on the Manchester workhouse, with job-creation schemes. In July 1847, Scholefield had chaired a meeting, supported by business inter-ests, to promote land schemes through the employment of able-bodied paupers. Chat Moss was mentioned as a possible site, and whether anything formal came of it or not, it is possible that Elijah did his bit by taking on paupers to assist in the labour-intensive work of draining the Moss and establishing the farm.

It is hard to imagine Elijah warming to the term 'gentleman farmer', but equally difficult to see how he could till the land in bucolic simplicity whilst overseeing an empire of industry which was still expanding, at Newton Heath.

The end of the Community scheme on Chat Moss was very different from the spectacular crash of O'Connor's Chartist land company, in 1848. Rather, by this time, the scheme on the Moss had simply faded away, leaving Elijah, as a man of property, in possession of land, ripe for agricultural improvement.

Accordingly, there is nothing of the Communard in Elijah's endorsement placed in the *Manchester Times* at the end of 1852, for a proprietary brand of fertiliser, imaginatively and euphemistically marketed as Sewage Guano. Reading its authoritative tone, you might think Elijah had been farming all his life. 'I used about a ton last spring, the greater part of which I sowed on one and three-quarter statute acres of oats, and on a quarter of an acre of white wheat.' Elijah went on to report that it also produced a 'beautiful crop' of peas, and all this on land 'first broken up from the raw moss state four years ago'.

There can be no doubt, however, that although it failed to become a utopian community, the Chat Moss venture gave expression to some of Elijah's deepest beliefs. One summer's day, fellow Chartist and teetotaller, Joseph Johnson, visited Elijah at Hephzibah, and Elijah explained his objectives with missionary zeal.[4] He saw the building of the farmhouse and the tilling of the waste as a parable, proving what might be done with unpromising material; how use might be made of what was apparently useless. Elijah talked eagerly and at length 'with fresh and youthful enthusiasm' on utilisation of wasteland in the context of his belief in Universalism. Whether, as Johnson pondered, Elijah was concerned 'either in things material or spiritual, either in waste lands or wasted lives', the image of him discoursing 'all the long summer day', sitting outside the farmhouse under the sunny skies of Irlam Moss, is one to savour.

Things were going well for Elijah and Martha. On 25 March 1852, their daughter Elizabeth, whose marriage to Thomas Ridgway in 1843 had been cut tragically short, was married to James Ogden, tailor and draper. Their marriage produced five children. Two weeks later, son Elijah Junior, now a 'traveller' for the firm, was married to Margaret Blackwell. Here, however, there was a whiff of scandal – earlier in the year, in Birmingham, Margaret had given birth to an illegitimate daughter, whom she named Judith *Dixon* Blackwell. Elijah got to know all about it, of course, but does not seem to have been greatly troubled, beyond, in later life, having to insert a clause in his will dealing specifically with Judith, to ensure her entitlement alongside other grandchildren. In May 1853, there was another happy event in the Dixon family, with the double wedding of daughters Ann and Judith. All the marriages were celebrated at the church of St Mary, Manchester. Judith's husband, James Harrop, was a book-keeper and partner at Taylor's Silk Mill in Newton Heath, and the couple later had three children. William Garner, already a farmer at Newton Heath, and wife Ann later moved to Hephzibah farm, and settled down to a life of farming on the Moss, where their progress was to be closely followed by Elijah. All their six children were born there, and baptised at St John the Baptist church, Irlam, where, in due course, William and Ann were buried. Although Elijah Junior died before he was forty, he and Margaret produced six children.

Elijah's sponsorship deals were not confined to fertiliser. Advertisements by way of endorsement became the cutting edge of marketing strategy for Victorian entrepreneurs, all the more effective when your product was endorsed by a well-known and respected personality. Given the kudos of the firm's appearance at the Great Exhibition, and the lengthy tribute in the *Daily News*, syndicated in several local papers, including the *Huddersfield Chronicle*, Elijah was in demand. Moreover, the publication of Archibald Prentice's memoirs in early 1851 reminded readers of Elijah's brave deeds as a reformer in 1817. In an endorsement for William Carter's 'Botanic Shaving Soap', appearing in the *Nottinghamshire Guardian* in June 1851, Elijah had said it is 'the best I have ever used' and elaborated on its excellent qualities, much in the way latter-day TV celebrities promote make-up or coffee. Elijah was very likely sincere in his praise, for the studio portrait shows a craggy visage adorned with mutton-chop whiskers, leaving the rest of his face clean-shaven. No mean task to keep that smart and trim with a cut-throat razor.

The fact that Elijah was happy to exploit his success and new-found status as a captain of industry, reflected the changing face of Manchester politics after the events of 1848. The Chartists suffered a defeat, but they did not go away. Rather, still led by O'Connor, but increasingly influenced by the charismatic Jones, they were re-forming and re-grouping; adjusting to changes in society, especially the emergence of the new class of skilled workers.

Against this background, and now that the Corn Law issues had been finally resolved in favour of the free-traders, old wounds were healing and new alliances were being forged. The fall-out from the rejection of the Chartists' third petition triggered the formation of a new body supported by the old-school Radicals; the Manchester Universal Suffrage Association, whose objectives were keenly supported by Elijah. But the middle classes, and skilled workers aspiring to the middle class, were drawn more to another new organisation, the Parliamentary and Financial Reform Association. The Radicals – and their private conversations can easily be imagined – determined that the mantle of reform should not thus be dragged from their backs. Abel Heywood was promptly joined by James Scholefield in setting up the Manchester branch.

The Manchester Irish returned to the Chartist fold. Even the leaders of the Lambs – Mick McDonough and John Finnigan – had reconciled behind O'Connor in expressions of unity at the St Patrick's Day celebrations in March 1848. Franchise reform was once again back on the main-stream political agenda, openly supported by the likes of Prentice and Cobden who, not long before, had wanted to keep the Radicals at arm's length.

All but the die-hards, both Whigs and Tories, were now coming to see that franchise reform had to go beyond the injustice of the 1832 settlement, and re-alignment in party allegiance was taking place along the fault-lines of this issue. Cobden was now in favour and John Bright, another leading Corn Law repealer (though no friend of Elijah's owing to his opposition to the Ten Hours Bill), was changing his stance. Indeed, Bright was one day to go so far as to write privately to Tory prime minister Benjamin Disraeli, urging the need for extending voting rights.

And what if Elijah, carried along on such a crashing wave of success, *did* enjoy his translation from demonic cart orator to wealthy businessman? As the employer of hundreds, he stood alongside, at least in social status, those of his foes who survived from the days of Church-and-King and, more significantly, members of Manchester's newer aristocracy, the cotton-kings and their acolytes, the bourgeoisie, so reviled by Engels. Unlike Engels, however, who foresaw only class conflict and revolution, Elijah clung to the hope that his life-long causes might be realised through peaceful agitation. And his words were still matched by deeds.

In 1847, a Ten Hours Act, drafted by Lord Ashley (later Shaftesbury) to regulate employment hours, especially those of women and children, finally reached the statute book. It had been opposed by many Lancashire mill owners, including the sainted Bright, and in 1850 their renewed lobby in Parliament sought to water down its provisions. This kind of behaviour certainly was grist to the Engels mill. In May, Elijah addressed a meeting of factory workers ('operatives' still the preferred term in the press) in the Corn Exchange urging them to stand firm against fresh efforts to dilute the Act. Some employers wanted get-out clauses to allow 'relay' (shift) working, and flexible provisions which it was feared would sabotage the central purpose of the Act. The situation was complicated by the fact that Ashley himself, thinking it would pre-empt further predations, was in favour of the employer-sponsored amendments, but Richard Oastler was not. Some manufacturers may have seen the amendments as a ruse to undercut them, but the *Preston Chronicle and Lancashire Advertiser* made much of the fact that the operatives' cause was backed by well-intended manufacturers. Among them were the chairman, Lawrence Pitkethley, and, of course Elijah, whom it described as 'formerly a factory worker, but now an extensive lucifer-match manufacturer.'

It was not long before Elijah's stand on tithes brought him into conflict with the local clergy. He had long maintained his belief in Disestablishment of the Anglican church and his contempt for the antiquated tithes system. In towns like Manchester, and even in still semi-rural areas like Newton Heath, tithes were becoming uncollectable from the growing, ever-changing, usually impoverished and mainly Dissenting or Catholic population. In rural areas such as Irlam, however, where the 'squirearchy' still held sway, it was worthwhile for church authorities to attempt enforcement. So, after a lapse of sixteen years, the Rev Marsden of Eccles took action, through his churchwardens. In May

1852, Elijah was summoned to appear before magistrates at the New Bailey, to show cause why the sum of *sixteen pence*, being the tithe owed in respect of Hephzibah, should not be paid. Whether or not an order was made, prior to distraint on Elijah's chattels, the protest was successful in attracting publicity for the anti-tithe cause. Prentice's *Manchester Times* reported the matter and attacked the church for 'an outrage of conscience and the disturbance of the peace of the parish'. Elijah had become a dab-hand at using the press; as well as believing in free speech, he had a knack for knowing what reporters of those days would see as a good story. He would also have been gratified by the fact that after a period of strained relations during the Anti-Corn Law era, he and the formidable Prentice were once again on the same side of the argument.

In so far as Elijah went back to the land to escape the smoke and grime of the town, he was part of a wider movement, encouraged by the growth of the railways, to seek rest and relaxation away from the mills and factories. In Manchester, Queens Park and Philips Park were opened in 1846, for the recreation of working class families in north Manchester (the latter named in honour of Mark Philips who had lobbied for its creation). At the same time, leafy suburbs were developing on the fringes of the town, in Crumpsall, Ardwick, Broughton, and Longsight, for the new class of skilled workers, engineers, draftsmen, foremen, warehousemen and clerks, who were to become known as white-collar workers. Railway travel broadened horizons and created new leisure pastimes. The same issue of the *Manchester Courier*, which in September 1850, reported on Elijah and Joseph Johnson speaking at a public meeting to condemn atrocities committed by the Austrian empire in Hungary, also reported on the more mundane activities of its readers. 'An immense party of pleasure-seekers' from the town had enjoyed a bank holiday trip to Alton Towers, seat of the Earl of Shrewsbury. The noble earl was not at his seat but 'the excursionists had a treat of no ordinary character'.

Elijah always had doubts about O'Connor's Chartist land scheme, eventually condemned by Parliament as a land 'lottery' and dogged throughout by poor book-keeping and vague ideology. Beset by court cases, it was a text-book lesson in muddled administration, and none of the four or five estates purchased from funds raised by O'Connor to endow settlements provided a workable template. Moreover, it was fundamentally flawed in that it failed to recognise that the real driver of economic progress was industrial expansion in the towns. The inevitable collapse of the National Land Company was marked in Manchester by a gathering of 3,000 people in the Hall of Science, among them investors in good faith who had lost money.[5] As Elijah himself was to discover, the object of acquiring land as a means of mass enfranchisement was fine in theory, but in practice the real impetus came from the need to provide housing for the burgeoning middle class – the sort of people who could afford to enjoy a day trip to Alton Towers.

Ever open to new ideas, ever watchful of events, Elijah must have followed the progress of more practical, more clearly focussed, hard-headed land schemes intended to benefit working people. One such, the Bradford Freehold Land Society, had the backing of Saltaire patriarch Titus Salt, and attracted support from Cobden and Colonel Thompson, both present at the second annual meeting, in February 1851. Cobden lauded the increase in value of land made to grow 'tall chimneys and cottages' when it had 'ceased to grow cabbages'. At a conference on land schemes in Birmingham, Cobden referred to discussions on the subject with Elijah, whom he described as his 'old Radical friend'.

In order to attract more members, the Bradford scheme copied O'Connor's idea of balloting for allocation of land. Elijah appears to have supported this, as against rights of seniority. Cobden quoted him as saying, 'I don't like your priority; it is the law of primogeniture introduced into your freehold land society.' Cobden agreed, and was clearly citing Elijah as an authority. His speech ended with a commitment to further parliamentary reform, and was another sign of the two men moving closer together on issues of the day. Their dialogue on how to develop land for housing cemented their mutual respect.

However, sadness also attended on the Dixons during their stay on the Moss. Brother Asa, seven years Elijah's junior, was recorded as resident at Hephzibah on 6 March 1851, the night of the census. Asa was perhaps the least settled of the brothers and had had his fair share of troubles. He had tried his hand at various jobs and ill-fated business ventures and had ended up doing menial work as a glass packer. In 1835, he had been made bankrupt, and in 1848 his wife Mary died, followed, less than a year later, by the death of his son, John. Asa's occupation on the census form is shown as 'ag lab' (agricultural labourer) – to all appearances working on the farm – but his stay with the Dixons might have been a case of shelter from the storm. At any rate, Asa died seven months later, back in Ancoats, in circumstances which warranted an inquest, and the Coroner made a formal finding of death due to 'insanity'. The likelihood is that he took his own life; the inquest was held at the Waterman public house, alongside the Rochdale Canal.

In August 1853, brother Hezekiah, five years younger than Elijah, died in Manchester, leaving Abner and Elijah as the last surviving Dixon brothers. Late in 1853 or early 1854 Elijah and Martha handed over Hephzibah farm to Ann and William Garner, and returned to Manchester. By then Elijah's plans for another, very different, land scheme were afoot.

Chapter Twenty

New Moston

Even though Elijah and Martha appear to have been happy during their rural interlude at Chat Moss, Elijah seems always to have been looking across the wide horizons of the Moss back towards Manchester. Dixon, Son & Company continued to flourish, and the challenge of steering its expansion through changing technologies and markets was irresistible. So, too, was Elijah drawn back to Manchester to progress a new land scheme, close to the centre of the firm's operations in Newton Heath.

In January 1850, together with others of like mind, including William Ricketts, James Gaskill, and Peter Potts, Elijah became a founder member of the Manchester Bridgewater Freehold Land Society. The broad objectives of the Society were plainly suggested in the title, and it is an interesting coincidence that the society's formation was more or less contemporaneous with the first annual meeting of the Bradford Freehold Land Society. Its aims were similar, with an obvious democratic ethos, specifically focussed on acquiring voting rights. It was intended that members would make weekly payments to a common fund, proceeds to be applied to the purchase of land to be divided into allotments, whose respective owners would thereby be enfranchised as 'forty-shilling freeholders'.

On 6 March the following year, the Society purchased fifty-seven acres of farm land a couple of miles north-east of Newton Heath, from the trustees of Samuel Chetham Hilton.[1] The land retained by the trustees was by far the largest estate in the area, including the ancient medieval halls of Moston, Great Nuthurst and Little Nuthurst. The land they sold off lay within the township of Moston, bordering Failsworth to the south and east and Chadderton to the north. Historically part of the ancient Chapelry of Blackley, the district remained, in 1850, essentially rural in character, although surrounded by mills and factories on all sides. At its eastern extremity it was contiguous with the Rochdale canal for a short distance, and the Lancashire and Yorkshire railway line between Manchester and Rochdale lay half a mile to the west. Flat and well-drained by streams running towards the river Irk, close to the rapidly expanding populations of Manchester and surrounding townships, it was ripe for development. The Society paid £2,900 for the land, although additional costs for building streets and sewers, as well as an access road, were estimated at a further £5,000. The plan was to divide the land to accommodate 230 'allotments', allowing plenty of room for gardens.

This was certainly a more practical scheme than Chat Moss, given economic realities. And just as Elijah had selected the savvy Nightingale to partner him in the match and timber business, his fellow-directors in the new joint stock company seem to have been chosen for their business acumen as well as their commitment to reform. James Gaskill (sometimes rendered Gaskell), as president of the Society, was a cotton spinner and minister of the Bible Christian church at Hulme. He had founded a Sunday school to cater for children of Radicals, barred from regular schools. William Ricketts, as secretary, was the Society's day-to-day administrator. He was variously described as loan society secretary, land agent and actuary and, as the owner of a temperance hotel and dining rooms, shared Elijah's teetotal views. Peter Potts, treasurer, was a baker and flour dealer in Chorlton-on-Medlock. Elijah, as chairman, was the guiding spirit.

The scheme encompassed six separate but adjoining plots of land, five geographically described in the Moston rates book for 1852 as 'top end of Moston'. The 1844 tithe map shows that the land purchased was previously tenanted by members of the Whitehead family (three brothers and a son) together with a part of Brown's farm, and a field held by James Carr, tenant of the adjacent Slater Fold farm, west of Moston Lane.

The upbeat report on the third annual meeting of the MBFLS which appeared in the columns of the *Manchester Times* on 29 January 1853 had all the marks of an advertising puff. Perhaps Archibald Prentice was doing Elijah a favour in printing a glowing account of the company's progress. The venue of the meeting, Ricketts' Temperance Hotel in Great Bridgewater Street, is the only clue as to the origins of the company's name. Formed before suitable land could be purchased, its promoters seem to have chosen a name suggested by the address of their meeting place – happily plagiarising the successful ethos of Manchester's first canal company.

The report illustrates the scale of the scheme, and work undertaken to put 'the estate at New Moston' on the map. The key to access was a new road, 'twelve yards wide', leading from the Oldham road in Failsworth, linking with existing highways further west and connecting with Moston, Harpurhey, and Middleton. According to the *Times*, the new road, 'now open and dedicated to public traffic' would provide 'one of the most healthy drives about Manchester'. In fact, before the arrival of the MBFLS the south end of Moston Lane, there named Morris Lane, was little more than a footpath down the steep side of a little valley, known as Morris Clough, to a wooden footbridge over the Moston Brook. To facilitate carriages and carts, therefore, the Society had to carry out culverting and infilling to support a wider and more level road to top Moston, leading down from Hardman Fold (Hale Lane) on the Failsworth side.

Here was the guiding hand of Elijah Dixon, pioneer environmentalist. The road to New Moston was to be an example of modern engineering, in contrast to the rutted, muddy lanes and streets of Ancoats and Collyhurst, about which Elijah had so often complained at Vestry meetings. Even on Chat Moss, Elijah would have had to ensure that roads were built to connect isolated farms, including Hephzibah, with Irlam and each other. Modern Ordnance Survey maps still show Twelve Yards Road running across the Moss.

In contrast with Chat Moss, there was nothing about the New Moston scheme suggesting its future as an alternative economic model. Rather, it anticipated an alternative way of life – happier and healthier – for ordinary people whose livelihood was inextricably linked to the growing industrial economy of the town. Its new road put it within easy reach of mills, collieries and factories all around, but the workers who lived in New Moston would have gardens to cultivate, pleasant views and cleaner air. Not exactly a garden city but certainly a garden suburb. It was not the model society envisaged by the younger Elijah in 1832, when he had spoken of cities as 'prolific sources of misery, crime, disease and death', but it was a step in the right direction. It was also a recognition that the development of industrial towns was inevitable, not the temporary aberration imagined by Spence and Cobbett. Elijah was perfectly placed to see that the future was being shaped by technology and industry, and once again his own role in events was defining the future of Manchester.

The blurb in the *Manchester Times* could hardly have been more helpful. It stressed the 'elevation' of the company's estate, no less than thirty-six locks up the Rochdale canal, well above smoky Manchester, 'auguring well for its salubrity and the enjoyment of health'. There was, however, no appeal for a new social order, nor any Biblical references. Rather, the MBFLS was pitching for the upwardly mobile family man – the man on the excursion train to Alton Towers – whose attention might easily be grabbed by the averment that 'when finished [the New Moston estate] will be one of the most valuable investments on record, in the phase of freehold land history'. But it must be said in fairness, that Elijah was probably confident, perhaps naively, that incomers were bound to avail themselves of the right to vote.

Accordingly, the MBFLS pressed on. In April 1853, the company placed an advert in the *Manchester Courier* for offers by tender to make up a further 3,000 yards of roads, 'twelve yards wide', for the 'New Moston Estate', allowing for sewering, as well as ballast, stonework and edging required. A couple of weeks later, there was an indication of upheaval in the lives of the tenant farmers whose freehold now reposed with the Society. Having, presumably, agreed compensation, the company invited offers for materials, including oak beams, made available by demolition of houses and outbuildings occupied by John Whitehead, James Whitehead, and Luke Barnes. Other farms and farmhouses remained undisturbed by their unincorporated landlords for many more years. But in due course, as the forming of new streets progressed, the company was obliged to make at least four applications to magistrates for permission to stop up ancient footpaths across the fields.

In June 1853, the rates book for Moston township gave its imprimatur to the name of New Moston, by so describing the situation of land and buildings owned and occupied by 'E. Dixon and others'. From then on, the name was gradually absorbed into the addresses of all properties at the 'top end of Moston', including many outside the Society's estate.

As for the road to New Moston through Failsworth, unforeseen problems arose. It was a case of the best laid plans of mice and men – together with a large dose of parochialism – which led to an outcry over the poor state of the new road between the bridge over the Moston brook and Hale Lane. The dispute reflected the anomaly of New Moston being culturally linked to Manchester, by virtue of its historic association with the township of Moston, whilst being nearer to, and more directly approached from, Failsworth, entirely outside the boundaries of Manchester.

In January 1857, Mr Trafford, the assistant surveyor of Failsworth, called a site meeting of ratepayers, evidently with the intention of getting himself off the hook. He reported that the landowner, Mr J.W. Hilton, had offered £20 towards the cost of immediate repairs, and that this had been matched by a further £20 on behalf of the ratepayers. Elijah diplomatically offered to pay the same out of his own pocket, but objected to paying more, given that the Society had already put in £1,500 to widen the road and to level the hollow down to the brook. Most Failsworth ratepayers took the view that, as the road was there to serve New Moston, they should not have to pay for it, and cheerfully passed a resolution that notice should be served on the Society to re-open the 'old road' to the Moston Brook.

Two years later, locals were still complaining that in the vicinity of the bridge the road was well-nigh impassable in bad weather, as well as lamenting the state of the easterly approach to New Moston over the Wrigley Head canal bridge, obviously taking traffic avoiding the route across the brook. To this day the Moston Brook remains a landsker, dividing a Lancashire village from a city suburb.

Chapter Twenty-one

Clough House

In spite of his adventurous New Moston land scheme, Elijah's centre of operations continued to be Newton Heath. The match works and timber business were still expanding, and other family members, besides Elijah and Job, were drawn in. Elijah Dixon Junior, some fourteen years younger than brother Job, was employed as a traveller, helping to develop the firm's growing export business, along with his uncle, Abner Dixon. Some time after the marriage of daughter Mary, in 1842, her husband George Evans, a millwright by trade, had joined the firm. His engineering skills would be valuable in a business heavily reliant on machinery, and his key role in the firm's development was confirmed in his later becoming a partner.

Whatever the demands of business, and in spite of the failures of Chartism, Elijah and Nightingale remained true to the cause. In the meantime, the old Chartists were dying off. Brave Scholefield, whose Every Street chapel had been a bastion of reform, died on 24 April 1855, aged 65, pre-deceased by his wife and five of their seven children. The death of Feargus O'Connor in August 1855 propelled Ernest Jones to the fore, and his settling in Manchester in 1860 meant that it once again became the centre of agitation for franchise reform.

Of all the bereavements suffered by Elijah and Martha, none could have affected them more deeply than the death of their son Job, on 28 November 1855, aged 40. George Evans registered the death, the cause of which was given as debility due to 'affection of the lungs'. Job was their eldest surviving child, and the bond between father and son is evinced by his being brought in as a founding partner of the firm, while still in his twenties. Elijah obviously hoped that Job would one day take over the helm. Job's early years encompassed the bleak days of 1817, his father's imprisonment in London, and a stay in the Manchester workhouse. His marriage to Matilda Marsh had produced eight children. He was buried at All Saints church ground, Newton Heath, on 3 December. Job's will, made six months before his death, left houses and shops in Newton Heath to Matilda; Elijah and Nightingale now faced having to reach an agreement with her concerning her inherited interest in the firm.[1] The partnership was formally dissolved in June 1856, with the firm presumably buying out Matilda's share, and making provision for the children. Six months later, a legal notice appeared in the *Manchester Examiner* to the effect that the firm was to carry on under the surviving partners, trading as 'Dixon and Nightingale' for a time. Shortly afterwards, George Evans joined the partnership and the firm became 'Dixon, Son and Evans', the 'Son' presumably now referring to Elijah Junior.

In June 1858, Elijah was among the mourners at the funeral of Lawrence Pitkethley in Salford. *Reynolds's Newspaper* explained that the funeral was private, 'with only about 20 of his most intimate acquaintances being present'. It placed Elijah at the head of the list, describing him as 'a very old Radical, of Hunt and Cobbett's time'.

It was, indeed, increasingly the case that Elijah's attendance at events invested them with sober purpose and respectability. A meeting at the Newton Heath Mechanics Institution, in support of Alderman Abel Heywood, standing as the reform candidate for Manchester in the general election of 1859, was presided over by Elijah and, with echoes of the old double act, Nightingale proposed Heywood as 'a fit person to represent the city in parliament'. For in 1853 the fair town of Manchester, the first powerhouse of industrial England, had fittingly achieved city status.

Most members of the Dixon family continued to live in Newton Heath, near to the firm's premises on Oldham Road, in spite of the new mills, factories and railway installations gradually encroaching on the farms and heathland of Elijah's youth. Elijah and Martha, once back from Hephzibah farm, appear to have settled at The Cloughs (now referred to as Clough House) – about which nephew William Hepworth waxed lyrical – adjoining the match works, and probably accommodating office space as well as living quarters. At least, that is the address Elijah gave to the 1861 census takers, and going by the number of other family members staying there, Clough House was headquarters for both family and firm.

Formerly the property of the Cathedral Chapter of Manchester, the building stood out as a grand architectural survival with medieval and Tudor features, and five ancient gables.[2] It was also home to Elijah's daughter Judith, her husband James Harrop and their children, Horatio Nelson and Thomas. Horatio was named after James's father, former landlord of the King's Arms on Great Ancoats Street. In addition, two other names were listed for Clough House on the night of the census (a Saturday, then as now), 7 April 1861; George Evans, now 'mill manager', and Hannah Dixon, aged 15, one of Elijah's granddaughters, daughter of Job and Matilda. Hannah is listed as 'domestic servant', but in the light of her death later in the year, she may have been ill, and living at Clough House to be looked after by her grandparents, leaving her widowed mother better able to cope with the other six children. The Evanses appear to have lived next door and, as there is no mention of George's wife Mary, she may have been away on a weekend visit. On the same night, William Marsh Dixon (Hannah's brother) stayed at the home of his aunt and uncle,

Elizabeth and James Ogden, an overall picture which suggests that members of the close-knit and gregarious Dixon clan were frequent guests in each other's homes.

The role played by George Evans was to be crucial, especially after the death of Edward Nightingale in July 1861. Nightingale was only 52 and following Job's death six years earlier it was a bad blow. Elijah had lost his trusted business partner and his closest comrade in politics. This came on top of the death of brother Abner Dixon, aged 66, in February that year, followed within a few weeks by Abner's wife, Mary. In the preceding year, their grandson Abner John had died, only two days old. Abner, Elijah's last surviving sibling, was also his last link with family life in Holmfirth.

Nightingale was buried in a family vault at Manchester General Cemetery, Harpurhey. Opened in 1837, it was the first privately-owned cemetery to provide burial space on a large scale, effectively relieving pressure on the overcrowded churchyards of the city and providing another alternative for Dissenters like the Dixons, whose last wishes certainly did not include a desire to lie peacefully within the curtilage of the Established Church. Although it was the first burial ground in Manchester to be run purely as a business, it was a model for the municipal cemeteries which came later.

Abner's burial was also at Harpurhey. To this day, an intriguing memorial stone lies amongst the graves there, its inscription clearly visible. It records the deaths of Abner and Mary, as well as that of their son, Benjamin, aged 13, and Abner's twin brother Hezekiah. Abner and Hezekiah are referred to as 'Twin Sons of Job Dixon of Holmfirth, Yorkshire'.[3] Whoever drafted the words, or paid for the stone, it is as though, in death, the Dixons are making a statement, that as a family they have survived the storm. Nothing loquacious, only a simple narrative, 'They helped one another'. No Biblical reference, just words expressing Jesus's commandment, in John ch.15, v.12, to 'love one another'. They might easily have been composed by Elijah.

In a letter of April 1862 to grandson Elijah Marsh Dixon, son of Job and Matilda, Elijah bequeathed an illuminating insight into his character.[4] Job's eldest son, just a teenager when his father died, was probably a bit of handful as Matilda struggled to bring up six surviving children. After Job's death, and with funds realised from his share of the firm, she had moved with the children to the fast-developing resort of Southport. Elijah Marsh, listed as a seller of calicoes, seems to have missed his father – and Manchester. He obtained work in Liverpool, but was soon back in Manchester, courting Eliza Carter from Newton Heath. Anxious to be a man, barely 20, and without a word to his mother, he married Eliza at Manchester Cathedral on 20 February 1862 by licence. He gave his occupation as 'cotton spinner' and the marriage was witnessed by Henry and Elizabeth Barnes. It was a typical manifestation of impetuosity; a love-lorn young couple heedless as to anyone else's feelings. Suffice it to say, Matilda was upset and worried. So who better to turn to for help and advice than grandfather Dixon?

Elijah responded, with a long letter – four sides of foolscap – to his errant grandson. It is a model rebuke, insofar as it was delivered with unimpeachable authority, yet tempered by grace and understanding. Most recipients of letters beginning with a Biblical quotation might squirm with embarrassment (or, these days, contempt), but not this one. Why else would the letter have been preserved – and not destroyed – had it not been read as a statement of love and concern?

Elijah, as always, spoke plainly: 'Dear Grandson', immediately followed, for best effect, by apposite words from the Chapter 3 of the Book of Revelations, 'As many as I love, I rebuke and chasten: be zealous therefore, and repent'. You have done wrong, Elijah says, straight off, adding, to emphasise the obvious truth, that no doubt Junior is already regretting the folly of his ways. The rebuke is directed not at the event of his grandson's marriage, but at his regrettable failure to inform the family, especially his mother. However, and here Elijah begins to soften: 'It is never too late to mend'. The rest of the letter is written more in a mood of man-to-man understanding, even sharing a confidence or two with hapless Elijah Marsh: 'I do not blame you for getting married … I married myself with only one Sunday coat to my back, and one working jacket'.

Unfortunately, Elijah Marsh has not only been profligate with his emotions, but also with money. Elijah points out that embarking upon marriage, 'and I presume that you may ere long be a father' was doubly thoughtless given that he was in 'straits' and would need financial support. If he were a father, would he not expect his son to acquaint him with the marriage arrangements 'before he became responsible for the maintenance of his children ?'

But the worst is over. 'Now I by no means intend to be severe with you…' The remonstrance was intended for his own good. A quotation from Psalms, 'Let the righteous smite me, and I will esteem it a kindness', followed by a prayer for everyone's salvation – including his own – lays the foundation for the rest of the letter, intended to get Elijah Marsh back on track. Redemption is at hand if he will only discharge his duty to wife, relations, friends, countrymen and all mankind. Between the lines, however, can be seen the personal crisis which Elijah Marsh had brought upon himself, no doubt exacerbating his mother's worries. What might he do next? 'Now dear Elijah, I hope you will not think for one moment of leaving your mother to mourn your loss, by any hasty arrangements, but stand your ground like a man of true courage…' Elijah concludes by inviting grandson and wife to dinner and signs himself 'Your affectionate Grandpa, E. Dixon'.

Alas, however, young Elijah Marsh held back on the full extent of his financial difficulties, having already borrowed money, including a sum from his uncle James Ogden, and was soon appealing to his grandfather for relief. Accordingly,

Elijah's second letter, only a week after the first, while also liberally illustrated with Biblical quotations, contains a hint of exasperation.[5] Elijah Marsh's excuse that it was shyness that got him into trouble prompted another homily from his grandfather, who recalled that his own shyness as a youth had caused him to hide away from the world. The lad was once more enjoined to seek God's guidance through prayer. If, however, he had thought of his grandfather as a soft touch, he had reckoned without Elijah Dixon, man of business.

Elijah agreed to settle the loans, but to take security for them against his grandson's expectations. Thus, Elijah Marsh had to provide an IOU to be exchanged for his shares in the New Moston land company (held in trust during his minority) upon his forthcoming 21st birthday. Moreover, he was only going to get the further advance of £30 which he had asked for on his next visit to Manchester. This letter ends with a rather cooler 'Your affectionate Grandfather, E. Dixon', and a postscript suggesting that the troubled Elijah and his wife were not yet settled; perhaps Elijah Marsh was still working in Liverpool and had not yet secured permanent accommodation back in Manchester. 'If you should see or communicate with your wife, remember [me] to her, with kind wishes'. The last three words, squeezed between the initials 'ED' were obviously added as an afterthought.

On 31 January 1863, Elijah and Martha celebrated fifty years of marriage – a fairly exceptional event for those days. Mr and Mrs Dixon marked the occasion by a visit to a photographer's studio, the resulting portrait being the only surviving photograph of either of them.[6] And there they are in sepia, suitably solemn; Martha, mother of ten children, seated, hands together, resplendent in bonnet, shawl and crinoline, and Elijah, short and stocky in stature, standing, in morning coat and waistcoat, hand outstretched to a centre table, upon which are placed a book and an ornamental box. Both exhibit ample girth, and a dignity befitting their extraordinary story of triumph over hardship. In neither their postures nor their expressions, is there anything to suggest weary old age. Rather, the opposite; Martha at 74, and Elijah at 72, fix the camera with a confident gaze, at ease with the technology of the new world which has come about during the years of their marriage, and determined to be part of it. No doubt, too, Elijah and Martha were happy with their growing brood of grandchildren – by 1860, Job, Elijah Junior, Judith, Mary, Elizabeth, and Ann had provided them with nigh on twenty, with another dozen to come.

Elijah was in his prime – the Congreve matches of Dixon, Son & Evans now familiar in every corner of the British Empire and beyond – but how easy it is to imagine the patriarch's furrowed brow, as he wrote this letter, struggling to temper the impatience of youth with the wisdom of age. In this endeavour, later events suggest that he was entirely successful. Elijah Marsh and Eliza settled down to a happy married life and by 1865, they had three children. In old age, following the deaths of all his siblings and sons, Elijah seems to have enjoyed a close relationship with his once-errant grandson, living proof of his lifelong belief in the universal availability of atonement and redemption.

In politics, too, Elijah Dixon had achieved the status of elder statesman in the Radical cause. It is hard to reconcile the industrial hegemony of Britain in the 1860s, and its reputation as workshop of the world, with its lack of democracy. Politicians of both main parties, now calling themselves Liberal and Conservative, admitted the need for change and knew it was coming. The Radicals, coalesced with reformist Whigs and renegade Tory 'Peelites' into the new Liberal party, saw the opportunity for a new campaign to extend the franchise beyond the pathetic gains of 1832. Elijah was ready to play his part and his skills as speaker and chairman were, as always, in steady demand.

Whatever reconciliations and re-alignments had taken place in the late 1850s, the tensions in the reform movement were never far below the surface. Indeed, Elijah and the Chartist rump believed it their duty to expose them, rather in the way they had disturbed Whig meetings in the 1830s and 40s by heckling, holding up banners, and moving amendments. Nightingale was gone, but Elijah found a new and esteemed comrade in Ernest Jones, now practising as a barrister in Manchester.

They determined to make their mark on the third national conference of the National Reform Association, held in the Free Trade Hall, Manchester, in April 1864. Their fear – which proved justified – was that delegates would agree on a watered-down extension of the franchise. Lord Palmerston, as Prime Minister, an old-school Whig, and more interested in foreign policy, was an unlikely leader of a Liberal party, supposedly committed to reform. Predictably, the meeting commenced with speeches urging 'unity of action' and delegates were asked to sink their differences in favour of a resolution limited to the extension of property-based 'manhood' suffrage (all males liable to pay rates), a re-distribution of seats, vote by ballot and triennial parliaments (the demand for annual parliaments having been railed back by this time). Jones and Elijah were not having it. Jones argued that anything short of manhood suffrage would not achieve unity of the working and middle classes, and promptly moved an amendment to that effect. Elijah seconded it.

Reminding his audience of his experience in 1816 and 1817, when he had supported universal suffrage, vote by ballot and annual parliaments, Elijah stressed that his principles remained unchanged. He recounted his part in preparations for the doomed Blanketeers march and clarified that as well as doing his share of cart oratory he had also been an organiser. He reminded his – initially unsympathetic – audience that the first Manchester meeting in support of parliamentary reform had taken place in 1817 'on the very spot where we are now assembled': St Peter's Field. This, Elijah disclosed, had been preceded by a meeting of seven working men in a bedroom, of whom he was one. Recounting how two of the seven had deserted in fear, and the remaining five had eventually been locked up for high treason, Elijah had his audience spellbound, then cheering. The fact that he was not going to be arrested for high treason this time represented a great improvement in the education of the country, but, unable to resist a Biblical reference, Elijah averred that without manhood suffrage, even Jesus 'with no house wherein to lay his head' would be denied the vote.

So much for the Manchester papers – the *Courier* and the *Times* – content to leave their readers with the impression of Elijah as a grand old man of yesteryear; something of a Manchester treasure. They had, in effect, censored one of the most powerful speeches ever made by a Manchester man in the cause of human rights. It was only thanks to the shorthand skills of the reporter from *Lloyd's Weekly* that readers of that worthy journal were treated to a full account of Elijah's excoriating attack on political complacency and *realpolitik* in the edition of 1 May. Covering the broad canvass of events since 1832, it was a speech sparkling with wit and sardonic contempt for those who had consistently ignored and exploited the working classes – landowners, mill-owners and, of course, the politicians they had elected.

Elijah began diplomatically enough; the 1832 Act had not even enfranchised all the middle classes, let alone the working millions. But the attack on privilege that followed surpassed even the polemicism of Engels. The whole weight of parliamentary interest was in the hands of the aristocrat and the capitalist. Land and money, composed of 'acreage, old family interests, cotton, iron ships, but not one labouring hand', ruled supreme in the House of Commons. Elijah continued, 'It cannot be said that there is a single member of the House of Commons who pretends to represent the interests of labour. This unjust state of things has been so often described from reform platforms, and with so little effect in the way of serious agitation, that the enfranchised have agreed to put aside the extension of the suffrage, vote by ballot, and triennial parliaments, as worn-out hobbies'.

Attacking three previous Prime Ministers, Lords Russell, Derby and Aberdeen, for dishonestly promising what they never intended to deliver, Elijah also poured scorn on the hypocrisy of the incumbent Lord Palmerston. Whatever their lordships had said through the Queen's Speeches of 1853, 1854, 1859 and 1860, could any working man be simple enough to believe that any of them seriously intended to remedy the inequalities of the representative system? 'They tilted at each other with reform lances. They saw that promising was "the very air o' the time". They used that which they were prepared to cast away, their fight for office at an end. The inequalities and shortcomings that roused their generous ire while the great battle for place was at its fiercest, disappeared from their minds, and therefore no longer haunted their consciences...'

As for Palmerston, Elijah warned: 'His lively lordship has held sway for some years now, and still seats are unequally distributed, registered voters are a little more than a million strong ... Parliamentary reform could not just now be of any use to him, nor has he been under the painful necessity of using it during his tenure of office, or we should have heard it from his lips'.

All this was in an effort to persuade his audience that Palmerston could not be trusted to deliver a proper reform of the franchise. And in this, Elijah proved to be dead right.

Yet, and not for the first time, Elijah's Radical stand was attacked as impractical and divisive. When a Liverpool delegate, J.R. Jeffrey, dared Jones and Elijah to say if they would enfranchise 'the soldier, the policeman, and the pauper', Elijah was up first. ' I beg to say that I would enfranchise every one of those', and Jones agreed. Jeffrey's subsequent remark expressing disdain for the man in the workhouse separated from his wife and children was surely made in ignorance of Elijah's own story. Had it not been, and had Elijah not been prepared to turn the other cheek, the insensitive Jeffrey might well have been asked to step outside.

Jones rose once more to say, as he was shouted down, that a rating franchise would be detested by all classes and would be an utter failure. For Elijah, very much in the minority, out-voted, but still defiantly speaking up for the working man, and catechising their betrayers, it was just like old times.

Chapter Twenty-two

Dob Lane

Elijah probably understood that however loud they shouted, and however much they demonstrated, the advocates of universal suffrage were never going to win victory in the prevailing political climate of the 1860s. Nor even would they succeed in securing manhood suffrage. The hereditary basis of the House of Lords would provide the landed aristocracy with a veto on reform for another hundred years, and the House of Commons consisted of a body of elected men, who in effect, had the power to choose their electors.

There were other causes dear to Elijah; Co-operation and Temperance in particular. By 1863 Elijah was chairman of the Temperance Provident Building Society (founded in 1852, possibly as an adjunct to the New Moston land scheme), with Abel Heywood as trustee. In the same year, he chaired a meeting at the Wesleyan School to inaugurate a Mechanics Institute for Newton Heath and Failsworth. Elijah, as president of the Institution, described how it was begun by only two or three people, but now had the backing of other wealthy patrons. Premises on Church Street had been found and Elijah had 'guaranteed the rent (£20 per annum) for two years'. Not all serious business, however; the meeting included recitations of works by Ben Brierley and Edwin Waugh, with a suggestion that musical entertainment should also be provided in future.

Reform, however, was still top of the domestic agenda, and now in his seventies, as a committee member of the Ballot Society, Elijah continued his efforts in support of the Radical cause. The death of Palmerston, in 1865, removed a powerful obstacle to reform, and new Prime Minister, Lord John Russell, introduced a Bill providing for lower property qualification and redistribution of seats.

The Manchester reformers mobilised yet again. On 9 May 1865, Elijah was on the platform with Ernest Jones and Alderman Abel Heywood at another great meeting in the Free Trade Hall, beating the drum for manhood suffrage. Jones was left to make the centrepiece speech on the theme that, if landed and capitalist interests were afraid of being swamped by workers who, if enfranchised, would have 'a preponderance in the representation', the working and middle classes should accept the challenge and exercise that preponderance. 'Labouring men,' he said, 'would send such representatives as labour had already sent: Lincoln, the wood-cutter, Johnson, the tailor, and Garibaldi, the sailor'. This was received with loud applause and the meeting shortly afterwards wound down, with Elijah seconding a proposal to send messages of condolence to the widow of Abraham Lincoln, who had been assassinated on 14 April, and to President Andrew Johnson, his successor.

At the works of Dixon, Son and Evans, no strangers to wood-cutting and now equipped with the best in up-to-date, steam-powered machinery, things did not always go smoothly. On Tuesday, 17 July 1866, Elijah's grandson, also named Elijah (and a son of Elijah Junior), tragically drowned while playing with a toy boat in the reservoir, referred to as Wood's Pond, within the Company's yard, an inquest being held the next day: he was only five years old. Later in the year, a young apprentice lost four fingers off his left hand, from contact with a powered circular bench-saw.

When, in 1866, Russell's Bill – which split the Liberal party – was defeated, the mantle of electoral reform fell on the unlikely shoulders of Benjamin Disraeli, Chancellor of the Exchequer under Conservative prime minister, Lord Derby. The Radicals were initially dismayed, and the fall of Russell's ministry provoked mass demonstrations in London and the industrial cities. Reformist groups sprang up in every locality, and in September Elijah chaired a branch meeting of the Reform League, at Dob Lane Unitarian Chapel school-room, Failsworth, to make preparation for local people to join a demonstration in Manchester later that month.

On Monday, 24 September, pro-reform demonstrators brought the city to a standstill. This time there was no question of troops being deployed against them. The city fathers themselves supported the principle of franchise enlargement, and the crowds were addressed by the great and good of the Liberal party, surrounded by aldermen, councillors, Members of Parliament, and clergymen. Many employers granted their workers a day off to take part. The event was planned and timed to put maximum pressure on the Derby administration when Parliament re-assembled.

In an expedient show of unity, members of the National Reform League, including Elijah, supporting manhood suffrage, joined forces with the moderate, household suffragists of the National Reform Union. Six disciplined processions, banners waving and led by marching bands, converged on Campfield (also known as Knott Mill fairground) from all quarters of the city, their numbers swelled by contingents arriving by train from surrounding towns. According to the *Ashton and Stalybridge Reporter*, a large group of reformers mustered at the infirmary esplanade was drawn from Rochdale, Oldham, Ashton, Stalybridge, Hollinwood, Woodhouses, Failsworth - and New Moston.

Elijah no doubt took satisfaction in this honourable mention for his new suburb, the slowly growing population of which resided, mainly as owner-occupiers, in little groups of newly-built houses, still surrounded by fields, along Ricketts Street, Jones Street and Dixon Street. By now there was even a beer house on Dixon Street, and although Elijah seems to have been sanguine about a pub on the street that bore his name, he might just the same have joined colleagues from several Temperance societies, who attached themselves to the column starting from New Cross.

It was a rainy day, but Manchester was en fête. Elijah would almost certainly have worn his trademark, wide-brimmed hat, perhaps in honour – but not imitation – of Henry Hunt, a distinct reminder to these new converts to reform of earlier struggles. While Elijah was hardly a *fashionista* himself (he had a reputation for being indifferent to fashion and other such unimportant conventions of society), many Radicals distinguished themselves by certain features of dress and style, typified by Henry Hunt's flamboyant appearance at Peterloo in top hat with green brim, and O'Connor's arrival in Manchester, wearing a fustian suit. Members of the Manchester Female Reform Society at Peterloo set a trend by wearing white. Even before the Chartist era, male adherents to the Radical faith had worn dark jackets of hard-wearing fustian (woven from stout twilled cotton) to symbolise their political allegiance – and, given its use as prison clothing, to show solidarity with imprisoned colleagues.

Elijah – bearing in mind his emphasis on the glorious constitution of 'King, Lords and Commons' in his petition of 1817 – would surely have eschewed the red white and blue tricolour cockades, evocative of Revolutionary and Republican France and favoured by many in the early years. They had made it easier for the authorities to bring charges of treason and sedition, and now, with the growing popularity of Queen Victoria, overt Republicanism was simply counter-productive. Alas, there are no surviving photographs or portraits showing Elijah's headgear, although shortly after his death it was said that his 'matchless wide-awake hat' (of felt, with rounded top and wide brim, Quaker-style) was the crowning feature of his appearance. Though hardly ostentatious, Elijah Dixon was never afraid to stand out.

Six separate platforms were constructed to enable speakers to address the various columns of marchers, and Elijah spoke to the gathering around Platform Six. Introduced as 'an old and well-tried friend of reform', he reminded his audience of the long history of the fight dating back to demonstrations of 1816 and earlier. The top table for speeches that day, however, was at the Free Trade Hall, where Jones was among those who prepared the way for John Bright, now – following his fall from grace as an opponent of the Crimean war – restored to great popularity, and in effect parliamentary leader of the reform cause.

No-one present at Campfield – with the possible exception of Bright – could have foreseen that the Bill shortly to be introduced in Parliament by Disraeli, would go further in extending the franchise than had been envisaged by Russell's Bill. Bright wrote privately to Disraeli, warning that reform was irresistible, and offering Liberal support for Derby's fragile ministry, provided it brought in acceptable reform proposals. But the real pressure came from mass demonstrations of working people, such as that at Campfield, and other similar events in

London and Glasgow. Up and down the land, in Co-operative societies, trade unions, and mechanics institutes – wherever working men met or organised – speeches were made, and resolutions for voting reform were passed. Elijah did his bit. No doubt able to exploit his connection with the 'white rose' county, as well as his Chartist pedigree, he travelled to Yorkshire, on New Year's Eve, to deliver a lecture in a warehouse at Clayton West in favour of manhood suffrage and vote by ballot.

To many people's surprise, Disraeli introduced his own reform Bill in February 1867. Its provisions fell well short of manhood suffrage, prompting a more serious outburst of demonstrations organised by the Reform League. A protest in Hyde Park turned riotous. Although the government had organised troops to stand by, they were held back, and Home Secretary Spencer Walpole resigned.

In Manchester, the Leaguers and Unionists held a conference at the Town Hall, in an effort to take stock of the progress of Disraeli's bill. 'Where are we up to?' was the tenor of the meeting. By now, Disraeli had made so many concessions to the Opposition – led by William Ewart Gladstone – that the Bill appeared more far-reaching than the one introduced by Russell, and many delegates obviously thought it was as good as they were going to get. Elijah and Jones made a last stand on behalf of the Leaguers. Their speeches to the conference in effect acknowledged defeat. Jones lamented that the franchise would still be property-based, and that the Bill did not introduce vote by ballot. Elijah said that household suffrage and a £10 lodger franchise was but 'an instalment' on the people's rights. Vote by the ballot, and manhood suffrage would still be demanded.

In fact, although a superficial unity prevailed, the meeting revealed what was fast becoming a fundamental difference between most of the old Radicals and these parvenu reformers. Elijah's creed of universalism meant he was naturally in favour of universal suffrage, although, for the sake of unity on that May day in 1867, he was prepared to go along with Jones in limiting the terms of the agreed resolution to manhood suffrage. The Reverend Samuel Alfred Steinthal, however, was not, and attempted to amend the resolution to support votes for women. This was condemned by delegate W. Stokes, in remarks which portended just how far the women's suffragist movement still had to travel, and the bitter struggles of the Suffragettes in the face of male chauvinism. 'Women', said Stokes, 'ought not to mend statutes, but stockings'.

Disraeli – who admired Ernest Jones – had indeed, as a popular cartoon of the day showed, caught the Whigs bathing, and walked away with their clothes. The provisions of his Bill made sufficient concessions to the reformist camp to take the sting out of the Radical campaign. In essence, the Representation of the People Act of 1867 enfranchised all male householders in borough constituencies as well as lodgers paying £10 annually for unfurnished rooms. It lowered the property qualification in the counties, and re-distributed 52 seats from rural towns to industrial towns. Manchester got a third seat.

Most Conservatives viewed the Act just as the Whigs had seen their 1832 Reform Act – as an expression of finality intended to stabilise the constitution. However, Elijah was right: it was but an instalment, and the demand for real reform remained unassuaged. The enfranchising of about a million men doubled the size of the electorate. But five million men and all women remained voteless. Moreover, Disraeli's limited re-distribution of seats ensured that the Conservatives, after losing the general election of 1868, were well placed to win parliamentary majorities in future. Aristocratic influence in government continued for the rest of the century, and the Act created a new phenomenon – the working class Conservative voter.

All in all, the little band of marchers from New Moston, who assembled on the infirmary esplanade before processing to Campfield on 24 September 1866, probably felt their efforts had been rewarded – if not to their full satisfaction – by the 1867 Act. For all its shortcomings, the Act meant that every man with hearth and home would have the right to vote. From now on that meant every man on excursion trains to Blackpool, as well as grander trips to Alton Towers. Times were changing. A few years later, on an August bank holiday Monday, 360 employees of Dixon, Son and Evans, many newly enfranchised as tenant householders, enjoyed a day-trip to Blackpool, courtesy of the firm.

Railways were now the main arteries of industrial transport and travel. New sidings, stations, yards and warehouses devoured land beyond the early lines. In 1871, the Lancashire and Yorkshire Railway, successor to the Manchester and Leeds, bought St George's-in-the-Field church, where Elijah's stepmother Mary and son John had been buried, so they could enlarge the Oldham Road goods yard.[1] The Company promised to re-inter the bodies, and paid for a replacement church on Oldham Road itself, near the corner of Livesey Street. This latter was built, though not completed until 1877, but had no burial ground. Moreover, a hundred years later, after the goods yard had closed, a stack of gravestones was discovered under supporting arches. Twenty years after that, during work on the foundations for a new Royal Mail sorting office, evidence of burials was discovered on the old church site. Once again, the same railway company had fallen short in its pledge to show respect for the dead.

At Walker's Croft, Elijah had attacked callous railway kings in their rush to build, whatever the cost, but now, as ever – if still a tad naive about unscrupulous railway companies – he was moving with the times; perhaps letting bygones be bygones. The people of the old township of Moston and its younger namesake the suburb of New Moston, were ill-served by the Lancashire and Yorkshire Railway, whose line between Manchester and Rochdale divided them geographically, but was bereft of a convenient station. Elijah to the rescue.

Accordingly, and ironically about the same time as the L&YR were demolishing St George's, Elijah began negotiations with the Company for a new passenger station at Moston.[2] A deed, preserved in the company's archives, records an agreement between Elijah, as partner in Dixon, Son & Evans, and two other parties, Mrs Sarah Harrison and Mrs Anne Close, acting jointly, whose addresses (in St Leonard's-on-Sea, and Antibes, France, respectively) reveal a further fascinating glimpse of changes in social mobility brought about the railways. While Matilda Dixon had moved to sunny Southport to open a boarding house, widowed Mrs Harrison was able to settle on the even sunnier south coast of England, and, thanks to the value of land and the advent of steam ships, Mrs Close went as far as the Cote d'Azur.

It seems that the hard-headed directors of the L&YR wanted to mitigate the risk of building a station in what was still an essentially rural location, set among fields and farms. The obvious site was land on Broad Lane, adjacent to the bridge over the line, and the main link between Moston and New Moston. Accordingly, they were able to extract a promise of payment of £150 per annum over a three-year period, at the end of which the company were free to close the station, should there prove to be insufficient receipts to justify retaining it. Mrs Harrison and Mrs Close became jointly liable for £80, and Elijah for the remaining £70. It was not just a case of altruism. The station, which opened in October 1872, was bound to increase the value of adjacent land and rents as well as being convenient for suburban commuters. Nowadays, although run down, Moston station continues to provide locals with a fast service to Manchester, as well as linking them with Leeds and the West Riding.

By this time, Elijah and Martha had moved from Clough House to their new home, Vine House, in Ricketts Street, New Moston. The new station was a good mile away, but until the building of the line from Manchester to Oldham via Hollinwood, it remained the nearest railway link for the new suburb. Yet it would hardly have been worthwhile for Elijah to commute to Newton Heath via Moston station. The journey by carriage, via Failsworth, was quicker, depending on the state of Hale Lane. Besides, by now Elijah was unlikely to be spending much time at the works. Son-in-law George Evans and grandsons Elijah Marsh and William Marsh could safely be allowed to manage the business on a day-to-day basis, while Elijah was near enough to keep an eye on them if need arose. And if the benefits of the new station accrued mainly to the residents of Moston and New Moston (including the Dixons), the L&YR lawyers appear not to have been troubled by the fact that Elijah signed on behalf of the firm. Nor, presumably, was George Evans.

Even at eighty, however, Elijah was involved in another rural adventure. For the last half dozen years of his life, Elijah attended Saturday night meetings at a small chapel in Whaley Bridge, staying overnight (possibly at the home of the local Baptist minister) before preaching a sermon the following morning. The airy moorland hills on the borders of Derbyshire and Cheshire were a long way to travel by horse and carriage, but the rail journey there from Moston involved two trains, inconveniently running to and from terminal stations separated by Manchester town centre. The health of wife Martha, two years older than him, may have begun to fail about this time. What better tonic than a country retreat like that at Chat Moss, only this time even further removed from the industrial city?

The line through Failsworth and Hollinwood arrived late into the railway age, but it appears that once again the Dixons had a hand in hastening its arrival. On 4 November 1871, the *Ashton Weekly Reporter* carried a brief item about the preparation of a Parliamentary Bill to authorise construction. It stated that the 'likely' route, branching off the Rochdale line at Newton Heath, would cross Dean Lane 'on the site of E.M. Dixon's residence' and 'thence behind Messrs. Dixon, Son and Evans's works'. Even if Elijah had by now taken a back seat at the firm, he would surely have been among the lobbyists in Newton Heath, Failsworth and Hollinwood who wanted the line. Quite apart from bringing the possibility of sidings and a new station on Dean Lane, convenient for the works and its employees, a station at Failsworth would be another boost for New Moston, providing its long-suffering residents could reach it over the bad road on the Failsworth side of the Moston Brook. In the event, the line was opened in 1880, but *without* a station at Failsworth, which was added a year later. Elijah Marsh Dixon, meanwhile, about to lose his home to the railway builders, would be happy to move from industrialised Newton Heath to settle with his wife and growing family in a more salubrious suburb, such as New Moston.

From now on Elijah pinned his colours to the mast of the Liberal party, though naturally, as a lifelong believer in votes for women, he was always to be found on its Radical wing. Universal suffrage was still more than fifty years and a world war away, and in the Manchester of the 1870s no Radical worth his salt could rest on his laurels. Elijah knew the way ahead but the Ballot Act was to be the last example of democracy by instalment that he would live to see.

Unwearied by age – apart from a little deafness – it was to be expected that Elijah's political engagements would become less onerous and more honorary. He was a natural chairman of meetings, a safe pair of hands who knew the rules of chairmanship backwards, and the obvious choice of local Liberal parties wanting to invest their meetings with gravitas. In 1868, he was elected chairman of the new Liberal Association of Newton Heath, whose first meeting was given over to the issue of party unity. Mr J.M. Elliott deployed flowery and obtuse quotations urging members to 'bear and forbear' to avoid internal conflict. On that occasion, Elijah's presidential role pre-empted a public objection to such remarks, obviously aimed at keeping the universal suffragists quiet. It would be surprising, however, if Elliott got home that night without hearing Elijah's opinion, privately put, and illustrated by ample quotation from the scriptures.

So too, when in the same year, a new Co-operative store was opened on New Road, Failsworth, Elijah was invited to preside at a celebratory tea party at the New Jerusalem School. The store, much rebuilt, is still open today (though no longer a Co-op) on what is now Oldham Road.

In politics as well as business, Elijah continued to make way for younger men. At the firm, the process had begun during the interlude at Chat Moss, when Job could be relied on to manage the works and Evans was at hand as engineer. After Job's death, first his brother Elijah (Junior) and later his son, Elijah Marsh Dixon, took on more responsibility (although he never became a partner) and by 1868 he was serving as one of two representatives of All Saints, Newton Heath, on the Board of Health, along with George Evans. When Evans resigned that year, the Dixons were anxious to replace him with a nominee, Edmund Wrigley, lest the position should fall to Robert Lancashire, of the same family that, more than 25 years previously, Elijah had berated for their self-serving administration of tithes.

In October 1869, Elijah was supported by George Evans in a letter written on behalf of Moston ratepayers to the Poor Law Board in London which appeared in the *Bury Times* on the 23rd. Moston was part of the Prestwich Union for the purpose of Poor Law administration, and Elijah and Evans were among Moston residents who complained that regular surpluses ought to be applied so as to reduce the rates. This had echoes of the old days when Elijah had attended Manchester leypayers meetings, ever watchful for misuse of public funds. The difference now was that there was no provision for representations to be made at public meetings. As Elijah had correctly predicted, the new Poor Law had become more bureaucratic and less accountable. The Poor Law Guardian for Moston accordingly expressed his outrage that the ratepayers had not consulted him and agreed to respond to Whitehall in terms of a letter which the clerk had already drafted. However, as if to prove Elijah's point, the terms of the draft were kept secret from the *Bury Times* reporter who covered the meeting. But at least the name and reputation of Elijah Dixon, businessman and Blanketeer, had given cause for officials in London to sit up and take notice of ratepayers' problems in faraway Moston - an altogether more favourable response than Elijah had received in 1817, when he had attended Whitehall in person.

Elijah was by now becoming acquainted with the rising generation of Liberal politicians in Manchester. Notable amongst these was Jacob Bright, younger brother of better known John, one of the three Manchester M.P.s returned in the general election of 1868. He and Elijah, both strong supporters of votes for women, became firm friends. Elijah was on equally good terms with Dr Richard Marsden Pankhurst, barrister and future husband of Emmeline. Both Pankhurst and Elijah were founder members of the Manchester Liberal Association, and Elijah, with his propensity for good causes, was surely a member of the National Society for Women's Suffrage, also founded by Pankhurst. Jacob and Elijah sat alongside each other on the platform for the annual soiree of the Newton Heath Ragged School, held at Culcheth in November 1870.

In July the following year, Elijah presided at a tea party to mark the opening of the new Ragged School in Queen street, Newton Heath, providing 250 places and replacing the now overcrowded one on Heath Street. All his life, the partially self-educated Elijah had been a believer in the value of education, and given the limitations of basic schooling provided by the Established church, his support for the Ragged School movement, which offered an alternative and broader education, was only natural. Very soon he would be gratified by a key reform in Gladstone's first ministry, the introduction of Board schools, the state's first foray into education.

Yet, however much he sympathised with the political principles of secularism, he supported the application of universal Christian values in everyday life. Why else, at this time, might he have put up a prize of £5 for the best essay on the subject of 'How shall working men and women spend the day of rest, called Sunday, so as to promote their own and the social welfare?' The competition was open to 'all working persons in receipt of weekly wages' in Newton, Failsworth, Moston and Droylsden. The winner in March 1871, was Joe Miller, from Newton Heath, who claimed to be 'born on th' common'. His 'Ploughboy's Poetical Essay' was chosen from twenty-four entries. Written in verse, 'i'th gradely Newton dialect', copies were later sold at a penny each to raise money towards a tea–party for (in Joe's own words) 'owd folk o'er seventy yer owd livin' on th' Yeth'. Nothing pretentious about Elijah's literary tastes.

At the age of 84, once again in the company of Jacob Bright, Elijah was on his feet at the Manchester Reform Club, to support a vote of thanks to John Morley, a future Irish Secretary in Gladstone's second administration, who spoke on the need for free schooling, and lamented the number of children denied education beyond the age of ten.

Because Newton had escaped incorporation into the borough of Manchester, its rating procedures continued to be administered independently, and right to the end Elijah seems to have kept a beady eye on expenditure. In August 1871, as chairman of a meeting of ratepayers, Elijah had the pleasure of hearing grandson Elijah Marsh denouncing what the meeting accepted was an excessive pay rise proposed for the Poor Rate Collector. Elijah Marsh, one of the Overseers, highlighted the fact that the increase had been mooted at a poorly attended Vestry meeting, and discredited it in an analysis of the Collector's duties and work-load. Grandpa Dixon must have permitted himself a wry smile when he heard the resounding cheers in response to the speech from his grandson, opposing the increase and commending civic frugality. Happily married Elijah Marsh was also playing an increasing role in managing the match side of the business.

By now the presence of Manchester's own Grand Old Man of Liberalism, had become de rigueur at Liberal party events, especially in Newton Heath and Failsworth. A guest lecturer at the meeting room of Newton Heath Liberal Association in Dixon Street paid tribute to Elijah, presiding, as 'one of the oldest reformers in England', before delivering a tub-thumping attack on 'Tory Fallacies'.

Elijah had campaigned for vote by ballot for more than fifty years. In 1872, notwithstanding the aristocratic elements that lingered inside the new Liberal party, Gladstone's first government passed the Ballot Act. It ensured replacement of the open electoral list with the now familiar secret ballot - thereby protecting tenants from blackmail and intimidation by landlords, a right they had assumed from time immemorial. It also shut down an obvious incitement to bribery. Nothing in all Elijah's long career of agitation and demonstration could have given him greater satisfaction. Vote by ballot had been called for by the Blanketeers and was the second of the Six Points in the People's Charter.

Chapter Twenty-three

Ardwick

Democracy is but Christianity applied to the politics of our worldly life.

Inscribed on the memorial to Ernest Jones, Ardwick Cemetery

IT WAS the premature death of Ernest Jones, on 26 January 1869, that dealt the most profound blow to the Manchester Radicals. Though he had resided in the city for barely a decade, he was a man who made firm friendships, and inspired great loyalty. His close links with Elijah went back to the boisterous meeting at Clerkenwell which preceded Jones's two year prison term, and in Manchester they had worked closely together in the Reform League and Co-operative movement. Jones shared Elijah's commitment to universal suffrage, and both men drew their spiritual strength from the well of Christianity. By the time of his death, both Jones and Elijah were active members of the Liberal Party.

In the crude terminology of modern politics Jones was well to the left of Elijah, more the ideologue; a brilliant speaker of the kind who these days might attract the jibe of 'never having had a proper job'. In a letter to the *Co-operative News* in the early 1860s, Jones praised the moral virtues of Co-operation in high-blown phrases and scorned 'competition' as a 'social poison', a 'bane to which Co-operation was the antidote'. As an entrepreneur, responsible for the employment of hundreds of workers whose jobs depended on Dixon, Son & Evans competing successfully in national and international markets, Elijah was unlikely to be seduced by such rhetoric.

Moreover, Jones had contact with, and was respected by, both Karl Marx and Friedrich Engels, whose theorising about history and materialism was far removed from Elijah's Christian egalitarianism. But Jones inspired many by his eloquence and, later in life, by his skill as a barrister, practising from chambers in Cross Street. His courageous but doomed defence of the 'Manchester Martyrs' – members of the Irish Republican Brotherhood, charged with murdering police sergeant Charles Brett – would probably have appealed to Elijah the Christian Universalist, though the act of murder would not. And anyway, in early life, Jones had indeed had a proper job – as secretary to the Leek and Mansfield Railway Company.

Elijah was a pall bearer for the burial service at Ardwick cemetery, after taking part in the funeral cortege, sitting alongside grandson Elijah Marsh in the fifth private carriage. Thousands lined the route from Jones's home in Broughton, and crowded into the cemetery. In what was seen as the last great Chartist gathering, the *Manchester Courier* and *Manchester Weekly Times* reported that four old Chartists ('all Peterloo veterans') led the procession but did not name them.

Elijah helped to organise a public subscription for a monument to Jones, and in April the following year was requested by the memorial committee to perform the unveiling ceremony. It was a very grand, if not extravagant edifice, twelve feet tall, and the announcement of the forthcoming ceremony in the columns of the *Manchester Evening News* presaged an unfortunate mishap on the day. Elijah arrived late. The reason was never given and no doubt Elijah offered embarrassed apologies when he arrived at the cemetery, but by this time Radical Unitarian minister, the Rev S.A. Steinthal, had stepped into the breach. Even so, Elijah was in time to add his own tribute to Jones. He had never known a man whose 'talents were so freely and distinctly sacrificed for the public good', and concluded, to cheers from the crowd, by echoing Jones's own words, inscribed in stone, that Christianity and freedom were one and the same thing. Had he lived, the recalcitrance of Liberal leaders to embrace a democratic franchise would almost certainly have led Jones into the nascent Labour movement. Might Elijah have followed? Might he have sublimated his natural suspicion of interfering, over-spending bureaucracy? It was becoming obvious to many that the Liberals could never be genuinely representative of the working man, but it took another 25 years after Elijah's death before the Labour party emerged as an independent force in parliament.

A few years later, Elijah was to preside at a meeting of Liberal Associations in Manchester which decided to establish a further, perhaps more enduring and useful, monument to the charismatic Jones. It took the form of a fund to publish and distribute a collected works of Jones's poetry and prose, as well as to hold an annual conference in his honour. The motion was supported by the Reverend Steinthal and Dr Richard Pankhurst, amongst others. Speeches in praise of 'democracy' were made in what today would be considered moderate and uncontroversial terms. Elijah, reiterating Jones's theme, said that democracy enjoined its citizens to 'love their neighbours as themselves'.

The following day, however, the *Manchester Courier* editorialised disdainfully on the 'decidedly democratic tinge' of Liberalism, which manifested itself, according to their interpretation of Elijah's speech, in 'an anxiety to despoil people of their property and to distribute it equally among those who are not burdened with any'. Equality, it went on to opine, was but a 'grim joke', supported only by the wild and fanatical 'rag-tag and bob-tail' faction of the Liberal party. Many years had passed since the newspapers had ridiculed Elijah the cart orator. And for all the gravitas of old age and celebrity status, he was still regarded by some as a dangerous Radical. He would have liked that.

Elijah also ensured the creation of another memorial to Jones in New Moston. The Freehold Land Society had given the name Jones Street to one of the main thoroughfares of its development, in honour of Manchester's adopted Chartist hero. If, however, he imagined it to be a permanent memorial to his friend, events – within a generation – were to prove him wrong.

A concomitant of longevity is the outliving of friends, colleagues and family members. One by one Elijah saw the passing of old comrades in reform. In April 1872, representing the National Reform Union, he attended the funeral of Samuel Bamford, at St Leonard's church, Middleton. Bamford had been a fellow detainee of Lord Sidmouth in the dark days of 1817. Although, with the help of Henry Grey Bennet, they both petitioned parliament the following year, they were lodged in different London gaols, and seem to have had little direct contact with each other after release, or indeed, during the long years of Radical struggle that followed.

Bamford had played a prominent part in the story of Peterloo – a part that remains controversial to this day. The six-thousand strong Rochdale and Middleton contingent, led by him, suffered heavy casualties. Bamford was a natural target for victimisation in the subsequent round-up orchestrated by Nadin, as a result of which he suffered another year's imprisonment. His activities and sufferings were publicised in his own writings, notably *Passages in the Life of a Radical*, in which he delighted in criticism of friend and foe alike. Like Elijah, he lived to a great age, and there is a nice irony in the fact that in spite of his gleeful crowing over seeing off contemporaries, some, including Elijah, outlived him.

The irony was all the richer given that Elijah himself had been on the receiving end of Bamford's caustic commentaries. In 1859, both men had attended an election meeting in the Free Trade Hall to support Abel Heywood. In his diary, Bamford, who liked the limelight, lampooned Heywood as 'Abel Anything', and poured scorn on Elijah's introductory remarks as chairman.[1] Elijah's reference to his own imprisonment in 1817, and subsequent labours in the cause of reform, provoked Bamford to aver that 'he has only laboured for himself to accumulate money'. Not long before the meeting, Bamford had boasted of being 'the earliest political sufferer now living' – overlooking Elijah. As a diarist, he was grudgingly, but privately, setting the record straight.

Just how grudgingly can be judged from a later passage in the diaries, published posthumously many years later. Commenting on the death of William Willis in 1861, Bamford refers to him as 'a great scoundrel, and one of the most bitter of my enemies', linking him with Nightingale, who died on the same day. They were, he said, members of the 'contemptible Elijah Dixon set'. Confident that the pair would 'enter the sulphurous regions hand in hand', it was a preface to further vitriolic comments on Elijah's erstwhile collaborators; 'enemies and false friends... slipping away before me'. Archibald Prentice, 'the Scotch mendicant', is accused of plagiarism and sponging. James Wroe, one of Elijah's closest comrades and one-time editor of the *Manchester Observer*, is recalled as 'little skinny, ignorant and impudent Jimmy Wroe ... about as fit for the business as a pig on a midden'. 'All are gone,' he exults. And yet for all Bamford's jealous bile, Elijah's little band of old contemptibles must take their place in history as deservedly as their detractor. Elijah was probably never aware of Bamford's attack on him, death pre-empting the Christian forgiveness he might otherwise have shown.

The death of another member of the old guard, Joseph Johnson, a few months later, brought about a curious re-examination of Elijah's part in the demonstration at St Peter's Field in 1819. Born in 1791, Johnson, a contemporary of Elijah and a fellow-member of the Manchester Patriotic Union, had served a year's imprisonment for his part in organising the demonstration. When the *Manchester Times* provided its readers with a brief obituary, it claimed that Johnson's death left Elijah as one of the last surviving veterans of Peterloo, only to carry a correction in the same issue, tendered by 'a correspondent', categorically stating that Elijah was not at the meeting that day – a stark contrast with William Hepworth's averment that his uncle received a sabre cut at Peterloo. The assertion that Elijah was older than Bamford was also corrected, and were it not for the fact that Bamford had pre-deceased Johnson, Bamford would surely have been prime suspect for the anonymous correspondent.

So what is the truth about Elijah and Peterloo? Was he there, in the crowd but not on the platform? Did he go into hiding soon afterwards, knowing that Nadin's men would be after him? Involvement in the MPU and with the Blanketeers had, after all, made him well known to the authorities. Was he ill or incapacitated, concerned for his wife and children, desperate to avoid their incarceration in the Manchester workhouse, unwilling to throw upon them the consequences of another term of imprisonment, so soon after his release from Tothill Fields? Wherever Elijah was on 16 August 1819, he was soon enough back on the scene as an activist in the Radical cause. Not so Johnson, whose wife died during his imprisonment and who thereafter took little part in Manchester politics, even, according to the *Manchester Times*, becoming 'petrified into Toryism of a type peculiar to himself'.

In his later years, Elijah's main political focus was the Newton Heath Liberal Association. The Liberals got a nasty shock in the general election of 1874 which brought an end to Gladstone's first ministry. Although they polled more votes than the Conservatives, they won fewer seats, thanks to the limited scope of Disraeli's reforms, prompting a good deal of introspection and a review of organisation. The parties were learning that what mattered on election day was getting the vote out – making sure your supporters actually voted. The party blamed apathy, and its poor performance in Lancashire and Manchester was typified by the defeat of Jacob Bright.

Accordingly, in February 1875, foregathered at the Association's meeting room in Dixon Street, Newton, Elijah presided as Newton Heath Liberals conducted a thorough post-mortem. In the 1830s and '40s Elijah had noted the importance of ensuring sympathetic voters got on the lists of eligible leypayers, so he was the obvious choice for chairman of a working party on voter registration, aimed at ensuring supporters paid their rates in time to qualify. The Association also decided to hold a series of lectures on political subjects the following winter.

Within the Liberal party, Elijah continued to support the National Reform Union – an umbrella pressure group intended to ensure that the next Liberal government would be a reforming one. In his last attendance at the Free Trade Hall, in December 1875, Elijah was on the platform at a grand conference to revitalise the Union through a new constitution. Dr Pankhurst sat alongside Elijah, and the *Dover Express* reported that 'several ladies were present' including those from women's Liberal associations. Whig grandees, still an influential part of the Liberal party, shuffled their feet for excuses not to attend, including Lord Granville, who wrote to say that while he did not concur with all the Union's aims, he welcomed healthy discussion and the fact that 'men of character and position' had put themselves at the head of it. Hardly ringing support for democracy, and although Elijah did not live long enough to see it materialise, the discontent among working class people that eventually gave rise to the Labour party can be imagined from imperious remarks such as these.

The Newton Heath Association was called into action earlier than expected, when in February 1876 it played its part in the successful by-election campaign to get Bright re-elected for Manchester. Elijah was present, and later took the chair (from George Evans), at a packed election meeting in Newton Heath public hall. The old campaigner, now 85, was no doubt delighted at Bright's success, and the vibrancy of political debate which characterised the meeting – probably enlivened, as Elijah would have conceded, by the presence of Tory hecklers and awkward questions – ranging through the whole gamut of issues facing Victorian England: trade unionism, land ownership, Disestablishment of the Church, slum housing, Sunday closing, Irish political prisoners, the County franchise, and expenses voted by Parliament for the Prince of Wales' visit to India. This was Elijah's last old-style political meeting and given the fundamental beliefs in universal suffrage and temperance, shared with Bright, it was a fitting swan-song.

On 17 April, Jacob Bright was the guest of honour at a soiree of the Number 2 Newton Heath Liberal Club. He took the opportunity to make a speech to the party faithful, catechising Disraeli's Tory government, ending by proposing a motion in favour of broadening the County franchise and 'a more equitable distribution of political power'. In seconding the motion, Elijah played out what was to become one of the last acts of his political career, preparing the reform agenda for Gladstone's second ministry. But it was a case of unfinished business. Eight years later, the 1884 Reform Act still left forty per cent of adult males – and all women – without the vote.

Chapter Twenty-four

The Atheneum

Old Chartist, old Blanketeer, that he was, Elijah's politics did not define him. His fight to change the distribution of power through agitation and demonstration was not the only means by which his life spoke. Politics and business were only a part of a life so infused with energy and faith that he felt bound to act in any rightful cause.

The early Radicals had been dead against foreign wars, supporting the French in their revolution against tyranny, and the American revolt against British rule. Those like Elijah, close to distress in the towns, objected to the cost of war, both in human and material terms, and blamed it for raising taxes and exacerbating distress. For their honesty they were persecuted by the Church-and-Kingers. Now they were in the age of Imperialism, during which British rule spread across the globe as an adjunct of its maritime power. Palmerston had gloried in gunboat diplomacy and Disraeli was soon to exploit the appeal of empire by creating the title of Empress of India for Queen Victoria. The tactic of drumming up patriotic fervour for the conduct of foreign wars won popular support – notably among newly enfranchised voters – but not amongst thoughtful men like Elijah, who suspected that the empire was being promoted by the same ruthless interests that had preserved slavery. Even Gladstone had supported the slave-owning American Confederacy, and – as John Bright, the Quaker, had learned to his cost during the Crimean war – there were political consequences for peace lovers.

However, along with Elijah, Jacob Bright (brother of John) was among those who attended a meeting at Manchester Town Hall in January 1872 to express views on a more enlightened form of resolving international disputes. A resolution supported by Elijah condemned the evils of war and called for the setting up of an 'international jurisdiction for the settlement of differences between states by appeals to justice instead of the sword'. Bright proposed a resolution calling on the government to adopt the principle of international arbitration, and the meeting made plans to form an association to promote its objectives.

A year later, a meeting convened by the northern section of the new Association, again held at the Town Hall, heard Elijah, in his eighty-second year, give a rollicking speech in favour of arbitration. What sort of madness was it for men to employ their time and ingenuity in shooting their customers? If people at home followed such a practice they would have to be 'taken care of' by their friends and put in a place of safety. Like the optimistic founders of the League of Nations and the United Nations, Elijah and Bright might be accused of naivety, and the extent to which the world eschewed their noble sentiments was to be well demonstrated down the generations. Yet Elijah insisted that until nations resolved to submit their differences to arbitration, peace and plenty would never reign throughout the world. In that at least, he was proved right.

Elijah had long believed in the need to break the link between the state and the Anglican church, and the growth of Liberalism encouraged hopes that this could be achieved – notwithstanding that Liberal leader Gladstone was himself a High Church Anglican. Elijah was on the platform at a meeting of Disestablishment faithful in October 1872, at the Free Trade Hall, again alongside Bright, Rev Steinthal and Dr Pankhurst. However, as with the parallel campaign to regulate the liquor trade, there were ramifications for any political party that had to answer to a diverse, pluralist electorate, however limited, on polling day.

Gladstone succeeded in pushing through Disestablishment of the Church in Ireland, where the issue was far more urgent. In England, however, it was more complicated because of the link to education. Most schools were still run as church schools, but Forster's Education Act, which set up Board schools, took the sting out of the issue. Their remit was to provide non–denominational religious education. Elijah, typically as a Non–Conformist Christian, might well have wished to break the constitutional links between church and state. But he, and most Liberals, would have baulked at the idea of purely secular education. Against this background, Gladstone cleverly steered his party away from denominational jealousy by leaving most Anglican and other denominational schools untouched. In contrast, Newton Heath Ragged School was soon to become absorbed into the system of local Board schools, leaving its teachers with the awkward duty of interpreting the Bible in any way they chose - provided it was not overtly that of any existing religious group.

Elijah never allowed his strong belief in Temperance to inhibit co-operation with old Radicals. He attended hundreds of meetings in taverns and beer houses, sitting alongside comrades who enjoyed drinking alcohol – occasionally or otherwise. His brother Asa had run the Highland Laddie beerhouse for a time, and comrade and business partner Edward Nightingale had been landlord of the Sir Ralph Abercrombie public house. The husband of Elijah's daughter, Judith – James Harrop – was the son of the erstwhile landlord of the King's Arms. At the same time, there were close friendships with Radicals prominent in the Temperance movement, such as Archibald Prentice, James Scholefield and a second Joseph Johnson (a lay-preacher, thirty years younger than the Peterloo veteran, who was to describe Elijah's career in his serialised memoirs). James Gaskill and William Ricketts, co-founders of New Moston, were also dedicated adherents to the Temperance cause. As with alcohol, so with faith;

difference of opinion did not stop Elijah from chairing a meeting at Failsworth in 1871 addressed by George Holyoake, staunch co-operator and secularist. The curious title of Holyoake's lecture was 'Prospects of the Ouseburn Co-operative Engine Company', and the October issue of *The Reasoner* reported that Elijah gave a speech 'of remarkable energy and eloquence'.

The ravages of the 'demon drink' in Victorian England, however, were as widespread and as well-known as they are in modern times. God knows there were enough reasons in those days for working and unemployed men to want to drown their sorrows, while poverty, and paucity of relief, made the consequences for them and their families all the more devastating. Moreover, then as now, brewers and distillers were a powerful economic influence, closely linked to the landed interest and generally supporters of Disraeli and the Conservatives. And in his abhorrence of social evils linked to drink, Elijah had at least one ally in the Irish community, with which he had often come to blows. It was said that Father Theobold Mathew, an Irish priest, administered 'the pledge' (to total abstinence) to at least 17,000 Mancunians.

Unsurprisingly, when Gladstone came to power in 1868, he came under pressure from Temperance adherents in his own party, including MPs such as Jacob Bright. Elijah was a member of the Independent Order of Rechabites, a friendly society promoting total abstinence, and founded in Salford in 1835 (there was, indeed, an Elijah Dixon 'Tent'). He was also an early patron of the Band of Hope, whose object was, and remains, to teach children the importance and principles of sobriety and teetotalism. In April 1868, Elijah presided at a meeting of Sunday school teachers and others at the Trevelyan temperance hotel in Corporation Street. In 1871, Elijah was listed by the 10 October edition of the *Manchester Evening News* as a private subscriber to a Temperance Guarantee Fund, and later the same month he presided at the inaugural soiree of the Newton Heath Pioneer Lodge of Good Templars. The Templars, a global, American-based organisation dedicated to promoting alcohol-free lifestyle, admitted men and women equally. Their mission arrived in Newton Heath under the auspices of Newton Heath Ragged School, thanks to the good offices of 'Bro. Elijah Dixon'. The *Ashton Reporter* informed its readers of the organisation's rapidly growing membership, locally and nationally. The *Pall Mall Gazette* of 28 February 1872 listed Elijah among the £50 donors to a subscription launched by the United Kingdom Alliance, whose aim was to outlaw the sale of alcohol for consumption entirely. The anti-drink wing of the Liberal party had reached its high tide of prominence and publicity.

The result of nation-wide pressure on Gladstone was the Licensing Act of 1872, which introduced the offence of being drunk and disorderly, and regulated closing times. The latter triggered an outburst of resentment in working class areas, and partly explained Disraeli's success in the general election early in 1874. Gladstone himself lamented that his government had been 'borne down in a torrent of gin and beer'. There were in fact other causes, and defeat for the Liberals affected neither Elijah's allegiance to the party nor his commitment to Temperance. In April, following the election, Elijah was a speaker at a regional conference of the Templars. It was well attended, and attracted delegates from across the north of England. Convoluted resolutions condemning the liquor trade and the 'drinking system' were carried, but the reality of Liberal politics henceforth was that any attack on the pleasures of the drinking classes might well lose you the next election. This was, however, a reality not yet understood by the supporters of Temperance, and they plodded on, hoping that a future Liberal government would introduce further curbs on the liquor trade.

Accordingly, Elijah threw his weight behind the parliamentary campaign for a Permissive Bill – which would allow local authorities to hold referenda on whether or not to prohibit the sale of alcohol. It might more accurately have been described as a Prohibition Bill, and although it was doomed to die a death – in spite of being introduced into parliament nine times – Elijah loyally supported its chief proponent, Sir Wilfred Lawson.

Though Elijah followed the campaign, the days of fiery rhetoric and heckling were behind him, and at the twelfth annual meeting of the Manchester and Salford Temperance Union, in January 1875, Elijah was content to take the chair. Preachy speeches delivered by clergymen expressed fears that Disraeli's government might reverse the limited gains of the Licensing Act and painted a Hogarthian picture of 'drinking and debauchery' in Manchester. Its solicitors had successfully opposed the granting of some licences, where the Union had identified the 'vice of intemperance', especially amongst women. It really wasn't Elijah's cup of tea, and perhaps he fidgeted uneasily, or even nodded off, as delegates recited reams of statistics about recruitment of affiliates to the noble cause. In March, at a meeting in the Atheneum Club, Elijah seconded a resolution calling for Lawson's Bill to be supported by petitions and public meetings. Another meeting there, the following year, was prompted by the return to parliament of Jacob Bright. Elijah, who was cheered loudly, seconded a resolution to the effect that Bright's re-election had 'preserved Manchester from the disgrace of giving its support to the Sunday liquor traffic', and all agreed it created a fair wind for Lawson's latest Permissive Bill.

The meetings at the Atheneum set the stage for Elijah's last speech, at the Manchester Reform Club, a few days later. The plan, which succeeded, was to get Lawson's Bill adopted as an official plank in the Liberal programme and, according to the *Leighton Buzzard Observer* of 7 March, Elijah 'the veteran Radical reformer' spoke 'nobly and earnestly' in the cause. It was, however, a lost cause. When Gladstone returned to power in 1880, he was consumed by his mission to pacify Ireland, and by foreign affairs, arising mainly from Britain's imperialist adventures in Africa and Asia. Given the disastrous election result in 1874, he was not prepared to risk another concession to the Temperance lobby

– except in Wales, where pubs were obliged to shut on Sundays. In England, it would take forty years and a world war before the government again felt confident enough to regulate drinking and drinkers.

Besides, the Liberal party already had a direct conflict of interest over the issue. Partly in response to the growth of Conservative clubs, the Liberals began building their own clubs, as a means of nurturing working class support. In Failsworth, Elijah was a founder member of the new club, opened in 1874 at Bridge House on Oldham Road. The press was assiduously informed that it was also for the benefit of supporters in Woodhouses and New Moston. It was a jolly occasion, enlivened by a procession, music from the Failsworth Brass Band, and recitations by local dialect poet, Ben Brierley. It was a place intended for the working man to rest and relax, to enjoy a game of billiards or bowls and a pint of beer. Any attempt by a do-good local council to deprive him of that, would have brought about imminent closure and a rash of applications to join the Conservative club across the road (at least, after its opening in 1886). Happily, the Failsworth Liberal Club, replaced in 1888 by a new, purpose-built club a little further south, survived for more than a hundred years, and as late as 1935 was still displaying a portrait of Elijah Dixon – over the bar.

Chapter Twenty-five

Windgather Rocks

In 1873, Elijah is shown on the electoral registers for rural east Cheshire as owner of a house and land 'near Wind Gather Rocks, Kettleshulme'. Hard up against the Derbyshire border it was, and is, a stunningly beautiful location, looking out over the green Cheshire plain towards the distant Welsh mountains, and protected from the worst of the weather by a spectacular rocky outcrop. It is difficult to imagine an English landscape in greater contrast to the industrial sprawl of Manchester and Newton Heath. The shrinking farmlands of New Moston and Failsworth – their meadows and lanes hemmed in by housing and mills – were nothing like the open moorlands and rippling hilltops on the borders of Cheshire and Derbyshire.

How are we to see this surprising development? Elijah, it might fairly be assumed, loved every aspect of the elemental beauty that he saw on his first, and thereafter frequent, visits to Windgather Rocks. Unlike the dream he had tried to live thirty years previously in the flat fenlands of Chat Moss, burdened by the theology of land schemes, was the Windgather venture simply the fulfilment of a personal project, a richly deserved indulgence, towards the end of a strenuous life?

Any man in his 70s or 80s is prone to reflect on the landmarks of his life, and if he has the time, health and the means to do so, free of want and pain, he is fortunate indeed. Of all the landscapes Elijah had known, the glories of Windgather most resembled the wooded Pennine cloughs and streams feeding into the Holme valley of his Yorkshire boyhood. He may also have had in mind that Martha, now herself in twilight years, might benefit from such surroundings.

Railways brought the means by which people could escape the towns to reach coast or countryside. Blackpool was all very well as a destination for the annual works outing for Dixon and Son, but richer men were moving from homes like Clough House – over the shop – to grand houses in the suburbs, old market towns, coastal resorts like Southport and St Annes, and to remote countryside. Also, thanks to the railways, those like Elijah who did not wish to quit the towns were now able to roam the countryside and be home in time for tea. Sunday schools were going beyond local parks with outings by train to coast and countryside. Manchester newspapers in the 1860s carried advertisements for, and short reports of, such trips; to Lytham, Southport and to places such as Hebden Bridge, Dunham, Disley, and Whaley Bridge.

Moreover, access to the countryside for the town's huddled masses had always been a bona fide Radical cause, taking the fight to landowners who sought to obstruct rights of way and ancient liberties. One unsung hero of these early battles was Elijah's friend from Chartist days, Reginald Richardson. Another was Archibald Prentice. Both played a part in reviving the Manchester Association for the Preservation of Ancient Public Footpaths. Quite apart from attending Chartist meetings with Richardson, Elijah would have been aware of his press campaign to protect paths from enclosure by Colonel Clowes on Kersal Moor, as well as similar activities in deepest Cheshire. Elijah had other connections with Richardson. In 1854 he had been appointed Clerk of Works to the Newton Heath Local Board, and in that capacity, acting as inspector of nuisances, he succeeded in ending the deadly 'slink trade' in diseased cattle.

The issue was only part of the bigger problem of nuisances, such as chemical discharges from factories, by which industrial pollution was degrading life in the towns. In the same year, Elijah (later to be president of the Manchester Building Trades Protection Association) had attended a meeting of manufacturers to discuss progress and enforcement of a Nuisances Removal Bill. They were concerned most about protection from 'vexatious and injurious interference', but were not, they insisted 'conservators of nuisances'.

It was a classic conflict of interest between Elijah the industrialist and Elijah the environmentalist, anticipating the perennial – and unresolved – dichotomy of industrial civilisation. Elijah was no different from any other manufacturer wrestling with the rights and wrongs of industrial life. Other captains of industry simply denied their responsibility to protect the environment. Their processes inflicted industrial disease on generations of workers who worked and lived under clouds of soot and smoke from factory chimneys, and besides streams and rivers polluted by chemical discharges and sewage. The results were infernal landscapes from which the upper and middle classes averted their eyes, and from which they fled at the first opportunity. In the Potteries, little different from some parts of Manchester, the miasma of furnaces and kilns belching fire and smoke prompted Queen Victoria to have the blinds of the royal train lowered whenever she traversed it.

So how does Elijah stand in any environmental audit conducted 150 years after his death? Then and now, as with all employers, he is entitled to claim credit for job creation. Wages earned by the 300–400 employees (possibly as many as 700 at the time of his death) put bread on the table in many Manchester homes. The firm took immediate action to switch from white phosphorous to red phosphorous once the dangers of the former had been identified. It was innocent of perpetrating the horrors of 'phossy-jaw' on its workers of which crime many competitors were guilty. Likewise, Dixon's took pride in the fact that its matches were safety matches, as featured prominently in its branding and advertising.

But were there toxic discharges from the premises of Dixon, Son and Evans, beyond its smoking factory chimney? Elijah attended a meeting of Manchester businessmen called to consider the effects of the Nuisance Removal Bill, to hear the chairman express incredulity that its terms would outlaw the discharge of noxious materials into watercourses. How, he said, could any dye works on the banks of the rivers Irwell and Irk be carried out in the face of such a law?

It is a fact that whatever chemicals were discharged from the premises of Dixon's into the watercourses of Newton Heath, they too were likely to join the murky waters of the Irk and Irwell as they flowed through the centre of Manchester. In 1860, a pickpocket was arrested for stealing the purse of a woman employee of Dixon, Son and Evans, on Newton Heath station. According to the *Manchester Courier* of 7 July, the prosecution proved its case by demonstrating that silver shillings paid in wages and found in possession of the thief 'were much discoloured by chemical action, as the coins coming from that establishment were represented as almost invariably being'. The discolouration probably came from handling sulphur, part of the match-head mix, which turns silver black. That said, match-making is largely a batch process with comparatively little continuous discharge. Waste would only arise if a bad mix was made accidentally, or if materials were over-ordered, leading to stock going off. Both scenarios might have necessitated land-fill dumping. On the box-making and timber side, however, off-cuts and sawdust could be readily sold or re-cycled as fuel.

Whatever the delights, and whatever peace he found in the landscape of Windgather Rocks, the purchase of a cottage at Windgather may well have been influenced by family considerations of a far more sombre nature. Until early 1868 son Elijah Junior was probably the lynch-pin of the firm's sales team. Elijah's only surviving son, he had been living with his wife and children in Manchester, working for the firm, occupation described as 'traveller'. He was the owner of property in Newton Heath, and the family had also enjoyed a rural pied à terre on Chat Moss, near to Hephzibah farm; at any rate Elijah Junior is shown as resident on the Moss in the 1861 census and two of his children were born there. However, following his death aged 37, on 7 July 1868 at Wye House, Buxton, the Death Certificate occupation column states 'Lunatic in Asylum'.

At the inquest the following day, the cause of death was recorded as 'brain disease'. Whether or not the underlying cause of Elijah's illness was ever diagnosed, it seems to have been incurable, and at some point the family – almost certainly through the offices of Elijah Senior – arranged for his admission to Wye House. And perhaps, given Buxton's growing reputation as an elevated spa town, a health resort, it might have been possible, for a time, to deflect unwonted enquiries – and even those of Elijah's children – by reference to the purported benefits derived by invalids from taking the waters at Buxton's natural mineral baths.

Built by the Duke of Devonshire in 1859-61, the prospectus of Wye House Asylum announced it as 'an establishment for the care and treatment of the insane of the higher and middle classes'. The fees would have cost Elijah a pretty penny, and by the standards of the time it was probably the best provision that money could buy. Its gabled facade gave the impression of a stately home. It was centrally-heated, 'furnished throughout on the most liberal scale', equipped with 'every necessary convenience', and views from the house and terrace extended over 'many miles of picturesque countryside'. At least, by offering 'treatment' it had held out some hope of a cure.

Elijah Junior's body was brought home for burial at Harpurhey. Henceforth, his father's hopes of a Dixon dynasty at the firm were limited to grandsons Elijah Marsh, William Marsh and (just) Marsh Dixon, and the Evans blood line through the sons of daughter Mary and son-in-law George. The circumstances of Elijah's illness and death must have had a devastating impact on the family. Then, as now, stigma and shame attached to mental illness, and there is no record of Elijah Senior ever speaking publicly about the episode.

The real reason for choice of Windgather as the Dixons' rural retreat remains a mystery. The railway did not reach Buxton until 1864, so if Elijah had cause to visit the town before then – perhaps to investigate the suitability of Wye House – he would have had to alight from the train at Whaley Bridge in order to take a horse-drawn coach or omnibus (the latter provided by courtesy of the London and North Western Railway). Whaley Bridge had been accessible by rail since 1857, so he could have been a regular visitor to the Derbyshire countryside even before Elijah Junior's illness.

However he came upon it, Elijah's first view of the cottage under the lee of Windgather Rocks, with its fresh moorland air, high above the unpolluted headwaters of the river Goyt, made a lasting impression. Far from the smoke and grime of Manchester, it must have appealed to him as a landscape of idyllic beauty, a desirable halfway house to heaven, God's purpose still discernible in its moorland grandeur; consolation, if that were possible, for the tragic end to a son's life, a few miles away on the other side of the hill.

Chapter Twenty-six

Vine House

W hen, some time around Elijah's eightieth birthday, he and Martha moved to their last home in Ricketts Street, New Moston, friends and neighbours may have smiled at the irony of its name – Vine House. Had they mentioned it to teetotaller Elijah he would have insisted that not all the grape harvest is fermented into wine.

In Vine House, built on the site of, or partly adapted from, a farmhouse previously known as Whitehead's, and perhaps incorporating some of its outbuildings for stables and a coach-house, Elijah and Martha found a comfortable, but by no means extravagant, home. The house name first appears on the census of 1871 and given its possible Biblical connotation it seems reasonable to suppose that it was bestowed by Elijah. He might even have had in mind the words he had heard fifty years previously from the lips of Robert Owen, looking forward to a golden age when 'every man should sit under his own vine'.

Vine House lacked the ancient provenance of Clough House but was probably far more convenient. Ricketts Street connected at its north end with paths and roads into Chadderton and Hollinwood. At the south end, there was a shortcut into Failsworth over the Wrigley Head canal bridge. However, given that the track had to negotiate the steep banks of the Moston Brook before the canal, Elijah probably preferred – as the lesser of two evils – the alternative carriage routes, via Dixon Street or Jones Street, thence along the road built by the Manchester Bridgewater Freehold Land Society.

Although most other plots owned by the Society at that time had been purchased for building, Ricketts Street was still largely surrounded by fields and working farms. In fact, sales of the Society's allotments were disappointing, so that in Elijah's time and beyond New Moston consisted mostly of fallow plots, the land dotted here and there with small rows of cottages and the odd tenement block such as Temperance Terrace.[1] Other early developments such as Holroyd's House and Brierley's Buildings were to disappear from the records, either renamed or demolished. Four cottages, two of which were attached to the side of Vine House and at first known as Dixon's Buildings were later renamed Vine Fold.

A notable incomer, however, and almost certainly to become an acquaintance of Elijah, was Robert Clarke, inventor of the tin whistle (also called a flageolet). Clarke, a farm labourer from Coney Weston in Suffolk, began making simple tin whistles with the help of the village blacksmith.[2] A typical immigrant to Manchester, Clarke was driven from the land by the indignities of feudal tenure; the story goes that the last straw came when he was paid short by his employer who falsely accused him of slacking. With his eldest son Robert, Clarke walked to Manchester, making and selling his whistles while staying overnight at various inns and farms on the way. They proved immensely popular and on reaching Manchester in 1858 he found a ready market for his whistles among the workers, especially the Irish, and so he settled at Bailey Street, off London Road, where the rest of his family joined him soon afterwards. Sometime between January and August 1862, he moved to New Moston, renting a cottage in Jones Street from Isaac Storey. He eventually came to own two cottages in Jones Street, one of which he used for making his tin whistles. As business boomed and 'penny' whistles were exported all over the world, Clarke was able to keep up with demand for his famous product by employing his family and other workers and, later, by building a two-storey workshop on land behind the cottages.

The Clarkes were to apply their growing wealth in the same way that Elijah had – by investing in land and building on it – and after Elijah's death they were responsible for some of the grand properties which slowly and surely changed the character of the area. Indeed, there were many similarities between Elijah and Robert. Both were Dissenters, both bridled under injustice, both were economic migrants, and both began cottage industries that employed local people and later expanded into mass production (a range of 'penny whistles' was introduced, offering different musical keys, and in spite of their nickname, in the early days the whistles actually cost a halfpenny; though no longer based in New Moston, Clarke whistles are still made today).

The area was attracting residents who wanted to develop their plots in ways that had not been foreseen by Elijah and his fellow promoters. Well-drained land, close to the canal and soon to be served by a new railway line through Hollinwood, had industrial potential, and the Bridgewater Society appears not to have been averse to selling plots to budding entrepreneurs. One of them was John Crossley, born in Failsworth, who in his fifties set up a Jacquard loom works adjoining a feeder to the canal, which he developed as a small wharf. By 1872, he was paying rates on a house in Potts Street, named Raven's Leach and by 1874 on 'a shed, engine and engine house' as well. Elijah would probably have been able to see the loom works across the fields from the back windows of Vine House. Crossley went on to own other plots of land on Dixon Street. Another plot, close to the junction of Moston Lane and Dixon Street, was bought by builder John Warriner, who erected a terrace of eight cottages, which he named Warriner Street.

Meanwhile, health and weather permitting, Elijah and Martha were in a position to make regular journeys to their country retreat at Windgather. However, for a couple of octogenarians, it was a fair old journey from New Moston. Given the awkward connections involved by rail, Elijah and Martha were much more likely to have travelled by private coach and horses, kept in New Moston. If Elijah was in the habit of attending Saturday evening meetings at a chapel close to Whaley Bridge station (possibly the Baptist chapel on Whaley Lane, now a private house) he must have got to know fellow worshippers well – because it appears that he began recruiting servants from among the congregation.

Also shown as resident at Vine House in the 1871 census return was Sarah Andrew, 'domestic servant', born at Whaley Bridge. Next door, at Dixon's Buildings, was coachman Thomas Hallam, born in the Hope valley, Derbyshire, and his wife Kezia, born in Kettleshulme. Of the three children residing with them, 18-year-old Samuel Hallam, born at Horwich End, a hamlet cheek by jowl with Windgather, was stated to be a 'farm servant'. Other evidence, including the birth places of the younger children, suggests that the Hallams may have moved to New Moston as early as 1867. They may therefore have led an itinerant life, going backwards and forwards between New Moston and the Whaley Bridge area, attending on the Dixons during the journey, and looking after them at journey's end. The other two Hallam children are listed as 'scholars' and may have been enrolled in school at Failsworth, or at the Methodist Sunday school that had been established in New Moston. In his census entry, Elijah has added 'slates and tiles' to his range of products and his match-making workforce is now up to 500. After 'manufacturer' he has appended '& farmer'. This may have been a nod to his former activities (or possible continued interests) at Chat Moss. There again, since Vine House at that time had an acre or two of land on its southern and eastern sides, perhaps he was growing a few vegetables; for the family, for sale locally, or simply as a hobby. There would have been land enough for Elijah to graze his coach horses, and maybe a donkey or two.

The previous (1861) census says Sarah Andrew was actually born in Taxal, close to Whaley Bridge, but gives the additional information that her father William, a farmer, came originally from Saddleworth. This throws up another possible explanation of Elijah's early exploration of the countryside on the Derbyshire/Cheshire border. He might have gone to seek out an old friend, perhaps a worshipper at the little chapel in Whaley Bridge.

Martha Dixon died at Vine House on 3 June 1873, aged 84, and was buried four days later at Harpurhey cemetery. The Registrar accepted 'old age' as the cause of death. The informant was her son-in-law, James Harrop, also living at Vine House, together with her daughter Judith and their children, Horatio Nelson and Annie Elizabeth (son Thomas having died in 1862). Perhaps Judith and James helped Elijah to care for Martha in her declining years. She suffered a gradual decline – from which fate Elijah himself was to be mercifully spared.

Indeed, everything known about the last years of Elijah Dixon – bereft of sons and wife – suggests that he did not go gently into death's goodnight. Rather he revelled in the good fortune of his longevity, to all appearances a template for the perfect finale to a worthy life. If only he had taken better advice on the subject of will-making...

Being a sturdy example of what the Victorians called a man of affairs, Elijah did not neglect to make a will.[3] On the contrary, he clearly gave the matter very great thought indeed. The result was a document, albeit written in the hand of a legal clerk, of great length and complexity, which reflected the diversity and extent of Elijah's estate. In fairness, he was hemmed in by the unsatisfactory state of the law at that time, as it applied to property ownership by women. This pre-empted what might have been done otherwise by way of an equal distribution between different branches of the family and obliged him to focus on his male heirs. The situation was further complicated by the fact that all his sons had pre-deceased him. The nub of the problem, however – as his executors were soon to discover – was not the identity of beneficiaries, but the identification of the property to be divided amongst them, and valuations he placed arbitrarily upon each individual property.

The real property – land and buildings – was of course extensive, quite apart from his share in the firm. Elijah seems to have succumbed to the temptation to recite it in detail – in the words of the Chancery Court judge sitting in St George's Hall, Liverpool, 'in much minuteness' – thereby raising a presumption against the estate being valued as a whole. A simple phrase, along the lines of 'all land and buildings that I may own at the time of my death' would have avoided the lawyers' holiday which was to arise. It turned out that after executing the will – then a codicil four days later – he had gone on to buy and sell several other properties, thereby rendering it, in the words of the Court, 'impracticable to give literal effect to the scheme'. He had, in effect, been meticulous to a fault, and the will was another example of Elijah's occasional urge to recite overpowering detail, as in the case of his Chat Moss census return. The upshot, in due course, was far more serious than a demand for sixteen pence in unpaid tithes. All six branches of the family represented by the Harrops, the Garners, the Evans's, the Ogdens, the children of Job and the children of Elijah Junior, were obliged to instruct separate legal counsel to get the court to sort out the mess.

Counsel for the Garners was none other than Dr Richard Pankhurst, who, one is inclined to think, might have waived his fee for the sake of his long-time connection with the Dixons. None felt more strongly than he about the injustice of inheritance law as it applied to women. A few years after Elijah's death, Pankhurst drafted the Married Women's Property Bill, which became law in 1882. What a pity that Elijah did not seek his friend's advice at the time he had made his will in 1870.

Looking at the terms of the will and codicil today, it does not require a trained lawyer to spot the folly of it all. No lawyer today could draft a will

– and then to compound matters, a codicil – shot through with ambiguity and uncertainty on such an industrial scale, without inviting a claim for professional negligence and a charge of misconduct. Even a signed disclaimer could not avoid liability. Imagine, too, the embarrassment of Elijah Marsh Dixon, whose unhappy lot it was to assume the role of plaintiff in the legal action which took the form of a claim against the other five families.

Meanwhile, Elijah lived out his life in blissful ignorance of the time-bomb he had bequeathed to his beloved family. In August 1875 he sailed to the Isle of Man, aged 84, probably in the company of a family member or servant.[4] Elijah stayed in accommodation at Ballaugh, in the north-west of the island, and his host may have been old friend Joseph Johnson, teetotaller and lay-preacher, who had moved to the island a few years earlier. He was naturally pleased with himself to have plodded up the long winding path of rock and scree to reach the summit of Snaefell, 2,034 feet above sea-level, although thick mist denied him the hoped-for view of what Manx folk call the 'six kingdoms' (Isle of Man, England, Ireland, Scotland, Wales and Heaven). Obviously proud of his achievement, Elijah wrote a letter addressed, somewhat oddly, to 'Dear Friends and Relatives' at Messrs Dixon, Son and Evans. With a touch of repetition Elijah informed his readership that he had only been capable of the feat because of 'total abstinence from all intoxicating liquors'.

In May 1876, Elijah attended a tea-party in Newton Heath. It was organised by local clergy for elderly residents, as a celebration both of longevity and the surprising fact that, despite its heavily industrialised surroundings, the township appeared to have more than the average number of aged survivors. Just how old 85 must have seemed to them can be judged from the fact that 70 was the cut-off point for the 200 or so invitees. Songs and speeches were heard, capped by 'humorous recitations' from Ben Brierley. The old township of Newton Heath, where Elijah had so often heard the chimes at midnight, was a fitting venue for his last public appearance, in spite of it being held in the Conservative Hall. History does not record whether on this occasion he wore his wide-awake hat – but you can believe it if you want to.

Elijah Dixon died of 'exhaustion' at Vine House on Wednesday, 26 July 1876, grandson Elijah Marsh Dixon at his bedside.

He was given a good send-off. Even before the funeral, an obituary appeared in the *Manchester Times* describing him as the 'Father of English Reformers'. Stressing Elijah's role in the events of 1816 and 1817, The *Times's* account of his career was the first of several contemporary tributes couched in the typical rotundity of Victorian monuments. Elijah, 'a very considerable personage', had left behind him 'a name for integrity and perseverance of the highest order'. The *City Jackdaw* was moved to tribute in verse:[5]

Write on his tomb, that when
Corruption swayed the lives of Englishmen,
He stood among the few,
Who hoped, and felt, and knew,
And suffered for their knowledge, that a day
Must come when purity would have her sway.
Write on his tomb, that now
Though still 'neath many a burden base we bow,
His labour beareth fruit;
For many a stout recruit,
By noble impulse and example led,
Reveres and follows the reformer, dead.

The *Manchester Courier*, as well as the *Times*, reported on the funeral on the Saturday, repeating the assertion that Elijah had been the Father of English Reformers, before describing the route of the funeral cortege. Twelve coaches of 'relatives and intimate friends' followed the hearse, which set off from Vine House at 12.30pm, for Harpurhey cemetery. The cortege would have passed places familiar to Elijah, probably taking the route along Dixon Street, down the Twelve Yards Road and over the Moston Brook into Failsworth. On Oldham Road, it would have passed Dob Lane Chapel, The Cloughs, the match works and timber yards, as well as Hope and Reeve Terraces, part of Elijah's grand property portfolio, soon to be disputed under the terms of his disastrous will.

Many of the cottages along the route were the homes of workers at Dixon, Son and Evans. From Hulme Hall Lane, the cortege was joined by sixty employees of the firm, deputations from Salford, Failsworth and Newton Heath Liberal Associations, the National Reform Union, various Temperance bodies, the Newton Heath Board of Health, and United Kingdom Alliance. An estimated 500 people joined the procession on foot, and two of the pall-bearers – employees of the firm – were Samuel and James Dixon, sons of Hezekiah. Among the mourners were Jacob Bright, Richard Pankhurst, Abel Heywood and Ben Brierley.

There were no eulogies or perorations at the cemetery as Elijah was lowered into the vault next to Martha; a simple service was conducted by the cemetery registrar James Fielding. A plain brass plate attached to the simple oak coffin bore the inscription: 'Elijah Dixon. Died July 26, 1876'.

Oddly absent from the official list of mourners published by the newspapers were representatives of the Co-operative movement. Yet they must have been present, because shortly afterwards, the *Co-operative News* published its own eloquent obituary, covering the broad range of Elijah's interests and achievements. Here at last was a well-earned eulogy for 'a remarkable man of a remarkable time'. Elijah's was a life 'gifted with powers rare and extraordinary, a life used with severe fidelity and unusual industry, a life prolonged and sustained, never idly, never aimlessly, but ever actively, and, to the last, full of purpose'. Like every good obituarist, the writer made his subject human; Elijah's 'native force and character' had expressed itself in a 'kind of half-disregard displayed to the conventional requirements of society, as if he did not quite know whether there was a fashionable world or not'. He ended by saying Elijah's had been a 'beacon life'.

Belgrave Road

What was left of Elijah for the world to remember him by? Grandchildren and great-grandchildren galore descended from his ten children by Martha. Two grandchildren followed him into politics, Elijah Marsh Dixon – whose hasty marriage to Eliza produced ten children, and who had once served alongside George Evans Senior as All Saints representatives on the Newton Heath Board of Health – became a councillor, and eventually an alderman for the City of Manchester. George Evans Junior was elected as a councillor for Newton Heath after its belated incorporation into the city, and he too became an alderman. His brother, William Thomas Evans served as a member of the Prestwich Board of Guardians.

At the time of Elijah's death, the great conglomerate Dixon, Son and Evans, with its range of products and processes was a textbook example of, to use economist jargon, horizontal integration. The business had grown like Topsy by virtue of Elijah's 'vagrant genius' and inventiveness. Still unincorporated, its structure as a family firm was not fit for purpose in the world of big business, and inevitably it was not long before there were changes. The confusion arising from Elijah's will did not help, and when it landed on the doorstep of the Court of Chancery – into which an earlier Dixon inheritance dispute had disappeared for thirty years or more – Elijah's heavenly groans must have been heard all over Newton Heath and New Moston. He might have groaned again to observe that the record of Dixons as a strike-free firm was tarnished within a year of his death.

In 1881, the London firm of Bell and Black issued a prospectus to take over three companies, one of which was Dixon, Son and Evans. In response to this, George Evans and Elijah Marsh agreed to sell only the match side of the business. In 1883, DS&E was formally dissolved; Elijah Marsh was offered a managership with Bell and Black and continued to live close to the works premises in Newton Heath, and later at Failsworth Lodge. The timber, joinery and box-making operations continued, now renamed George Evans and Sons, and for the next year or so Bell, Black and Co and George Evans and Sons were listed next to each other on Oldham Road, in trade directories. Eventually, Bell and Black was itself taken over by giants of the match industry, Bryant and May, and the match works at Newton Heath was closed.

That did not, however, sever the Dixon connection with matches. Elijah Marsh, and his youngest brother Marsh, moved south to take up new posts as managers with Bryant and May. Marsh moved to West Ham and became manager of the box and splint works, while Elijah Marsh bought a home at Heather Hall, Woodford Green, on the edge of Waltham Forest, part of London's rapidly expanding commuter belt. His son William Hepworth Dixon (named after that other illustrious forebear), having inherited his great-grandfather's interest in science, became chief chemist at Bryant and May until retirement in 1949. B&M themselves were later acquired by Swedish Match, whose constituent company archives are held at Hackney on their behalf and proved an invaluable research source.

Upon settlement of the court case, Elijah Marsh inherited and remained owner of Windgather Cottage, until his death in April 1896 aged 54. Surely, in spite of the distance from London, he would not have neglected opportunities for family rest and relaxation in the cottage? It must have been valued not only for its beautiful hillside location and surroundings but also for its memories of happy visits to Grandpa Elijah.

George Evans Senior died in 1888, leaving sons George, Excelsior and William Thomas to continue the timber business, and, indeed, to expand it. The timber yards and sawmills were extended across the match works site, and during the 1890s, new houses were built on Oldham Road to replace Clough House and Heath House, once the home of Edward Nightingale, on the corner of Oldham Road and Droylsden Road. Perhaps in a nostalgic acknowledgement of the huge contribution made to the local community as employers, a new twin-gabled four-house terrace built next to the works entrance was named Clough Place.

Although plaster and box-making seems to have fizzled out by the early 1900s, the timber business continued, and in 1931, George Evans and Sons agreed to a merger with John and William Bellhouse, another long-established Manchester timber firm. Evans Bellhouse, the merged company, closed its Newton Heath yard in the late 1970s, but is still trading from premises in Chester and Liverpool.

The loosening of family ties with the business inevitably prompted a gradual diaspora of Dixons. With whatever funds could be salvaged from the lawyers after Elijah's will was clarified, some headed for warmer, cleaner climes of coastal resorts, and southern England. William Marsh Dixon, brother of Elijah Marsh, emigrated to Australia, and died in Melbourne in September 1891. Those who had already moved out of town, thanks to Elijah, were happy to remain in the country. The Garners stayed on at Hephzibah Farm until 1888, when they sold it and retired to Liverpool Road, Irlam.

At the same time, the Moss prospered, albeit in a way that searchers after modern-day Shangri-las might eschew. It was years before Manchester and

Salford cured their woeful provision for sanitation in the slums, and night-soil dumping on the Moss continued well into the twentieth century. Farms begun in Elijah's era remain on the Moss, producing mostly potatoes and, as in the case of Hephzibah, lawn turf for garden centres. With the building of the Manchester Ship Canal, starting in 1887, Irlam grew from a village to a town, as the banks of the canalised Irwell and Mersey spawned new indus-tries. The Canal provided more landing points for night soil, distributed by an extensive narrow gauge railway system, as well as more outlets for produce. In 1928, only a mile or so from Hephzibah, on adjoining Barton Moss, Manchester Corporation began constructing a municipal aerodrome, from which, in 1930, a thrice-weekly service to London and the Midlands began operating. Later superseded by Ringway, Barton Aerodrome (now City Airport) survives for pilot training and commercial charters. Another, more recent development on the Moss, equally unimaginable in Elijah's day, is the controversial exploration for shale gas by way of 'fracking'.

Shortly before the outbreak of the Second World War, Windgather Cottage was opened as a youth hostel, being well-placed for Manchester ramblers, a development which might have pleased Elijah and old Chartists and reformers such as Reginald Richardson and Archibald Prentice, who loved the country-side. Likewise, when it closed through lack of support in 1983, these old cam-paigners might have shaken their heads to reflect wistfully on opportunities spurned by modern youth which they had been denied. Was the climb from Whaley Bridge too steep for modern hostellers? The facilities too basic? How would they have coped working twelve hours a day as little piecers?

Elijah's birth place, the little town of Holmfirth, is no different from the great city of Manchester in that it has no recollection or remembrance worth mentioning of its heroic Radical son. It has other claims to fame, of course. Thousands of tourists visit the famous location of television series *Last of the Summer Wine*, and rather fewer to see the old printing works of Bamforth and Co, early cine-film pioneers and originators of the saucy seaside postcard. There is just one tenuous link with Elijah. Now standing on end, close to the church, is the gravestone of Elijah's grandfather Richard, father of Job, who died in 1787, buried alongside his 'amiable' wife Mary and son David; last but one of the clothier dynasty.

Because it was for so long neglected by the authorities, the landscape of New Cross and Ancoats, familiar to Elijah, changed little for a century or so after his death. The layout of back streets, with only a few renamed, remains remarkably unchanged, but of the houses, shops and inns that once jostled for space on their margins there are only fragmentary traces, overshadowed by high-rise developments. Elijah's Manchester disappeared fast with re-de-velopment from the 1980s onwards. Even so, crumbling brickwork from ancient hearths and cellars can still be seen, here and there, tucked in behind railings and boarding erected by the developers of Manchester's fashionable Northern Quarter.

Incredibly, at the heart of the Northern Quarter, on the exact site of Elijah's first business enterprise, number 42, Great Ancoats Street, there stands a distinctive renovated building retaining typical angular features of the Georgian era. Contrasting with multi-storey buildings all around, and now re-numbered 87, it is a few doors away from the site of the King's Arms and James Wroe's bookshop. Nowhere in Manchester is there a building with such strong evocations of the city's Radical past, or Elijah's contribution to it. So too would our Radical forefathers approve the present use of old number 42. It is the home of 42nd Street, a mental health charity which helps young people by involving them in creative and artistic projects. Inspired by the pioneering work of philanthropist Thomas Horsfall, founder of the Ancoats Art Museum in the late nineteenth century, they are developing the shop as a gallery.

While statues of those such as Cobden and John Bright, who enjoyed the city fathers' stamp of approval, adorn Manchester's Squares, there is nothing at all to commemorate the heroes of Ancoats and New Cross – Elijah Dixon, James Wroe and James Scholefield – men who lived in the workaday fringes of the city, and who, together, made a unique contribution to freedom and our island story.

After a century of disuse, the name New Islington has been revived to suggest a similar area in east London, reclaimed from the working class by conversions of old mills and warehouses into stylish apartments and trendy waterside bars, overlooking restored canals and a new marina. The New Islington Free School stands opposite spacious apartments on the banks of the Rochdale Canal. What would Elijah have made of its controversial political provenance? Other landmarks of Manchester's Radical past survive. The classical facade of the old Town Hall in King Street, scene of many a fray, was removed to Heaton Park in 1912. Today, most of the buildings fringing Stevenson Square are drab warehouses dating from the late Victorian era after Elijah's death. Yet, just a little cluttered with street furniture, the small rectangle of enclosed space remains and it is not hard to imagine Elijah's rowdy encounters on the hustings, and punch-ups at Anti-Corn Law meetings. Likewise, the furious Chartist activity of the 1840s in Clerkenwell is redolently evoked by its later claim to fame as the meeting place of Vladimir Lenin and Joseph Stalin, the presence of the Marx Memorial Museum (a valuable archive of socialist records) and the annual May Day parade on Clerkenwell Green, scene of Elijah's 'Manchester Man' speech in 1848.

Of all the districts of Manchester, Elijah most identified with Newton Heath. It was home not only for Martha and himself, but also most members of the Dixon family, who lived close to the works in its heyday. Many of the shops and cottages on Oldham Road, dating from the1850s and '60s – within living memory of highwaymen on the ancient heath – were either built by Elijah or with materials supplied by him. Most were swept away within thirty years of his death, but at the same time, the area enjoyed a resurgence, spurred by railway expansion – a locomotive shed and a carriage works – and an increase in population.

Indeed, the railway created its own community, with the 'loco' at its heart and produced perhaps the most iconic sports club of all time. In 1902, Newton Heath Lancashire and Yorkshire Railway Football Club became Manchester United.[1] In turn, the railways and the presence of an energetic, adaptable labour force attracted heavy industry, with firms such as A.V. Roe (forerunner of British Aerospace), Mather and Platt, and Eyres Iron Foundry, employing generations of family members in the twentieth century. No wonder that, recalling its great steam locomotive shed, a curate living in the parish during the 1930s wrote of 'inescapable dirt', lamenting that 'the freshness of a sheet of notepaper did not last for even so long as it took the pen to reach the bottom of it.'

Yet the Dixon name – and Dixon blood – persisted for the best part of a century in Newton Heath. Still trading proudly on Oldham Road until 1971, under the name of W.H. Dixon, greengrocer, was another William Hepworth Dixon, the great-great nephew of Elijah's literary nephew! It was just a stone's throw from the site of a temperance bar whose doors remained open until the 1960s.

In recent times the decline of heavy industry, presaged by the scaling down of the loco at the end of the steam age, contributed to social deprivation and decline. The site of Newton Heath market, once the hub of a vibrant community, beside the towpath of the Rochdale Canal, lies empty and accusatory of official neglect. Likewise, much 'brown field' land, once industrialised, lies abandoned and overgrown. Yet nowadays, Newton Heath's reputation, first for overcrowding and pollution, then later decay and dereliction, is being reversed by another revival. Prompted by a growing population of migrants from all over the world, there is new social housing. Farmfoods sits on the site of Edward Nightingale's house, and Poundstretcher on land which was once the Evans Bellhouse timber yard and reservoir.

For all the changes, and with most of the shops, churches and pubs of Elijah's day long gone, you may still find defiant remnants of Elijah Dixon's Newton Heath. The handsome edifice of Newton Silk Mill, built in 1832, is a listed building. With its large windows, which once illuminated rattling spindles, it has been cleverly renovated for office use. The distinctive All Saints church, its present building dating from 1816, still stands (though sadly in need of restoration) dominating the skyline along the course of the old Roman road from the city. Gifted by James Taylor, the church's resplendent stained-glass window serves as a reminder of Elijah's battle to wrest control of Vestry finances from the powerful Lancashire family. Newton Heath Cemetery (All Saints new burial ground) was cleared for a recreation ground in 1975, but at least there is a plaque at the entrance on Orford Road. The name Dixon Street survives in a sign affixed to the side of the late-Victorian RBS bank premises on Oldham Road, close to where Job Junior owned shops and cottages.

Vine House, one of the older buildings in New Moston, was partly destroyed by fire a few years after Elijah's death. Rebuilt, it defies architectural classification, standing out from the semi-detached houses built nearby in the 1930s and '50s. Its main entrance fronts Parkfield Road North, and on its northern side is a little lane at right-angles to the road. Vine House extends back along the lane, where its brick walls are darker and older. In line with Vine House, and joined to it, are smaller dwellings, probably the site of Dixon's Buildings, home to Elijah's coachman and family. They have been named Vine Fold. Land at the back, once the site of the coach-house and stables, was later used as a builder's yard, before the erection in the 1990s of a terrace of 'town houses', made from bricks reclaimed from the old buildings, fronting a cobblestone cul-de-sac. Two new houses behind Vine House were added in 2003-5. All told, the combination of big house and little knot of secluded homes clustering round it, creates an atmosphere of mystery, begging the question, 'Who lived here?'

Elijah's last home stands directly opposite the second New Moston Co-op store, now used as a dance centre, and as the headquarters of NEPHRA, the local residents' association, as well as by a spiritualist and followers. The slow growth of New Moston during Elijah's lifetime, meant that, much though he would have approved of it, no Co-op store was built there until 1889. The first was in Eastwood Road, originally named Jones Street, after Ernest Jones. A larger replacement, on the corner of Ricketts Street (opposite Vine House) was built in 1895-6. It contained grocery, butchery, drapery and greengrocery departments and a large first-floor room for public and social events. Acquired by the Failsworth Industrial Society in 1927, it closed, as a co-op, in 1968. Along Eastwood Road, once tree-lined from end to end, there is a disparate collection of properties. Built about four years before Elijah's death, three remaining dwellings, once part of Temperance Terrace, appear as perfect expressions of Victorian arrivisme. Very different from the modest but enfranchised properties Elijah envisaged for New Moston, but even they may have been intended as tenements for workers, rather than for middle-class 'Pooter' suburbanites. At any rate, this grand three-storey building would not look out of place on the front of any Victorian seaside town.

There are other large houses, one a former nursing home, and an evangelical church. Opposite are modest semi-detached homes, and a picture-postcard patch of greenery leading to Rose Cottage and Moss Cottage. These date from Elijah's lifetime, probably the 1850s, and would have perfectly matched his idea of cottage allotments, each with surrounding land for a garden-cum-vegetable patch and even a cow or two.

At the bottom end of Eastwood Road, opposite Bannatyne Close (the site of the penny whistle works) is the Community Garage and next to this are the

Scout huts, a newer one built from pre-cast concrete in the early 1950s, and an older, attached brick-built one, which once stabled the horses for Co-op delivery wagons. The newer hut also serves as one of two polling stations for New Moston; the other, for many years based at the Junior School, has recently been moved to Broadway baths and leisure centre. The tin-whistle works disappeared in the 1970s, the company relocating to Kent, but Clarke's penny whistles, which inspired the musical career of flautist James Galway, amongst others, are still world famous.

At the junction with Moston Lane East is a pie shop, an architecturally distinguished pie shop, which once boasted a turret and finial. It had long been home to a baker and confectioner, but also housed the post office, from around 1914 until 1928. There stands on this corner one of the last Victorian pillar boxes in Manchester, bearing the cast iron motif VR. It was transplanted by Post Office engineers to replace a newer (GR) one damaged by the errant driver of a road vehicle in the 1970s, a rather fitting, if fortuitous, imprimatur with reference to New Moston's unique history. It is also the location of a well-known and well-exhibited photograph featuring a little group of girls with a dolls pram against the backdrop of tree-lined Eastwood Road, a serene evocation of the pre-motor car age. Standing in the middle of the road, clear of the horse-dung, the children have no fear of passing traffic, let alone speeding motorists mounting the pavement.

The photograph, taken about 1910, suggests massive expansion of New Moston during the 1890s, following incorporation into the city of Manchester, and an explosion of house building at the turn of the century, and into the Edwardian age. At the time of Elijah's death, there were 48 occupied households in New Moston; in a survey of 1994, counting only the same streets, there were over 480. The expansion continued at a furious rate up to the outbreak of war in 1914, pushing out the boundaries traced by the original six streets. Before then, there was only farmland between Moston Lane East and the railway to the west, but bit by bit the land was sold off as the countryside retreated, field by field. During this period also, with the building of large houses (some like The Elms and The Cedars on Moston Lane East, very large) with room for servants and ample grounds, New Moston moved up-market. It became more middle-class, with mill-owners, bank managers, engineers and doctors enjoying suburban life only a short distance from workplaces in the city.

Parallel to Eastwood Road is the former Dixon Street, now Belgrave Road. It too exhibits a mix of styles: Victorian terraces, the New Moston Inn (so named since at least 1871), detached houses, including a splendid example of late art deco, and, where an orphaned gatepost remains from the demolished Moston House, a 1960s development of maisonettes, facing green open space. The pub, though much altered, is one of the few buildings dating from Elijah's time. The irony of its survival down the years would not be lost on Elijah. At Belgrave

Road's north-eastern end, Northfield Road, the erstwhile Potts Street, no longer has its industry. The loom works (latterly home to Jackson's ladder works) was demolished in the late 1960s and now hosts private flats (Ashley Court), although the original works–owner's house still stands. The former canal wharf was gradually filled in to form a play area, recently converted to allotments. Only one shop is still trading; there were at one time six, and a petrol station.

Even during his lifetime – and as in the case of the scheme on Chat Moss – the noble ideals of the Bridgewater Freehold Society were overtaken by events; changes in society unimaginable at the beginning of the nineteenth century. The enthusiasm of fellow directors waned, and the value of shares fell. They were shrewdly bought up by Elijah, adding to the value of his disputed estate, but the beneficiaries, once their shares had been defined by the court, gradually sold off their plots. In 1890, along with Newton Heath and other outlying districts (Blackley, Crumpsall, Droylsden, Kirkmanshulme, Openshaw and West Gorton), New Moston, as part of Moston, was incorporated into the City of Manchester.

Streets in New Moston suffered name changes on 7 May 1900, when England was ablaze with Boer war patriotism. Gallant officers and tales of derring–do and empire stirred the imagination of the public more than remembrances of reformers. Names redolent of lordly squares and leafy lanes beyond the city, appealed more to New Mostonians than their dowdy inheritance of streets. Frost Street (combined with Scholes Lane) became Hawthorn Road, Potts Street became Northfield Road, Ricketts Street became Parkfield Road (North being appended in 1969) and Jones Street became Eastwood Road. In 1904, the extended Warriner Street became Circular Road, only to be changed again fifty years later to Chauncy Road. Dixon Street was changed to Belgrave Road. Now there are no 'streets' in New Moston.

The name changes, co-ordinated by Manchester Corporation and the General Post Office, and so far as is known endorsed by the residents without protest, were largely intended to eliminate mis–directed post by getting rid of duplicated street names. Nothing wrong with that, except that it was *this* Dixon Street that was consigned to oblivion, and others with far less distinguished provenance were spared. Surely, had it not been for the fact that only 25 years after his death Elijah's achievements had already been forgotten, it would have been possible to come up with Elijah Dixon Street. Or even, if the word street was anathema to upwardly mobile New Mostonians, Elijah Dixon Road.

The substitute name, Belgrave Road, added insult to injury, albeit unintentionally. All his life, Elijah held to the belief that the landowning aristocracy was at the root of injustice and inequality. Belgrave was, and is, a small Cheshire village at the entrance to Eaton Hall, seat of the Grosvenors, Dukes of Westminster, whose subsidiary titles include the viscountcy of Belgrave, and who, as owners, were able to bestow the derivative title Belgravia on the most expensive and fashionable area of London. With supine ignorance and indifference, the worthy burghers of Manchester demeaned all that Elijah stood for by coming up with a name oozing deference to the aristocracy. But Elijah would have no ill will towards one member of the landed Grosvenors. On 27 February 1818, Richard Grosvenor, second Marquis of Westminster, model landlord, devout Christian and embodiment of the Whig ascendancy, had introduced into the House of Lords the petition of Elijah Dixon, Blanketeer, 'carried to London in double irons', praying for redress and reform.

What, however, explains the collective amnesia of Manchester people towards brave men like Elijah Dixon who risked all on their behalf? Was their ignorance a by-product of rampant nationalism during the Boer War? Was it that the good citizens of New Moston were enwrapped every bit as much as the rest of the country in May 1900 by jingoism (a term coined by Elijah's acquaintance and fellow Co-operator George Holyoake) as newspaper readers followed seven months of day-to-day reporting on the siege of Mafeking? Ten days after Dixon Street became Belgrave Road, the papers carried front-page news of its relief, and, in common with the rest of the country, Manchester went mad. One newspaper reported, 'Never in the modern times have individual households been as generally awakened. From the head of the family to the juvenile in the cot, the outside enthusiasm was disturbing.' Indeed, it was a disturbing and mindless distraction which obscured the far more deserving achievements of men like Elijah Dixon and Ernest Jones whose lives had been dedicated to lifting the siege of tyranny at home.

Edwardian jingoism and gentrification in New Moston would have disappointed Elijah, but he might have approved later developments which brought about a more mixed social composition. Many medium-sized houses and shops, as well as side streets and avenues, were added to the existing streets, as large plots were sold to developers. The district expanded also into the spaces left by the last adjoining farms – Slater Fold, Rushes Gate and Crimbles – allowing for the building of Nuthurst Road in the 1890s, followed by schools and a park. In the 1920s and 1950s remaining open spaces were purchased for building private semi-detached houses, typical of the era, as well as council estates. When Broadway, one of the first dual-carriageway roads, was built to accommodate motorised traffic in the 1920s, it was later adorned with a classic period piece 'road-house' pub by the same name. Broadway's wide central strip was intended to accommodate tram lines, though these were never actually built. And, as in Newton Heath, Dixon blood clung to the soil; Annie Elizabeth Harrop (married name Ingham), Elijah's granddaughter, died at Vine House on 9 September 1940.

Today, older residents of New Moston remember a golden age of local shops before they were driven out of business by supermarkets, and other thriving examples of community life, now alas gone; girl guides, church brigades, a tennis club, a golf course, and – in a quaint manifestation of middle-class DNA – a long-defunct cricket club which staged matches in which players were required to wear top-hats. And yet, with its higgledy-piggledy mix of different styles and ordinariness, the place defies lumpen classification as between working class and middle class. Its residents, be they families in grand houses with acres of gardens, or terraced houses and council homes scattered between them, enjoy a life-style free of want and suffering beyond anything Elijah could have imagined as a young family man in Georgian Manchester. And although New Moston developed in a way very different from Elijah's vision of a semi-rural artisan community, divergent from its egalitarian ideals, there is probably little that would offend or surprise him today, other than an unexpectedly high number of Conservative voters. Most residents would proudly own to being working-class, though some would not. In any case you would be hard put to label New Moston as a whole by any single term of sociologist jargon.

Where they were mapped out by the Bridgewater Freehold Society, the streets of New Moston are unusually wide, and some, with echoes of distant days, are still partially tree-lined. The scourge of child-labour is unheard of, and the incidence of disease and infant mortality once commonplace is mercifully rare. There are schools nearby, for every child. The first Board school opened in 1902, followed by a primary school, added in the 1930s, which still survives. New Mostonians find employment in the factories, shops and offices of Manchester or Oldham, generally heated and well-ventilated, where the hours of work are regulated by parliament. For those who cannot work, or cannot find work, there are social security payments.

There is a chemist and a well-attended doctors' surgery, a less well-attended St Chad's Anglican church (whose amateur dramatics society once used the only surviving portraits of Elijah and Martha as props!), a Full Gospel (originally Primitive Methodist) church, and St Margaret Mary's Catholic church. The New Moston Club (founded in 1911), no longer a men-only retreat, has taken in the little war memorial rendered homeless by the closure of the British Legion Club. The butchers' shops, the greengrocers, fishmongers, ironmongers, cobblers and the optician, have gone, but now, as well as several convenience stores, there are sun-tan shops, hairdressers and cafes. Broadway Baths was added in 1932. Two of the former five fish-and-chip shops are still in business, joined by other more recent fast-food outlets. There is still a post office, although it has retreated to the very edge of New Moston, on the Chadderton boundary. There are no cellar dwellings.

In one respect New Moston remains as it has been from the beginning – a no-man's land. Manchester has never really recognised its most easterly suburb, a narrow salient of the city protruding into Oldham. For local government purposes it remains as it was in Elijah's time, 'top of Moston', acknowledged as a part of Moston at election time. An illustrated history of Manchester's suburbs, published in 2002, lists no fewer than thirty districts, from Wythenshawe in the south to Blackley in the north, but makes no reference to New Moston. Only two old-fashioned road signs show the way to New Moston; cast-iron black and white finger-post relics from the 1930s, situated at the Failsworth end of Broadway, fitting reminders of its historic links with the upstart suburb on the other side of the Brook.

It is a short walk from Vine House to the Scout hut. On polling days, it a short walk for everyone in New Moston to a polling station. Yet only one in three can be bothered to vote, by post or in person. Once the enemy of democracy was an alliance of privilege, the landed classes and the bourgeoisie. Now it is apathy. Elijah Dixon, clapped in double irons for demanding the right to vote, would be far from content with that.

Chapter Twenty-eight

Harpurhey

*'... the growing good of the world is partly dependent on unhistoric acts,
and that things are not so ill with you and me as they might have been, is
half owing to the number who lived faithfully a hidden life, and rest in
unvisited tombs.'*

George Eliot (1819-90), *Middlemarch*

It is wrong to assume that Elijah would be shocked or even surprised by contemporary apathy and its corollary, ingratitude, towards those who made sacrifices in great causes for the common good. He lived long enough to witness hundreds of thousands of working-class men, newly enfranchised by Disraeli, voting Conservative, partly in a frenzy of jingoism and partly so as to conserve their status as skilled or propertied workers, one up from the hoi polloi. Moreover, as we have seen, the achievements of Elijah Dixon and other members of his 'contemptible set' were largely forgotten, even by the people of Manchester, by the turn of the twentieth century. Even at the time of his death, one of Elijah's obituarists noted in the *Co-operative News*,

> 'How little appreciated by us of this generation is much of that we inherit: how little is known of the great conquests made for us by our fathers in the battle-time of new liberties and the death struggle of hoary wrongs; how little we feel and know now of the sacrifices and the sufferings which they have borne on our behalf.'

Written in tribute to Elijah Dixon 140 years ago, these words support an assertion, as true today as then, that events of the period 1816-76 made a special mark on English history, and that Elijah's role in those events made him 'a remarkable man of a remarkable time'.

Inevitably, Elijah's platform appearances in the cause of franchise reform attracted more press coverage than his behind-the-scenes work as a Co-operator. Yet the astonishing expansion of the Co-operative movement, during his lifetime and afterwards, alone nullifies any suggestion of grandiloquence in this assessment of Elijah's pioneering contribution and demonstrates how enduring have been the benefits of his shoulder work.

Elijah's vision and influence as chairman of the First and Third Co-operative Congresses in 1827 and 1831 was made in the feverish climate of political activity which preceded the 1832 Reform Act, and during a difficult patch in his own business career. Elijah himself must have carried his pioneering efforts in co-operation with great modesty, given that his presidency of the First Congress was unknown even to his obituarists, and only surfaced some twenty-five years after his death thanks to Holyoake's burrowing in the archives.

Many grandiose agrarian and utopian schemes, like the one at Chat Moss to which Elijah subscribed, fell by the wayside. The Owenite and O'Connorite models of investing huge sums of money to draft people into ready-made communities was too much of a gamble and too paternalistic for most ordinary working people. And for all the country air that settlement schemes might offer escapees from satanic mills and crowded slums, settlers risked losing not only their individual skills as, say, weavers, but also their existing networks of family and friends. At bottom, the schemes did not recognise the fundamental difficulties of achieving a division of labour, or trading with the outside world, without imposing communistic control over people's lives. Certainly, textile towns such as New Lanark and Saltaire, and, in a purely capitalist form, railway towns such as Swindon, were success stories, but only for as long as the single enterprise upon which all depended remained profitable.

Yet dreams of a self-sufficient utopian good life persist. There are waiting lists for allotments, which survive from the days when governments (even before they urged the people, in wartime, to Dig for Victory!) encouraged local authorities to provide land for garden-starved town-dwellers. There are even a few, usually environmentally-focussed communities, still trying to live the dream. And some might argue that in the heartland of capitalism, the American Amish have succeeded.

In contrast, the early Congresses chaired by Elijah, as well as his early shop-keeping partnerships run on co-operative lines, laid the foundation for the more worldly and outward-looking co-operationist model established by the Rochdale Pioneers in 1844. Their famous co-op store in Toad Lane departed from the impractical Owenite model by tempering idealism with sound business practice. Allowing for nothing on credit, concentrating on staple foodstuffs and reliable quality, it perfected the 'divvy' as a prototype scheme in customer loyalty.

When, in 1863, the Co-operative Wholesale Society was founded for the purpose of co-ordinating supply, warehousing and distribution to affiliated stores, it was an echo of the decision taken at the meeting, presided over by Elijah in the Spread Eagle Inn, Salford, in 1831 to form a General Union of Co-ops, and to acquire a warehouse in Liverpool.[1] A fire insurance department which opened in 1867, initially for the needs of stores, eventually became the Co-op Insurance Society, and a loans and deposits section, opened in 1872, grew into the Co-op

Bank, both based in Manchester. Factories producing processed foods, clothing and household goods followed, all with the CWS brand name. Further organic changes in the twentieth century saw a decline in the manufacturing arm, but in spite of set-backs, the co-operative model successfully adapted to modern retailing. In 1942, the Co-op opened the first self-service store in England; in 1965, it issued the first dividend stamps; in 1999, it started Britain's first internet banking service. The Co-operative Group, formed by a gradual agglomeration of smaller Co-op societies, now operates over 2,800 outlets throughout the British Isles, more than any other retailer, and there are still several independent societies in addition to the Group. No wonder Co-operation grew to be a global phenomenon, its principles copied in many countries, including the USA and Japan.

It was not, and is not, of course, just a matter of successful business practice. The idealism which inspired Elijah Dixon, Robert Owen, Captain Barlow and others in the 1820s may have been refined by the course of history, but it was never extinguished. Although in a form which could not have been foreseen by the pioneers of Chat Moss, the CWS came spectacularly close to realising Elijah's early utopian ideas, by purchasing land and establishing Co-op Farms, at one time the largest landowner in Britain, after state and church. The Co-operative Party, which to this day sponsors MPs in alliance with the Labour party, was created as a section of the Co-operative Union, a body set up during Elijah's time to advise and educate members on setting up and running co-operative enterprises. The Union's headquarters in Manchester, appropriately named Holyoake House, still receives delegations and visitors from across the globe.

The Co-op never abandoned its commitment to universal education. Its reading rooms and public halls became community institutions, an expression of its core belief in social justice and opportunity for all. The Co-op was the first British business to ban animal testing on its products, the first to include Fairtrade products in all stores, and the Co-op Bank the first to introduce an ethical investment policy. Elijah the businessman knew the benefits of large-scale operation; the price advantages of bulk-buying, economies of scale in production, and marketing. He would never, however, have subscribed blindly to the aphorism that 'big is beautiful' to the exclusion of small independent concerns. How pleased he would be to learn that, among the independent societies, there are still three stores in the Holmfirth area owned by the Wooldale Co-operative Society.

As for Elijah's belief in education for all, he would no doubt observe, looking at the growth of opportunities over the last 140 years, that today the young are privileged beyond all the hopes of Victorian reformers, especially in the choice of subjects for study. He might also observe with disapproval that there has hardly been a decade since 1876 when schooling and higher education has not been a political football, kicked to and fro between various parties, and a plaything of maverick ministers. Churches of different denominations remain involved in the delivery of state-funded schools; arguments about selection and grammar schools have persisted for seventy years; the replacement of free higher education by fees and loans has actually restricted opportunities for some working-class youngsters. In any case, not all progress was attributable to governments and churches. It was concerned individuals – including employers, and clergymen like James Gaskill and James Scholefield – who saw the need for education, and who were able to provide it at an elementary level on a surprisingly wide scale. Even in 1825, eighty-five per cent of children from five to fifteen in Manchester and Salford were in receipt of basic education.[2] In the same vein, and with Elijah's support, Mechanics Institutes, the forerunners of technical colleges, were an attempt to provide knowledge and skill in up-and-coming disciplines such as engineering and chemistry. Elijah's practical approach was likewise witnessed, in 1871, by his donation of land in Newton Heath, upon which a new Board school was eventually built, in 1901.

But how Elijah, campaigner for enlightened poor-law provision, would marvel in disbelief at today's welfare state. Ground-breaking progress was made by the Liberal government of 1906-14, which introduced an Old Age Pensions Act, and a contributory scheme of national insurance, providing relief during sickness and unemployment. Half a century later, war-time Britain, still smarting from the privations of pre-war slump, was promised post-war relief from the evils of 'squalor, ignorance, want, idleness, and disease' by the Beveridge Report. Many of its recommendations, including the setting up of a National Health Service, were enacted by the Labour government elected in 1945. All this, too, has become the meat and drink of politics, but generally the battlegrounds lie around the margins of its scope, not the principle. Benefits for those who cannot work, however, remain controversial and there are still many who, like Whigs of old, would deprecate all in need as 'undeserving'.

Likewise, how would Elijah, champion of the working man, campaigner against child exploitation, view the plethora of regulation in every industry, in the century following his death? Consolidated by the Health and Safety at Work Act of 1974, as amended and enlarged, its provisions – particularly those prompted by Britain's membership of the EEU – have become the target of complaints against over-regulation and the butt of jokes. But look at the facts and figures of industrial accidents in Elijah's day, and later. Then ask any worker if he or she would wish to be without such protections, and the argument is at an end.

In contrast to education, welfare and safety at work, latter-day politicians have stepped lightly round issues surrounding the consumption of alcohol and with good reason. Gladstone's Licensing Act of 1872 may have represented a triumph for the Temperance lobby, in which Elijah played his part, but it was a disaster for the Liberal party at the next general election. Fifty years later, the complete failure of the American Prohibition Act delivered a knockout blow to the hopes that a democracy – any democracy – might achieve a total ban on booze. Shakespeare's Sir Toby Belch exemplified the risk of ridicule attendant on censorious authority attempting to deny simple pleasures. 'Dost thou think', he raged at pompous Malvolio, 'because thou art virtuous, there shall be no more cakes and ale?' Today, only authoritarian and theocratic regimes seek to impose virtue.

Examining Elijah's role in the Temperance movement in the 1860s and '70s, it is possible to sense that it was, above all, a statement of genuine conscientious belief, having seen for himself the miseries inflicted by drink on working class Manchester. He was, as his Quaker friend, Jacob Bright, might have said, letting his life speak. And while governments have fought shy of total prohibition, there has since 1872 been a general acceptance that although - like prostitution - alcohol can never be eliminated, it must be regulated. Today, though issues are usually decided in Parliament by free vote, unfettered by party whips, licensing laws and drink-driving laws reflect universal acceptance of the state's duty to curb excess.

And if Elijah were to return amongst us to observe the rising rates of alcohol abuse and alcohol-related disease, he might politely invite us to join him for a sarsaparilla or two in England's last temperance bar at Rawtenstall, Lancashire. There, wearing an exasperated smile, and wagging a benign finger, he would be entitled to boast once more of his epic ascent of Snaefell; adding, with furrowed brow, 'I told you so.'

Elijah's demonstration of support for arbitration of international disputes was a prescient warning against war-mongers. There is no evidence that he was a pacifist in the manner of the Quakers, but experience and hard knocks taught him that conciliation, reconciliation and negotiation could achieve more than clamorous ultimatums when it came to solving disputes.

No point in asking the question: to what extent was he heeded? Look at the stats. Twenty million people died in or as a direct result of the First World War; maybe 55 million in the Second World War; at a conservative estimate 160 million deaths – including those of civilians – were caused by war and genocide in the twentieth century. Elijah may have understood the power of the arms industry in late Victorian England, but he underestimated the credulity of ordinary people when it came to their natural patriotism. Mafeking Night was followed, in 1914, by scenes of cheering crowds, and queues outside recruiting offices. Yet the world today seems hardly chastened by recent slaughter. The League of Nations which emerged from the Treaty of Versailles utterly failed in its objectives; easily circumvented by evil men. The United Nations has credits to its name, but every television news bulletin belies its declared role of international arbitrator and peace-maker. Again, in his commitment to peace, Elijah was far from naive: wars disrupt trade; there is no sense in shooting your customers. Moreover, for all its failures, arbitration by the United Nations and intervention by international peace-keepers remains the world's only hope of mitigating the scourge of war.

Following the desecration of paupers' graves, Walker's Croft was lost forever beneath an avalanche of new developments heralding the railway age. Even so, the nation's conscience may have been pricked by this and similar episodes, since a series of Burial Acts, passed between 1853 and 1859, included rules that specifically outlawed building on disused burial grounds without strict consultation and controls, such as allowing a minimum number of years since closure and the re-interment of bodies elsewhere. Yet even today, similar battles, with similar outcomes, may be in the offing; a section of the parliamentary Bill sanctioning future work on new High Speed rail links provides for the 'disapplication of powers contained in other legislation', including those relating to 'listed buildings, ancient monuments and burial grounds'.

Of all the great causes to which Elijah lent his weight, none was more pervasive and all-consuming than the right to vote. Only the certainty that he was right, and that history was on his side, would have consoled Elijah in his declining years, given that Disraeli's 1867 Reform Act had delivered a franchise that was neither muckling nor mickling. It took the best part of another 50 years before Britain arrived at anything like a realisation of the Chartists' Six Points, and another 20 years on top of that before parliament finally broke the link between ownership of property and the right to vote. In fact, the Chartists themselves eventually realised that their third point – annual parliaments – was unworkable, and later changed their demand to triennial parliaments.

The 1884 Representation of the People Act was another case of tweaking the safety valve; while it extended the £10 rental, property-based voting qualification in the towns to the countryside, and established the principle of one-member constituencies, all women and forty per cent of men were left without the vote.

Indeed, it was the absence of any votes for women that continued to outrage the honest democratic faith of Elijah and those of his friends, such as the estimable Dr Richard Pankhurst and his wife Emmeline. It took another 40 years and the First World War, before *any* woman was allowed to vote. Even a century later the delay in granting voting rights to women besmirches the democratic credentials of Britain, and had he lived longer it is surely likely that Elijah would have followed the Pankhursts out of the Liberal party and into the Labour party, as the only party committed to universal suffrage.

One episode in particular might have been the last straw. On a beautiful Sunday morning in July 1896, Emmeline Pankhurst and four other women, attending a rally in favour of votes for women in Boggart Hole Clough, a park bordering Moston, were arrested and charged with public order offences.

Very much on home territory, therefore, these events would have been of great interest to Elijah, given his close friendship with Emmeline's husband, and his dedication to universal suffrage. James Keir Hardie, a founder member of the Independent Labour Party, and others described by the press as 'socialists' also had their collars felt. The charges were, in the event, dropped and the parks committee decided that such open-air meetings should, in future, be permitted. Yet, almost exactly ten years later, another meeting at Boggart Hole Clough turned nasty. Suffragists, Adela Pankhurst among them, and again supported by Keir Hardie, were mobbed by exuberant young men, some members of a local football team. They charged downhill at the protestors, wielding sticks. As panic set in, and the crowd attempted to get away, some of the men linked arms to prevent the women escaping. Female speakers in particular were singled out, grabbed by their arms, subjected to insult and abuse, dragged round the park, clothes half ripped off, and beaten across the face. Blood was spilt, though admittedly not on the scale of Peterloo.

It was not just that bringing charges against the organisers of the meeting – most of which were dropped – amounted to a travesty of justice. Following the humiliations suffered by women at Boggart Hole Clough, their protests became more militant and violent. They chained themselves to railings, broke windows, and when imprisoned, went on hunger strike and were force-fed. In the period leading up to the First World War, Christabel Pankhurst, Emmeline's daughter, urged Suffragettes to intensify their campaign by way of secret arson attacks. In Lancashire, Edith Rigby admitted burning down Lord Leverhulme's house in Rivington and planting a bomb in the Liverpool Cotton Exchange.

Elijah would have been shamed not only by events in Boggart Hole Clough, but also by the slow, grudging progress towards female emancipation in Britain as a whole. The Municipal Franchise Act of 1869 had been welcomed as a step in the right direction, granting the right to vote to single women ratepayers in local elections. Then to have witnessed the delay until 1918 for some but not all women over the age of thirty to be allowed to vote, and a further twelve years before they could vote on the same terms as men, would have strained Elijah's patience with the Liberal party to breaking-point. And how he would have rung the bells for provisions in the 1948 Representation of the People Act which finally abolished plural voting rights for university graduates and business owners.

Yet it must be said that contemporary feminists troubling to read through the labyrinthine provisions of Elijah's will might recoil in horror at the limited income provision for wife Martha; 'thirty shillings per week'. But Martha pre-deceased him so that aspect of the notorious will, at least, escaped litigation. Perhaps more shocking was the exclusion, from a bequest to daughter Judith of all household goods and furniture, of 'printed books and manuscripts'! No reason is given, but if on this slim basis, you are tempted to shout the man down as misogynistic, pause for a moment to consider his early support for women's suffrage, when even fellow Radicals were unconvinced. In Elijah's defence, given that he probably anticipated Judith and husband James caring for Martha in the event of her outliving him, thirty shillings a week for personal use was not an unreasonable sum; likewise, it is still common practice for testators to leave the distribution of books to the discretion of executors, as personal mementoes. In any event, how interesting it would be to know the contents of Elijah's library of books and manuscripts.

Of course, no electoral system perfectly meets the objections of those who point to its anomalies and inequalities. Fast moving changes in population make it hard for parliament to keep up with its statutory duty to equalise constituency numbers, and the debate continues on issues upon which the Electoral Reform Society has campaigned continuously since 1884 – forms of proportional representation as opposed to first-past-the post. Suffice it to say that standing back from the fray, Elijah might have gone along with an aphorism once quoted in Parliament by Winston Churchill, that in a world of sin and woe no-one can pretend that democracy is perfect or all-wise. It is simply 'the worst form of government – except for all the others'.

Though his name crops up in history books as a footnote here and there, Elijah was soon forgotten. Others, no more devoted to their cause than he, took on starring roles and earned their places in history. Richard Cobden and Edwin Chadwick have their statues; Sam Bamford and Ernest Jones their blue plaques; Peterloo is commemorated by a red plaque. Richard Pankhurst's widow Emmeline achieved a status so iconic as to render plaques in her honour superfluous. Abel Heywood – Bamford's *Abel Anything* – was mayor of Manchester at the time of Elijah's death. When the new Town Hall was opened the following year, the eight-ton bell in its handsome tower was fortuitously named *Great Abel,* ample consolation for being snubbed by Queen Victoria, who refused to be received by a miscreant Radical. More recently a boutique hotel and pub opened in the Northern Quarter, bearing Heywood's name. And there are still pubs in almost every town in England whose names celebrate the reformers' arch-enemy, the Duke of Wellington.

However, you would search in vain for memorials to Elijah Dixon and the Blanketeers. There are none; no statues, no plaques, no portraits hung in hallowed halls, no pubs or restaurants named after Elijah; and nothing to commemorate the bravery of the Blanketeers. Of course, society cannot live in perpetual remembrance. There is no reason for Elijah Dixon to be revered or canonised – but there is every reason to remember him.

Elijah and Martha lie at rest together in what is now an unmarked grave. Whatever adornments in marble or other stone once marked the family vault have long since perished. But at least their graves, unlike those of Jones at Ardwick, and Scholefield at Every Street, lie undisturbed. And not being honoured in stone, Elijah did not suffer the ignominy of Jones and Hunt. A dozen years after Elijah's death, Hunt's monument at Every Street was dismantled, on the pretext that it could not be made safe, and those who had witnessed his great meeting there were left to write despairing letters to the press. Ernest Jones's elaborate monument was swept away in 1960 when Ardwick cemetery was converted into playing fields. Ben Brierley, who became a local councillor, suffered mixed fortunes in posterity. He had a Moston pub named after him, its strategic location spreading the name to a bus terminus. Brierley's grave at Harpurhey can still be identified, but barely two hundred yards away, in the adjacent Queens Park, stands the bare plinth which once supported his statue, before vandalism preceded its removal. A casting was made, however, and the good citizens of Failsworth rehabilitated their local hero with a new statue close to its famous Pole.

Only a couple of miles from the scene of all the great battles fought for the people of his adopted city, you may pilgrimage to Elijah's grave in Harpurhey cemetery. And there, in a little pool of urban serenity, away from the drone of traffic on nearby Rochdale Road, you may still hear the soft whispers of Elijah Dixon, appealing for a better world.

Endnotes

Chapter One: Holmfirth

1. *Daily News*, 19 September 1850: 'Mornings at the Mills', article by W. H. Dixon

Chapter Two: New Cross

1. *Hansard*, 27 Feb 1818: Petitions re Suspension of Habeas Corpus Act. The Deputy Constable is not actually named in Elijah's petition, but is named in others.
2. *Annals of Manchester to 1885* (re 1818), W. E. A. Axon

Chapter Three: Westminster

1. *Historical Sketches and Personal Recollections of Manchester*, Archibald Prentice, 1851
2. *Hansard*, 27 February 1818
3. *Hansard*, 9 February 1818 and 5 March 1818

Chapter Four: St Peter's Field

1. There are many published accounts of the 'Peterloo Massacre', as the events at this meeting became known; individual sources have not been quoted here, but are a composite of contemporary reports and more recent research on casualty numbers.
2. *The Peoples History of Manchester*, John Reilly, 1859
3. *The Age of Reform 1815-1870*, Ernest Llewellyn Woodward, 1963

Chapter Five: Great Ancoats Street

1. *The Trial of Henry Hunt*, T. Dolby (publisher), 1820
2. *Quarter Sessions*, Lancashire Archives, item QSB1/1823/Apr/pt6/48
3. *Annual Register for 1821*, Baldwin, Cradock & Joy (publishers), 1822
4. *Quarter Sessions*, Lancashire Archives, item QSB1/1826/Jan/pt5/70

Chapter Six: Store Street

1. *History of Co-operation*, Vol.2, G. J. Holyoake, 1906

Chapter Seven: Town Hall

1. *Hansard*, 23 February 1830
2. *Absalom Watkin Journal Extracts (1814-56)*, A. E. Watkin, 1920

Chapter Eight: Camp Field

1. *Manchester voters' list*, 1832

Chapter Nine: Stevenson Square

1. *The Age of Reform 1815-1870*, Ernest Llewellyn Woodward, 1963

Chapter Ten: The Manor Court Room

1. *The Match Industry: Its Origin and Development*, W. H. Dixon (great-grandson), 1925

Chapter Eleven: Collyhurst Bridge

1. *The Age of Reform 1815-1870,* Ernest Llewellyn Woodward, 1963

Chapter Thirteen: Carpenters Hall

1. *Condition of the Working Class in England*, Friedrich Engels, 1845 (English edition 1886)
2. During a revolt in Upper Canada, between 1836 and 1838, British seamen were secretly authorised by the government to raid rebel homesteads and hold hostage, or murder, suspected participants (some were merely civilians, including several from America). The government denied this until an assassin was caught in Feb 1838 and the truth came out at his trial.

Chapter Fourteen: Walker's Croft

1. *Manchester Courier* and *Manchester Guardian*, both 11 May 1839 (re 9 May)
2. St Michael's burial ground was also discussed, after which Elijah again mentioned a brother's burial, but no evidence of a related burial there has yet come to light.

Chapter Sixteen: Newport

1. *Manchester Times and Gazette*, 1 February 1840 (re 27 January); it also carried a report of an Anti-Corn Law meeting the same day, at which similar sympathies were expressed by many of the same attendees.
2. *Condition of the Working Class in England*, Friedrich Engels, 1845

Chapter Seventeen: Clerkenwell

1. *Manchester Historical Recorder*, pub. John Heywood, 1875. George Russell executed 15 September 1798. It also says that James Burrows was hanged here in 1866, but later says this was actually at the New Bailey prison.
2. Manchester Rates Books and Trade Directories; also *Historical and Literary Remains* Vol.72, Chetham Society, 1867
3. Hackney Archives, Item D/B/BRY/1/1/10, Copy of partnership agreement
4. *Chartism and the Chartists in Manchester and Salford* (p.126), Paul Pickering, 1995

Chapter Eighteen: Newton Heath

1. *Great Exhibition, Juries Report*, 1852
2. *Society of Arts Journal*, Vol. 1 No. 17, Letter from Charles Tomlinson, 8 March 1853
3. *The Match Industry: Its Origin and Development*, W. H. Dixon (great-grandson), 1925

Chapter Nineteen: Chat Moss

1. *History of Co-operation Volume 2*, G. J. Holyoake, 1906
2. *Manchester's Narrow-gauge Railways: Chat Moss and Carrington Estates*, R. W. Nicholls, 1985
3. Although the farm is not named in earlier Censuses (all the entries just appear as 'Irlam Moss'), it is shown as such from 1871 onwards, when the Garners were in possession, and by reference to neighbouring farms it is clear that it was the same farm as established by Elijah.
4. *People I Have Met*, J. Johnson, c.1900
5. *Chartism and the Chartists in Manchester and Salford*, P. A. Pickering, 1995

Chapter Twenty: New Moston

1. *A History of the Ancient Chapelry of Blackley*, Rev J. Booker, 1854

Chapter Twenty-one: Clough House

1. Hackney Archives, Item D/B/BRY/1/1/11 (Will dated 17 July 1855)
2. *History of Newton Chapelry*, H. T. Crofton, Chetham Society, 1904
3. The burial records state that Abner was actually interred in the public ground, not the family grave, despite being commemorated on this.
4. Hackney Archives, Item D/B/BRY/1/1/11 (Letter dated 17 April 1862)
5. Hackney Archives, Item D/B/BRY/1/1/11 (Letter dated 23 April 1862)

6. Exact date not stated, but the photograph is a carte-de-visite, a small print format that became popular from the late 1850s for handing out to family and friends. Since the marriage date appears at the bottom, it suggests an anniversary commemoration, and thus the golden anniversary (1863) would seem most likely.

Chapter Twenty-two: Dob Lane

1. *Lancashire and Yorkshire Railway Volume 2*, John Marshall, 1970
2. National Archives, Kew, Ref. RAIL/795/561

Chapter Twenty-three: Ardwick

1. *The Diaries of Samuel Bamford*, Edited by M. Hewitt & R. Poole, 2000

Chapter Twenty-six: Vine House

1. *Manchester Rates Books* and *Census Returns*
2. *The Story of Robert Clarke*, George Goddard, published in the *Oldham Evening Chronicle*, October 1953; also *History of the Tinwhistle*, Norman Dannatt, 1993
3. UK Government: Wills and Probate Service (will dated 16 June 1870; codicil 20 June 1870)
4. Hackney Archives, Item Ref. D/B/BRY/1/1/11 (Letter dated 16 August 1875)
5. *A Glimpse of New Moston*, Bernard C. Savage, 1998

Chapter Twenty-seven: Belgrave Road

1. There were two railway football teams: *Newton Heath LYR*, for carriage works staff, and *Newton Heath Loco*, for enginemen. The former had a ground on North Road (now Northampton Road) and merged with other local teams to form Manchester United. The *Loco* played at a pitch off Warden Lane and remained a non-league side until c.1970, after which the ground fell into disuse, but could still be seen, heavily overgrown, until the 1990s. Houses now cover both sites.

Chapter Twenty-eight: Harpurhey

1. *The CWS in War and Peace*, Sir William Richardson, 1977
2. *History, Gazetteer and Directory of Lancashire*, Edward Baines, 1825

Appendix 1

People

Addington, Henry (1st Viscount Sidmouth)

British Tory Prime Minister 1801-4; Home Secretary in Lord Liverpool's government 1812-22. Born Holborn, 30 May 1757; educated Winchester and Oxford, where he studied law. Became Speaker of the Commons in 1789, on Pitt's recommendation. In 1801 became Prime Minister, after George III asked him to help remove Pitt, whose support for Catholic emancipation was opposed by the king. Following discussions, Pitt agreed to stand aside. Sidmouth negotiated Treaty of Amiens with Napoleon in 1802 but was felt to have made too many concessions; hostilities resumed in 1803. Was criticised for poor handling of war against France, and William Pitt returned as PM the following year. Later, as Home Secretary, Sidmouth was tasked with suppressing increasing social unrest; introduced many restrictive and punitive acts of parliament, including Habeas Corpus Suspension Act of 1817, passed in February of that year and renewed in June. During this period, he issued warrants for the arrests, without charge or trial, of Radical protestors suspected of revolutionary tendencies, conducting many interviews with the detainees personally. Eventually, even his own colleagues criticised his ineptitude, especially after *Peterloo*, and he stood down in 1821, being replaced by Robert Peel. Continued in the House of Lords for a few years and retired from politics after voting against the 1832 Reform Act. He died 15 February 1844 in Richmond, Surrey.

Bright, Jacob

Younger brother of John Bright (below) born on 26 May 1821 at Green Bank, near Rochdale, a son of Jacob Bright, Quaker and owner of a cotton-spinning mill, and Martha Wood. Educated in York, joined his father's business as a manager. Married Ursula Mellor in 1855. Became interested in politics, and supported Chartism and the Radical section of the emerging Liberal party. After incorporation in 1856, became first mayor of Rochdale municipal borough. Though not particularly religious, he was a campaigner for peace and universal suffrage. Stood as unsuccessful Liberal parliamentary candidate for Manchester in 1865, but won by-election in 1867, retaining his seat the following year, and serving for another six years. Served again as MP for Manchester from February 1876 (attending Elijah's funeral in July) and for Manchester South-West from

1886-95. On retirement, moved to Goring-on-Thames, Oxfordshire, where he died on 7 November 1899. Cremated at Esher, without a service.

Bright, John

Brother of Jacob (above); born at Green Bank on 16 November 1811. Followed his father, both into the cotton-spinning and carpet manufacturing business, and as a practising Quaker. Married Elizabeth Priestman of Newcastle in 1839; she bore him a daughter, Helen, who died in 1841. Remarried in 1847, to Margaret Elizabeth Leatham of Wakefield, a marriage which produced seven more children. Speaking at a meeting in Rochdale, his forthright delivery so impressed Richard Cobden that he invited him to speak at an Anti-Corn Law meeting in Manchester. The two founded the Anti-Corn Law League in 1838 and on this, and free trade, became virtually a double act. Bright became MP for Durham in 1843 and Manchester in 1847. Although broadly a believer in social justice, and much admired as an orator, he was less enthusiastic about universal suffrage, improved factory conditions and trade unions, tending to take the side of the manufacturers. He was also reputed to be over-sensitive, taking criticism badly and even falling out with Cobden on occasion. His 'Angel of Death' speech, criticising Palmerston for taking Britain into the Crimean War, lost him his seat in 1857. Re-elected for Birmingham soon after, a seat he retained for the rest of his life. By the 1860s he was arguing for parliamentary reform, but was content with the provisions of the 1867 Act, whereas most Radicals were not. There is no direct evidence of discourse between John Bright and Elijah, but they must have attended the same meetings on many occasions. Died in Rochdale on 27 March 1889.

Candelet, Peter Turner

Fellow reformer, police commissioner and member of Northern Political Union committee. Born c.1797 in Stockport, Cheshire. A linen draper in 1822, Candelet started a subscription at his shop (31 Market Street) to pay for David Ridgway's defence at the latter's trial for selling Carlile's *New Year Address*, and he and Elijah stood as surety on his release a year later. When Carlile's sister, Mary Ann, was also imprisoned in April 1822, Radicals, both male and female, raised two guineas and sent goods to help her; among supporters were Mrs Ridgway (who donated a frock) and P. T. Candelet (who gave a frock waist). On 25 February 1824 he married Sarah Sutcliffe (of Manchester), at Manchester Collegiate church, and after her death he married again - to Mary Sutcliffe (of Halifax), on 13 May 1830 (it is not known whether Sarah and Mary were related). When James Wroe died suddenly in 1844, Candelet started a subscription for Wroe's widow, Alice, supported by James Scholefield, Abel Heywood,

Elijah and others. Owner of property in Heaviley (Stockport), and Queen Street, Bowling (Bradford) but later became an auctioneer, selling property for Dixon, Son & Co in the 1850s. Lived, latterly at Holme House, Broughton, Salford, where he died on 4 January 1861; buried on the 10th at St Mary CE, Stockport.

Carlile, Richard

Born in Ashburton, Devon, on 8 December 1790. After working briefly for a druggist in Exeter, he was apprenticed to a tinsmith for seven years, an occupation he detested, and by 1813 he was in London with his wife, Jane. After several unsuccessful attempts to get articles published, the suspension of the Habeas Corpus Act in 1817, which had a dampening effect on sales of Radical journals and pamphlets, prompted him to try selling books himself. Borrowed money from his employer to buy 100 copies of the proscribed *Black Dwarf*, and walked around London persuading news vendors to take a few each. His offer to publish the *Dwarf* himself was declined, but the publisher of *The Republican*, W. T. Sherwin, liked his style and offered him the editorship. He encouraged Sherwin and other publishers to be bolder and began publishing works by Tom Paine and others.

Carlile was invited to address the meeting at St Peter's Field in Manchester in 1819, but the arrest of Hunt and subsequent massacre prevented this; he escaped and was hidden by Radical friends (notably James Wroe) before taking the mail coach back to London. By now, he had six indictments against him, and in November 1819 was sentenced by the King's Bench court to two years imprisonment (which he served in Dorchester gaol) for 'scandalous, impious, blasphemous and profane libel'. Even then, he continued publishing and producing pamphlets; one was ostensibly a serialised report of his trial, but included Paine's *Age of Reason* in instalments. Both his wife and sister, taking the same defiant stand against injustice, continued to publish and sell his works while he was detained, and both also suffered imprisonment. The relationship with his wife was rather strained, however, and they mainly lived apart after 1819, being formally separated by 1832.

By the time of his northern tour in 1827, Carlile was a committed atheist, causing him to be vilified, even demonised, by the pious. However, it provided the basis for lengthy and friendly discussion with Elijah, in the columns of *The Lion*, after the latter's conversion to Christian *Universalism*. There was mutual fascination, and each took it as a challenge to try to convert the other. Despite a dogged boldness when occasion demanded it, Carlile was, according to his friend George Holyoake, retiring by nature; he abstained from alcohol and rarely ate meat. Like Elijah, he was tolerant, and once said of himself 'I have no wish to force my opinions on any man - if he wishes to have them, he must either buy them or challenge me to defend them; and, in this last instance, it must be some one whom I consider worth contending with, before I would open my mouth.'

Carlile died on 10 February 1843 of bronchitis, at his home in Bouverie St, Fleet Street, London; he left three children by his wife (Richard, Alfred and Thomas Paine Carlile) and three (Julian, Hesphatia and Theophila) born after separation from Jane, to a partner whom he only referred to as 'Isis'. His last wishes provided for dissection of his body at St Thomas's hospital before a group of friends and medical students, and his remains were buried 16 days later at Kensal Green Cemetery. His wife died a few months later and was buried with him.

Cobbett, William

Born in Farnham, Surrey, on 9 March 1763, son of a farmer and publican, he became a farmer himself but from his youth opposed the unfairness of the parliamentary system. Obtained work as a clerk in London and moved there in 1783. Joined the army in 1784, eventually becoming a corporal, serving in Canada, but was accused of troublemaking when he attempted to report theft of army funds by a quartermaster. Newly married, he fled to France with his wife and later went to America, teaching English to French refugees. He returned to England in 1799, becoming a leading reformer and opponent of the Corn Laws, founding the *Political Register* newspaper in 1802. After imposition of newspaper tax in 1815, he changed the format to a (much cheaper) pamphlet and it became the most widely-read news sheet among workers, with a circulation of over 40,000. The *Register's* anti-government stance made him a target for Sidmouth and to avoid detention after the Blanketeers episode he returned to America where he lived from 1817-19. Stood unsuccessfully as parliamentary candidate for Honiton (1806), Coventry (1820), Preston (1826) and in 1832, Manchester, but later became M.P. for Oldham. Elijah, said to have a similar, direct, manner of speaking, was a strong supporter. Died at his farm in Normandy, near Farnham, 18 June 1835.

Cobden, Richard

Well known as co-founder (with John Bright) of the Anti-Corn Law League and advocate of free trade; born on 3 June 1804, Heyshott, Sussex, settled in Manchester, 1832. Strong supporter of incorporation for Manchester, persuading the majority that it would be better than the antiquated manorial regime under the Mosley family. Equally opposed to feudal control, Elijah, Wroe and others disagreed, arguing that a council elected by a handful of qualified voters, under the flawed 1832 Reform Act, was less democratic than the former churchwardens and leypayers' committees, on which any rate-payer could serve. Many

Chartists were dubious about Cobden's motives, suspecting him of being more interested in glory than principle. Elijah crossed swords with him on more than one occasion, but there were points of agreement such as land scheme allocation. Died in London on 2 April 1865.

Condy, George

Born c.1787 in Ireland. After being called to the Bar at Gray's Inn (11 February 1828), moved to Manchester and lived at various addresses around Norfolk St, Pall Mall and Spring Gardens, practising as a barrister and becoming a commissioner of bankruptcy. Entered into partnership with Mrs Jane Leresche as letter-press printers and publishers of the Radical *Manchester and Salford Advertiser* at 78 Market St (Mrs Leresche was also an importer of Chinese tea). Condy was a correspondent for the London *Times,* a theatre critic and dramatist, publishing a five-act play *Camillus* in 1837. Also wrote a childrens song containing the lines *We shall have the Ten Hours Bill, Or the land will ne'er be still.* By 1841 was living in Cheetham, at Mount Pleasant. Leading campaigner for rights of factory children; described by many as an intellectual, sharply intelligent in the courtroom, outspoken and often sarcastic as a journalist, yet good-humoured and easy-going in his social life. On the announcement of his death, on 4 November 1841, aged 54, the *Manchester Courier* printed a brief obituary the next day, praising his honesty and affability, despite admitting they did not share his political views. Buried on 10 November at All Saints, Chorlton-on-Medlock: a monument, proposed by his friends, was never erected.

Gaskill, James

A cotton spinner from Hulme, born c.1800, became a Bible Christian and assisted at Christ Church, Hulme, where he co-founded a Sunday school in 1819 with close friend Joseph Brotherton. It was specifically intended to welcome Radicals and their children who, at the time, were often barred from regular schools for wearing the white hats and green ribbons favoured by Hunt supporters. Took over as minister at Hulme, after James Scholefield had left to found his new chapel in Ancoats. In 1850 became vice-chairman to Elijah in the Manchester Bridgewater Freehold Land Society and held plots in the New Moston estate, although, unlike the other committee members, he did not have a street named after him. He was a founding member of the United Kingdom Alliance (abstinence society, 1853) and started a building society in Hulme. Remained a spinner and schoolmaster all his life, living close to the church on Queen Street, before moving to Stretford Road where he died on 17 August 1870, aged 70. He never married. Part of his estate was used to found the James Gaskill Science Scholarship at Owens College (now part of Manchester University).

Harrop, James

Born Ashton-under-Lyne c.1825, James had moved to Manchester with the family by 1829, when his father, Horatio Nelson Harrop, became landlord of the Kings Arms public house at 45 Great Ancoats Street (later renumbered first 85 then 93), three doors away from Elijah's first shop. Married Elijah's daughter Judith at St Mary's church, Manchester, on 11 May 1853, by which time James was a partner in Harrop, Taylor and Pearson, proprietors of Newton Silk Mill. Over the years, his occupation was stated variously as 'silk manufacturer' or 'book keeper'. He also owned shares in the New Moston estate, as well as houses around Newton Heath. Later lived with Elijah and Martha at Vine House, New Moston, and continued living there after Elijah's death in 1876. The house suffered a serious fire around 1880 (said to have been started accidentally by one of the children playing with fireworks) and was extensively rebuilt. James died intestate on 6 August 1892, the estate passing to his daughter Annie Elizabeth, Judith and two sons having pre-deceased him. Annie, by then the widow of William Walter Ingham, was the last of the line in New Moston, when she died at Vine House in September 1940.

Heywood, Abel

The son of John and Betty, Heywood was born in Prestwich, near Manchester, on 25 February 1810 and baptised at St Mary's church on 22 April. After his father's death two years later, the family moved into Manchester and he started work in a warehouse at nine years of age. In 1831 he became a bookseller and agent for Hetherington's *Poor Man's Guardian* at a shop on Oldham Street. Persistently refused to charge the stamp tax on publications he sold, and accrued fines because of this: from March 1832 he served four months imprisonment in the New Bailey for non-payment. Was prosecuted twice more before the government reduced the duty in 1837. Later began publishing and printing books, at Oldham Street, as did his older brother John (born 27 August 1806), based in Deansgate (John Heywood & Co remained in business until the 1970s). Although a Chartist and supporter of Co-operation, Heywood split with Elijah and other Radicals, in his strong support for Incorporation. Elected as a councillor in 1843 and alderman in 1853 and 1859; stood twice, unsuccessfully, as a Liberal parliamentary candidate.

Heywood was Mayor of Manchester in 1862-3 (during the cotton famine) and 1876-7, instigating and overseeing design and construction of the present Town Hall, performing the opening ceremony himself, after Queen Victoria had refused an invitation to do so. As a friend, and representative of the Liberal Association, he was among the mourners at Elijah's funeral in 1876. Died on 19 August 1893 in Bowdon, Cheshire, and was buried at Philips Park Cemetery on 22nd. The eight-ton bell in Manchester Town Hall's clock tower was named *Great Abel* in his honour, inscribed with the line from Tennyson: *Ring out the false, ring in the true.*

Houldsworth, Thomas

Born 13 September 1771 at Hagg Farm, Gonalston, Nottinghamshire, son of Henry Houldsworth. In 1793, with his father and brothers, Henry and William, founded a cotton spinning mill in Manchester at 58 Little Lever Street, later extended along Newton Street, bearing his name only. Houldsworth was Elijah's employer at the time of his arrest in 1817 and allowed him to return after his release. In 1818, became Tory M.P. for the vacant seat of Pontefract, an ideal constituency for an ardent horse-racing fan. From 1830, he held the rotten borough of Newton (-le-Willows) for two years. The seat was abolished under the 1832 Reform Act, and Houldsworth became M.P. for North Nottinghamshire, retiring at the 1852 general election. Died on 1 September that year. Not to be confused with nephew William Henry Houldsworth who, in 1863, founded mills at Reddish - still standing. Newton Street mill was demolished in 1906, the site being used for a postal depot.

Hunt, Henry

Born on 6 November 1773, in Upavon, Wiltshire, Hunt became a farmer, and early on was attracted to Radicalism, denouncing both Whigs and Tories as complacent and self-serving. A follower of Francis Burdett; soon became known as a prolific and rousing public speaker. After meetings in London in 1816, was dubbed 'Orator' Hunt by opponents, a term meant to be disparaging, but which enhanced his reputation. Radicals nicknamed him 'King Harry the Ninth'. Invited by the Patriotic Union Society of Manchester to address the meeting at St Peter's Field on 16 August 1819, he was the chief target of the magistrates, at whose bidding the bungled actions of the local yeomanry during his arrest led to the Peterloo Massacre. Served thirty months in Ilchester prison following this, during which time the Great Northern Union was formed in Manchester (Elijah being a member) to support his cause. This was the germ of what later became the Chartist movement. Attempting to recoup his fortunes on release, he began manufacturing and marketing various products: breakfast powder, synthetic coal and shoe-blacking with political slogans on the packaging, causing suspicion (and even friction, particularly with Carlile) and many Radicals felt he had watered down his principles. His popularity diminished still further when he refused to support the Reform Bill, although his argument was that it was too limited. Nevertheless, he was still revered as one of the pioneers of Radicalism, and was feted on a visit to Manchester on 19 August 1830. After his defeat at the Preston election of 1833, he retired from public life to Whitchurch, Hampshire, where he died of a stroke on 15 February 1835.

Johnson, Joseph (brush maker)

Born c.1791, possibly in Didsbury, he became a brush-maker in Manchester, at 17 Shudehill. Joined the Hampden Club formed by John Knight and in 1818, along with Knight, John Thacker Saxton and James Wroe, started a Radical newspaper, the *Manchester Observer*, and later the Patriotic Union Society, which organised the meeting at St Peter's Field on 16 August 1819. He was arrested after this and sentenced to 12 months' imprisonment at Lincoln, during which time his wife became seriously ill and died. The prison authorities denied his request to attend her funeral. This affected him deeply and after release in 1821 he withdrew from political activity to a large extent. Died in Northenden in 1872. Not related to:-

Johnson, Joseph (auctioneer and biographer)

Born c.1823 in Manchester, he followed his father, Samuel, to become a book-seller and stationer at 10 Market St, although residing at Cheetham Hill. Father worked at the same mill as Elijah and in his limited spare time sold books at a shop near Store Street. The book business proved lucrative, so Johnson left the mill and moved to Market Street, later joined in the business by sons Joseph and Thomas. Following visits to the Isle of Man, Samuel retired to Douglas. About 1867 Joseph joined him and became an auctioneer, while Thomas remained in Manchester, running a book shop on Corporation Street. A strong advocate of political and social reform, Johnson was also a teetotaller and lay preacher. Contributed articles to newspapers on the Island and in Manchester, and wrote several biographies and educational books. His serialised memoirs, which contained chapters on Elijah, Henry Vincent and George Holyoake, were published in the *Isle of Man Times* and later in book form (*People I Have Met*). Elijah may have visited Joseph on his trip to the Island in 1875. In 1905 Joseph moved to Waterloo, Liverpool, where he died on 7 March 1907, following a serious operation. Buried three days later at Kirk Braddan, Isle of Man.

Jones, Ernest Charles

Last of the Chartist leaders, also a poet and lawyer (and no mean artist). Jones was born in Berlin on 25 January 1819, son of Major Charles Jones, equerry to the Duke of Cumberland. The family returned to London in 1838 where Jones studied law and became a barrister in 1844, by which time he had also become a follower of Feargus O'Connor and the Chartist movement. He and Elijah probably first met in Clerkenwell in 1848, to discuss the rally at Kennington the following week (after which Jones was arrested), although Elijah may well have heard him speak at an earlier Chartist 'camp' meeting, near Blackstone Edge. Jones was also a strong supporter of Co-operation, being a committee member, with Elijah, of the Manchester and Salford Co-operative Society. Elijah, a pall-bearer at Jones's funeral, was a great admirer and firm friend, naming one of the five original streets in New Moston after him (the other four being Dixon, Frost, Potts and Ricketts Streets). Died on 26 January 1869 and buried at Ardwick Cemetery; his grave was later marked by a 12-foot high memorial, raised by public subscription.

Knight, John

A handloom weaver from Quick, near Mossley, he was baptised on 9 December 1762 at St Chad, Saddleworth and after apprenticeship in Manchester, settled in Oldham. Despite relative prosperity, he was frustrated by the existing political system and was influenced by the writings of Tom Paine. In 1794, was arrested at a meeting in Royton, for a seditious speech, and sentenced to two years imprisonment. Organiser of the Manchester meeting in 1812 which led to the arrest of 38 weavers by Joseph Nadin; Knight, and co-defendants, were accused (on the basis of Nadin's statements *alone*) of administering oaths and pledging to destroy power looms. Nadin's evidence was disbelieved by the jury, and all were acquitted. Knight founded Manchester's first Hampden Club in 1816, Elijah and David Ridgway being early members. On 30 March 1817, he was dragged from his bed by Nadin, during the Habeas Corpus Suspension, and, like Elijah, despatched in irons to London to be questioned by Sidmouth. Knight, however, was moved from prison to prison, serving time at Tothill Fields, Reading, Salisbury and Worcester. Released in January 1818, he co-founded the *Manchester Observer* and Patriotic Union Society. It was Knight's idea to invite Major John Cartwright and Richard Carlile to address the meeting at St Peter's field in August 1819, but Henry Hunt deputised for Cartwright, unable to attend. Knight was leader of the Oldham contingent, was on the hustings and arrested, but acquitted; re-arrested on 15 November, after a 'seditious' meeting in Burnley, and sentenced to another two years imprisonment. Later became organiser for the National Spinners Union and campaigner for the Ten Hours Bill. In August 1838, aged 76 – said to be as lively a speaker as ever – chaired meeting in Oldham in support of Stalybridge cotton workers dismissed for attending services at the chapel of Joseph Rayner Stephens. Died at his home on Lord Street, Oldham, a few weeks later. Buried on the 9 September 1838, 2,000 mourners followed his coffin on foot from Oldham to St George's churchyard, Mossley – a distance of five and a half miles.

McWilliams, David

Son of Robert and Agness McWilliams, born in Manchester in 1797 and baptised on 22 November. Married Mary Arrowsmith at the Collegiate church on 7 January 1821. Listed as cotton-spinner at 2 Ryton Street (1822-5) 58 Canal Street (1830) and Edge Street (1841) as well as other addresses around London Road, Chorlton Row and Hulme; was a committee member of the Northern Political Union in the 1820s. Described as journeyman spinner, acted as a fugelman (guide) directing crowds from the dicky seat of one of the landaus conveying Henry Hunt and entourage during Hunt's visit to Manchester, on the eleventh anniversary of Peterloo. Joined Elijah in drapery partnership at Prestolee, near Radcliffe, but was declared bankrupt in November 1831. The following year he was running a Co-operative store on Swan Street, where Elijah had previously been in partnership with Jeremiah Hanmer. Later became a commercial agent, living in Chorlton-on-Medlock by 1870, where he died aged 73.

Nadin, Joseph

Born in Fairfield, near Buxton, in 1765, he was employed as a cotton spinner in Stockport, but made a name for himself by reporting fellow workers to the authorities during riots and machine-wrecking episodes. Moved to Manchester by 1792, where he married Mary Rowlinson, a widow. By 1794 was a flour dealer at 7 Turner Street and by 1797 was listed as a special constable for St Paul's district, gaining notoriety as a thief-taker. He was appointed Deputy Constable of Manchester in October 1802, a position he managed to retain, through reappointments, until resigning in 1821 - becoming a constable for the Salford Hundred and a market inspector for the Court Leet. Succeeded as Deputy Constable by Stephen Lavender, whose daughter Louisa married his son Thomas. In partnership with brother, Joseph Nadin Junior, Thomas was a solicitor at 48 King Street, when he instigated David Ridgway's arrest.

Nadin had a reputation for brutality, corruption, wrongful arrest, employment of paid spies, false witnesses and agents provocateurs, to which the authorities, over many years, turned a Nelsonian blind eye. Although not mentioned by name in reports of Elijah's arrest in 1817, he was the only Deputy at the time and personally arrested most of the other Blanketeers. Hated by Radicals and dubbed 'the real ruler of Manchester', it was at his insistence that the military were ordered to assist in the arrest of Henry Hunt at St Peter's Fields, so the responsibility for the ensuing Peterloo massacre might fairly be laid at his door. Made a small fortune and retired to a country estate near Cheadle, Cheshire, where he died on 4 March 1848; buried at St James's church, Charlotte Street, Manchester.

Nightingale, Edward

Born 30 August 1808 in Manchester, son of William and Ellen. Married Mary Hallsworth, 24 December 1829, at Manchester Collegiate church; occupation given as bookbinder. Elected as a police commissioner in 1837 - at that time described as an iron dealer of Lees Street, Ancoats. Early involvement with the reform movement gained him a reputation for strong, sometimes offensive, language and strong-arm tactics. Was suspected of accepting money from the Tories to disrupt Whig meetings, an accusation never proved. Later took a back seat in politics, except for local government in Newton Heath. Partner in Dixon, Son & Co from 1841, while still running the Sir Ralph Abercrombie public house on the corner of Great Ancoats Street and Lomax Street. Later moved to Oldham Road, Newton Heath, near the timber yard and, from 1856, to a large house, Heath Hall, on the corner of Droylsden Road, where he lived until his death on 17 July 1861. His widow carried on the partnership until it was formally dissolved in January 1862. Buried in a family vault at Manchester General Cemetery, Harpurhey.

Oastler, Richard

In some ways, a mainstream 'ultra Tory' – an admirer of Wellington and totally opposed to parliamentary reform. Born Leeds on 20 December 1789, youngest child of Robert Oastler, linen merchant and Methodist community leader, and Sarah Scurr. His adopted Church-and-King views were mitigated by a firm rejection of laissez-faire views widely supported by manufacturers, leading him to take up strong interventionist policies on social evils such as slavery, oppressive working hours and Whig notions of poor law reform. Strong supporter of friend and fellow Tory, Michael Sadler. Formed a sometimes uneasy alliance with the Manchester Radicals and often referred to as a 'Tory-Radical' - a description of which he disapproved.

In 1838 he was a major contributor to the fund for the defence of Rev J. R. Stephens. He permitted and even organised anti-poor law demonstrations on the Yorkshire estates, for which, unsurprisingly, he was dismissed. From December 1840, Oastler spent three years in Fleet debtors prison. Released in February 1844 after friends raised a subscription to pay the debt. Thereafter, took more of a back seat in politics, Chartism having largely superseded the factory reform movement as the pervasive issue. Following the death of his wife, moved to Guildford in 1845 but died of a heart attack in Harrogate on 22 August 1861; buried in Kirkstall, Leeds.

O'Connor, Feargus

Christened Edward Bowen O'Connor, but called Feargus by his father Roger, he was born into a Protestant Irish family in Castletown-Kinneigh, County

Cork, Ireland, on 18 July 1794. Father exiled from 1801-3; schooled in London, and later, Dublin; may have studied at Trinity College but did not take a degree. Studied law, being admitted to King's Inn in Dublin and later Gray's Inn, London, but despite being called to the Irish Bar in 1830, did not practice for long. Political career launched in 1822 with the publication of *The State of Ireland* focussing on local government corruption. During the reform agitation of 1831-2 became known as a rousing speaker, both in Ireland and England. At first a member of Daniel O'Connell's Repeal party, the two gradually grew apart over O'Connell's laissez-faire beliefs, his refusal to support repeal of the Union and antagonism towards trade unions. Through his untiring tours of England, especially the north, O'Connor became the first great Chartist leader, seen as a unifying force among a disparate mix of opposing factions.

He founded the Radical *Northern Star* newspaper in 1837, based in Leeds, with Bronterre O'Brien as its main leader writer, and O'Connor himself writing a weekly front-page letter. Served several prison sentences for his Radical views. In 1846, founded the Chartist Co-operative Land Company, with members paying a regular subscription and plots being allocated by ballot. The scheme was not a success and was eventually declared illegal, the excuse being that it was a form of lottery. Became M.P. for Nottingham in 1847, but repeated failure to get the Charter through parliament, and of the land scheme, not helped by heavy drinking, caused increasing friction with colleagues. Rumours of mental health problems came to a head in 1852, first with an embarrassing tour of America and then after he assaulted three fellow M.P.s in the House of Commons. Following arrest, his sister arranged for him to be admitted to an asylum in Chiswick; after two years he was allowed to live at her house in Notting Hill. Never married, but believed to have fathered several illegitimate children, through various relationships. Died on 30 August 1855; buried on 10 September at Kensal Green, an estimated 50,000 mourners in attendance.

Owen, Robert

Born 14 May 1771, Newtown, Montgomeryshire. Apprenticed to a London clothier, was offered a supervisory position at a Manchester cotton mill c.1790. Impressed by his ability, employer Peter Drinkwater promoted Owen to manager, later becoming a partner. Persuaded the firm to acquire the New Lanark mill, on the upper Clyde, founded in 1785 by David Dale. He married Dale's daughter, Caroline, in September 1799. Knowledge of the atrocious conditions endured by workers in Manchester mills led him to adapt the New Lanark mill to create a much improved workplace, providing housing with central heating, a school and a factory shop that sold good quality food at a fair price. His belief in, and lectures on, model communities based on Co-operation and profit-sharing inspired many devotees, including Elijah. Though by no means the first 'co-operator' (an honour that might be fairly due to Woolwich shipwrights who founded their own flour mill and bakery in 1760) he was regarded as a father-figure in the movement. Several other attempts at ideal communities failed, however, because for many they were too ambitious.

Attended the first Co-operative Congress, chaired by Elijah, in Manchester in May 1827, joined on the panel by William Thompson of Cork, Rev J. Marriott, J. Finch and William Pare, whose notes of the meeting were discovered by George Holyoake over seventy years later. When the Rochdale Society of Equitable Pioneers set up shop in 1844, they began retailing with meagre capital and supplies, following the 'gradual build-up' approach advocated by Dr William King of Brighton, who founded *The Co-operator* journal in 1828. Owen was very disparaging, opining that at least £20,000 of capital investment was required to begin such a venture. The Pioneers model, however, essentially a consumer co-operative, stood the test of time. Nonetheless, Owen's visions of social improvement, fairness and mutual help have remained an inspiration. Died in Newtown on 17 November 1858.

Pankhurst, Richard Marsden

Almost universally referred to simply as 'Dr Pankhurst', he was born in Stoke-on-Trent in May 1834, son of Henry Francis Pankhurst, and wife Margaret. Henry was a Conservative and Church of England supporter who changed allegiances, and became a Liberal and Baptist. The family moved to Manchester and, from an early age, Richard attended Baptist Sunday schools before entering Manchester Grammar School and Owens College. Studied law in London, becoming Bachelor of Law, with honours, in 1858 and receiving his Doctorate in 1863; called to the Bar in 1867 at Lincoln's Inn, joining the Northern Assize Circuit. Founder member of the Manchester Liberal Association, as was Elijah, and started a national society for womens' suffrage. He also drafted the Bill which was later to become the Married Womens' Property Act, granting wives full control over their earnings and possessions. Other issues he campaigned vigorously for included free speech, free education, state ownership of land, home rule for Ireland, disestablishment of the Anglican church and abolition of the House of Lords, which he called 'a public abattoir, butchering the liberties of the people'.

In 1879 he married Emmeline Goulden, 24 years his junior. Richard and Emmeline Pankhurst later helped found the Womens' Franchise League and Independent Labour Party, accusing the middle-class Liberal party of failing to meet the needs of working people. Political associates included James Keir Hardie, George Bernard Shaw, Annie Besant and William Morris. Stood unsuccessfully for Parliament in 1883 and 1895. Died on 5 July 1898 in Manchester and was buried with his parents at Brooklands Cemetery, Sale.

Potts, Peter

Treasurer of the Manchester Bridgewater Freehold Land Society. Potts Street, in the New Moston estate he helped found, was named after him (renamed Northfield Road in 1900). Born in Macclesfield, Cheshire, in 1816 and baptised at Christ Church there on 25 August. Married Elizabeth Mellor of Hulme on 13 February 1837, at which time he made a mark instead of a signature. Baker and flour dealer at 17 Oxford St, Chorlton-on-Medlock, later in partnership with Charles Parkin, though his home address was in Sale. Elizabeth died on 13 April 1859; married Agnes McGuffie a few months later, at St Martin, Ashton-on-Mersey. Died on 19 July 1896, aged 80, at Priory Mount, Sale, and buried at Brooklands Cemetery. Agnes died two years later and was buried with him and daughter from the first marriage, Ellen Alice.

Prentice, Archibald

Born in Carnwath, Lanarkshire on 17 November 1792, he moved to Manchester in 1815 to work as a clerk for a local textile manufacturer, Thomas Grahame. Lived on Islington Street, Salford in the 1820s and wrote for *Cowdroy's Gazette*. Co-founded the *Manchester Guardian* in 1821 with neighbour and fellow-writer John Edward Taylor, but following differences over editorial style, in 1824 Prentice bought the *Gazette*, renamed it the *Manchester Gazette*, and edited it until January 1828. After financial difficulties, friends formed a joint stock company and the paper was incorporated into a new journal, to become the *Manchester Times and Gazette*. This gradually declined in circulation, however, especially after the rival *Manchester Examiner* was started in 1846; Prentice sold his business to the latter a year later, the amalgamated paper becoming the *Examiner and Times*. He was a Presbyterian, an active reformer (one of the so-called moderates), teetotaller and founder member of the Anti-Corn Law League, although, like Elijah, he did not entirely trust Cobden. Later lived at Moreton Street, Strangeways (1841). Often sided with Elijah and other radicals on points of principle, but sometimes disagreed over approach. He favoured free trade and the Incorporation of Manchester, becoming a councillor with particular responsibility for the gas department from 1845 until his death on 24 December 1857.

Ricketts, William

Born in Rochdale and baptised on 20 May 1804 at the church of St Chad, the son of William, basket maker, and Ann of Toad Lane. Initially followed his father's trade, but had moved to Liverpool by 1823, where he married Mary Hignet on 26 November at St Nicholas' church. Of several children born to them in Liverpool, some died in infancy. By 1841 he was in Manchester, still making baskets and living on Deansgate. Later listed variously as secretary to a loan society, land agent and actuary at 4, Great Bridgewater Street, which premises he also opened as a dining room and Temperance hotel, from around 1847. Secretary of the Manchester Bridgewater Freehold Land Society, Ricketts Street (now Parkfield Road North) in New Moston was named after him. Died 24 February 1871 at Great Bridgewater Street.

Ridgway, David

Fellow Radical and partner of Elijah in the manufacture of pill-boxes, syringes and diachylon (an early form of sticking-plaster). Born c.1790 in Macclesfield, Cheshire, had moved to Manchester by 1806, where he married Martha Tepton at the Collegiate church on 20 January. Listed as a fustian-cutter at 46 Back Chapel Street, Ardwick (1807) and 7 Swarbrick Street, London Road (1808-25) but also selling coffee, tobacco and other goods, while his wife sold thread, childrens' books and 'Mother Shipton' (prophecies). In 1816, he kept a subscription book for the new Hampden Club at his house-cum-shop. Like Elijah, was a searcher for religious truth, some of his children being baptised twice, at Wesleyan or Bible Christian chapels, as well as at the Collegiate church. Arrested in 1821 for selling a copy of Carlile's 'New Year Address to the Radicals', sentenced to 12 months' imprisonment at Lancaster and bound over on release. During the trial in 1822, Richard Carlile appealed from his own prison cell, through the *Republican*, for a subscription from Radicals to pay for Ridgway's defence: Peter Candelet received the subscriptions at Market Street and he and Elijah provided surety on his release.

Was living at 3 Baker St, New Islington, when his wife Martha died in November 1834, aged 48, and that year's trade directory shows him in partnership with Elijah as 'Dixon & Ridgway, New Islington'. Moved to Newton Heath in September 1837 and shared a house with Elijah, claiming a rates rebate for part of the year. On 19 August 1838 his daughters Margaret and Mary Ann, still at Baker St, married William Steele and Rankin Wright respectively, in a double wedding at St Mary's church, off Deansgate. Ridgway was listed as 'traveller'; both grooms were mechanics. The partnership was dissolved in June 1841, when Elijah formed 'Dixon, Son & Co' and Ridgway entered a separate partnership with his son-in-law, William Steele, and Samuel Mather as pill-box makers and suppliers of druggist sundries: this was also in Newton Heath, not far from Elijah's works. The split with Elijah appears to have been amicable: Ridgway's son, Thomas, later married Elijah's daughter, Elizabeth, with William Steele as a witness. In 1851 he was lodging with the Young family in Leeds, occupation 'plaster manufacturer'. Ridgway, Steele & Co stayed in business until at least 1853, but nothing is known of what became of Ridgway after this.

Ridgway, Thomas Preston

Born at 7 Swarbrick Street, Bank Top (near London Road) on 20 November 1820 and baptised both at Christ Church, Hulme (Bible Christian), on 5 March 1821, and at the Collegiate church on 29 April 1821; son of Elijah's long-standing friend and business partner, David Ridgway, and his wife Martha. Named after Thomas Preston (1774-1850), London Radical who organised meetings at Spa Fields and was involved in the so-called Cato Street Conspiracy of 1819-20. Thomas was the first husband of Elijah's daughter, Elizabeth, whom he married at the Collegiate church on 29 January 1843, when living on Oldham Rd, Newton Heath. His occupation is given as 'pill-box maker', like his father. Died of consumption on 13 July 1843, aged only 22, less than six months after the wedding. No known children from this marriage.

Scholefield, James (Reverend and Doctor)

Born 6 April 1790 in Colne Bridge, Huddersfield, Yorkshire, and baptised 6 May at Kirkheaton. Became assistant to William Cowherd, founder of the Bible Christians, at Hulme and Salford, and married Charlotte Walker at St John's church in Manchester, 20 February 1821. Established his own chapel (Christ Church) on Every Street, Ancoats, which opened in 1824. He was a vegetarian and dispenser of homeopathic remedies, listing himself as 'surgeon' in the 1841 census. Arrested in 1842 for permitting a Chartist congress at the chapel (for which Feargus O'Connor stayed at his house the night before) and later founded a monument to Henry Hunt in the north part of the burial ground, completed the following year. O'Connor gave the foundation address. One of the more Radical Chartists, along with Elijah, James Wroe and Edward Nightingale, he later took a more pragmatic view on Corn Law repeal and the Incorporation of Manchester. After this came about in 1838, he put his name forward as nominee for councillor and was elected twice, preferring to keep an eye on the running of the new corporation from within. He died on 24 April 1855, of 'slow effusion of the brain', and was buried in the family vault beneath the house, together with his 'amiable' wife and five of his children. A gravestone, removed to the main burial ground by the Baptists some years after his death, can still be seen against a wall, close to the remains of the chapel in what is now a park.

Stephens, Joseph Rayner (Reverend)

Born 8 March 1805 in Edinburgh, the son of a Cornish-born father, John Stephens, and Essex-born mother, Rebecca Rayner. Came to Manchester in 1819, entering the grammar school, and later receiving tuition from a Methodist school in Leeds. Taught for a time in Cottingham, Yorkshire, becoming a Methodist preacher in 1825. Sent as a missionary to Stockholm, where he stayed for three years, becoming fluent in Swedish. Ordained as a minister and sent to the Cheltenham circuit in 1830, then Ashton-under-Lyne in 1832. Suspended in 1834 for supporting disestablishment, but chose to resign. Became a campaigner for the rights of factory workers and ardent supporter of Chartism; known as an advocate of 'physical force' - though he always denied this. His ringing - often intemperate - speeches were said to be clearly audible to open-air audiences of up to 20,000. On 13 November 1838, he spoke at a meeting in Leigh, Lancashire, deemed to be unlawful; arrested in December and sentenced to eighteen months imprisonment, which he served at Chester Castle, being bound over for five years after that. On release in 1840 he settled in Ashton and preached as an independent Methodist. Produced several journals, including the *Ashton Chronicle* in 1848-9. In 1852, moved to Stalybridge, preaching at King Street chapel, continuing to agitate over local issues almost up to his death on 18 February 1879. Buried at St John's churchyard, Dukinfield, there is a monument to him in Stamford Park, Stalybridge.

Wroe, James

Born in Manchester, baptised at the Collegiate Church on 11 January 1789, the third child of Thomas and Ruth, he followed his father and brother working as a house painter but began selling books and sheet music from a stall on Port Street. Listed as both painter and book-seller in 1818, at 49 Great Ancoats Street. With John Saxton, Joseph Johnson and John Knight, started the *Manchester Observer* on 3 January 1818, and with the last two named, formed the Patriotic Union Society the following year. Was present at the St Peter's Field meetings in July and August 1819, and coined the term 'Peterloo' in a series of pamphlets printed at the *Observer* office - ensuring his detestation and subsequent victimisation by the authorities. Indicted on eleven counts of seditious libel for his articles about the massacre (being scathing about the part of the yeomanry) and for selling Sherwin's *Political Register*, one edition of which contained comments about the Prince Regent's speech. For the latter, he served six months in Lancaster gaol. Such was the paranoia of the authorities, even his wife Alice and ten-year-old brother David were charged merely for selling copies of the newspaper. David was advised to plead guilty and was fined sixpence (justice was seen to be done!). Wroe moved across the road to 218 Great Ancoats Street (later renumbered 92), where he accommodated Richard Carlile on his Manchester tour in August 1827. The two had first met in London in December 1818 and Wroe helped Carlile get away after Peterloo. He was strongly supportive of Elijah on suffrage, local accountability and anti-incorporation but, like James Scholefield, when incorporation became a reality he accepted it and stood as councillor for New Cross Ward, becoming surveyor of highways, in which role he was highly regarded. Died of 'chronic inflammation of the liver' on 4 August 1844, aged 55, his son James present. Should not be confused with the Christian Israelite proponent, John Wroe of Bradford, who was unrelated.

Appendix 2

Places

Notable Manchester buildings and venues mentioned in the text.

Bridgewater Arms

One of Manchester's principal coaching inns in late eighteenth and early nineteenth centuries, from where the London mails were despatched. Opened in 1789, it stood on the east side of High Street, close to the corner of Market Street. When the railway age brought about the decline of stagecoaches, limiting them to local routes, the inn itself declined amid competition from other taverns and hotels; demolished in the 1840s and replaced by shops and offices. The present Debenhams store (originally Rylands) was built partly on the site in the 1920s and the only reminder of the inn's existence today is the back street behind the store, named Bridgewater Place.

Carpenters Hall

Nickname given to the Hall of Science in Campfield, on the corner of Tonman and Byrom Streets, off Liverpool Road. It was the brainchild of the Owenite Co-operative movement, who wished to follow the example of the Mechanics Institutes in providing free education to workers. Whereas the Institutes tended to concentrate on engineering and chemistry, courses offered by the Hall of Science offered a broader range of subjects, including politics and social philosophy. Foundation stone laid by Robert Owen on 5 August 1839, addresses being given by himself and Abel Heywood; completed in January 1840. Its familiar name arose because the woodwork was constructed by local carpenters, freely volunteering their skills and time. When Friedrich Engels visited the Hall in 1843 he was surprised at hearing 'the most ordinary workers speaking with a clear understanding on political, religious and social affairs'. Referring to it by yet another popular name – the Socialist Hall – Engels recounted that with a capacity of about 3,000 it was 'crowded every Sunday'.

However, rifts within the movement led to its being sold in 1850, and two years later Manchester's first Free Library was established there, Dickens and Thackeray attending the opening. By 1877, it was deemed unsuitable for the growing volume of books and, after the opening of the new Town Hall in Albert

Square, the library moved into the old town hall building on King Street. The original Tonman Street building was demolished soon afterwards and the Free Library, now known as Manchester Central Library, moved to its present location in St Peter's Square in 1934. An iron and glass market hall, later the City Hall exhibition centre, was constructed roughly on the Hall of Science site in 1879; this is now the Aerospace section of the Museum of Science and Industry, so not inappropriate.

Christ Church, Ancoats (Bible Christian)

Founded in 1822 by the Reverend Dr James Scholefield, after leaving the Bible Christian church at Hulme, this stood near the southern end of Every Street, on land formerly belonging to the Mosleys at Ancoats Hall. The chapel, circular in plan and fronted by his house (later numbered 20 Every Street), was opened for services on 29 February 1824 and contained a schoolroom in the cellar and a separate surgery at the rear. On three sides it was surrounded by an extensive non-denominational burial ground, opened before the chapel was completed. A tunnel under Ancoats Grove gave access to the largest section of the graveyard on the eastern side, reaching down to the banks of the River Medlock. Either side of the steps to the house doorway were two cellars, the right-hand one used as a family vault by the Scholefields. In 1842-3, in the northern part of the burial ground, a red sandstone memorial to Henry Hunt was built, topped by a miniature statue of him. The vaults below it were intended for the remains of Chartists, whose names were added to a plaque on the obelisk above; in the event only five burials took place there. After Scholefield's death in 1855, the chapel was taken over by the Baptists, who reinterred the Scholefields in the main burial ground.

Closure of the burial ground in 1867 was followed by that of the chapel itself, about 1880, after which it became a Salvation Army hostel. The Hunt obelisk, said to have become unsafe (though this was disputed), was demolished late in 1888. A reply to a newspaper query about the church, in 1889, mentions one of the surviving gravestones bearing the inscription 'In memory of Martha, daughter of Elijah and Martha Dixon, who died Ocr 15, 1823, aged 2 years and 11 months'. The respondent, a Mr F.L. Tavare, added in parentheses 'A child of the Father of English Reformers and Peterloo Veteran'. In 1895 the site was acquired as part of the Manchester University Settlement, a gymnasium being built on the northern part of the burial ground, and in 1928 the Round Chapel was extensively rebuilt, though mostly retaining its outward appearance, to become the Round House Theatre. In the 1940s a ballet club and café were added. In the 1960s it was used as a store for the education department, but lay derelict by 1975. The house was demolished the following year and, in spite of its Grade II listing, the chapel by 1986. The southern part of the burial ground was left as a small park with the lower section of the chapel wall and a few token gravestones retained, including Dr Scholefield's, cemented upright against an adjoining wall. The sad fate of the Hunt memorial and the Round Chapel neatly demonstrates what commentators have called the 'collective amnesia' of Manchester towards its Radical past.

Collegiate Church

Familiar today as Manchester Cathedral, the 'Collegiate and Parish Church of St Mary, St Denys and St George', to give its original full title, has a long and complex history. A new parish church was completed in 1215 on the site of an older (c.900) church dedicated to St Mary. Local noble families, particularly the Greslets and De la Warres, extended and added to the buildings, culminating in 1421 when Thomas De la Warre donated his manor house as a college for the priesthood, by licence from King Henry V and - this being pre-Reformation - Pope Martin V. A free grammar school was later added, between the college and church, opening in 1518. In 1653, from a bequest by Humphrey Chetham, the college was bought and opened as a free library and blue coat school. This is still open and is Britain's oldest free public library; the school is now Chetham's School of Music. In Elijah's time, the church was still the main parish church for Manchester and any resident was entitled to be Christened or married there. The vestry rooms were used for meetings of churchwardens and leypayers (ordinary citizens who paid the poor rate). The churchyard, with burials from the 1500s onwards, surrounded the main building, but was gradually reduced in size by selling bits off and extending surrounding streets across it. Burials in the main ground ceased in 1819, except for the interment of a Bishop in 1866. Only a small section now remains. Between 1767 and 1788, part of the adjacent college garden was used as a paupers' burial ground, and in 1815 another 'overspill' ground was opened alongside Walker's Croft, on the north bank of the River Irk between Hunt's Bank and Miller Street. This cemetery is now covered by the suburban platforms of Victoria Railway Station. The church became a Cathedral in 1847, when a new diocese of Manchester was formed, as a step towards the town being granted City status in 1853.

Corn Exchange

The original building, designed by architect Richard Lane, was opened in 1837 in the roughly triangular area bounded by Hanging Ditch, Cathedral Street and Fennel Street. Its full title was the Corn and Produce Exchange. This building, however, was demolished in 1897 and replaced by the existing one, built in two phases between then and 1903. The trading floor ceased to be used after 1945, the building becoming a venue for exhibitions and later home to many small traders, especially in second-hand and collectors' items. The exterior-facing rooms were also used for retail outlets, including Harry Hall's Cycles and Manchester's first computer shop. The nearby IRA bomb of 1996 caused much damage and forced most traders to relocate. Now renamed The Triangle, the refurbished Victorian and Edwardian buildings house multiple food outlets.

Free Trade Hall

The current hall, the third of this name, was built in 1853-6 in Italian palazzo style by Edward Walters, and is on Peter Street, roughly on the site of St Peter's Fields, scene of *Peterloo*. The land was given by Richard Cobden. An earlier wooden pavilion of 1840 and a brick replacement of 1842 were both deemed inadequate. By 1858, Sir Charles Halle had made it the regular home for his orchestral concerts and the building (and the Halle orchestra) achieved international fame. The hall was gutted in the bombing blitz of December 1940, but reopened in 1951 after an extensive rebuild, retaining two sides of the original facade. A 1950s state-of-the-art polished wooden baffle system was installed behind the stage, providing unrivalled acoustic qualities. It continued as a major concert venue for rock bands and singers, as well as staging classical music and theatre productions. The Halle orchestra moved home in 1996 to the new Bridgewater Hall on Lower Mosley Street and the Free Trade Hall has since been converted into a hotel.

Manchester Athenaeum (or Atheneum)

Designed in the palazzo style by Sir Charles Barry, the building on Princess Street, close to the corner of Mosley Street, was completed in 1838 for the Athenaeum Society, whose aims were the 'advancement and diffusion of knowledge', although membership was by subscription only. It contained coffee and news rooms, a library and lecture hall, the latter often used for public meetings. Richard Cobden gave the opening address; famous guest lecturers over the years included Charles Dickens and Benjamin Disraeli. The Society declined in the 1930s and the building was acquired by the Corporation in 1938. Since 2002 it has been connected by an atrium to the adjacent art gallery, to which it now forms an extension. It is Grade II listed by English Heritage.

Manchester Town Hall (first)

Replacing the old Police Office on King Street, Manchester's first purpose-built town hall was opened on the same street in 1825, on the corner of Cross Street. Designed by Francis Godwin, much of the construction work was undertaken by the local building firm of David Bellhouse (whose descendants would later merge their timber business with that of George Evans, Elijah's grandson). It contained offices for the Boroughreeve, constabulary, town clerks and other officials on the ground floor, with the first floor housing the Assembly Rooms. By the 1860s, the administration of the still-expanding city had outgrown it and a new hall was commissioned by the Mayor, Abel Heywood. Designed by Alfred Waterhouse, this was constructed between 1868 and 1877 in Albert Square and is still in use today. After closure in 1877, the King Street site housed the Free Library, but was demolished in 1912, a bank being built on the site. The Ionic columns from the facade were dismantled and re-erected beside the boating lake in Heaton Park, where they can still be seen.

Manor Court Room

Home of the Court Leet, part of the Mosley family's manorial estate, it stood on Brown Street, off Market Street. As late as 1839, minor misdemeanours were still being handled by Court Leet officials appointed by the Lord of the Manor, Sir Oswald Mosley, 2nd Baronet (1785-1871). The manor was also responsible for civic amenities such as water supply and highways. Given the massive population growth of Manchester, this basically feudal system was one of many archaic institutions that were crying out for reform. Sir Oswald, who had offered to sell the manor and all rights to the Manchester inhabitants in 1815, but was turned down, eventually transferred the estate in 1846 to the Corporation for £200,000 and was thus Manchester's last Lord of the Manor. His great-great grandson, also Oswald, the 6th Baronet (1896-1980), was the infamous fascist leader. In 1839 the old courtroom became the Borough Police Court, a post office being added a year later. It was replaced by the Assize Courts at Strangeways in 1866. Spring Gardens Post Office, completed in 1884 and still open, though with 1960s additions, now covers the site.

Open Spaces

Manchester's open spaces, once common as meeting places, or for sport and recreation, have gradually moved from the centre to outlying districts, spurred by the creation of public parks from the 1840s onwards. In medieval Manchester, there were five main 'fields' used for common grazing, agriculture and markets, of which only two survived by 1800: Camp Field and Castle Field, whose names give clues to their ancient usage. Of the others, Acre's Field, occupied by St Ann's church and Square from 1712 onwards, was still talked about by a few, but Parsonage Field and Dole Field had long gone, the latter surviving only as a street name, off Deansgate. To these were added newer 'fields' surrounding the eighteenth century churches of St George (1798) and St Peter (1788).

Camp Field - this occupied an area roughly bounded by Liverpool Road, Deansgate, St John's Street and Byrom Street, and saw many changes from the 1820s onwards. St Matthew's church (1823-5) and the Hall of Science (1839-40) were the first buildings to be established here, and part of the western end had disappeared under the Liverpool Road railway station in 1830. By the 1850s, large buildings on Deansgate began to cover parts of the site and, St Matthew's having been demolished in 1952, most of the area today is occupied by the Museum of Science and Industry, with a few adjacent modern houses and flats.

Castle Field - before the extension and widening of Priestner Street to create Liverpool Road, around 1810, this was south of, and contiguous with, Camp Field, and surrounded the site of the Roman fort of Mancenium (later Mancunium or Mancestre), completed in 82 AD. From 1761, the name was more readily associated with the area around the Bridgewater Canal wharves and gradually the field was decimated by access roads, warehouses and offices, which multiplied after 1804 by the conjoining of the canal from Rochdale. Later still the area was criss-crossed by railway viaducts and up to the 1970s the whole area had a cluttered, down-at-heel appearance. However, many of the buildings survived and, now renovated and used for residential or leisure purposes, have become a notable cultural centre. The reconstructed Roman fort and nearby Science Museum, based around the world's first 'Inter-City' railway station, are among the attractions that are frequently supplemented by fairs, canal festivals and street entertainers.

St George's Field - not the small churchyard itself, but the large grassed area surrounding it, which once occupied the site between St George's Road (now Rochdale Road), Lees Street (Thompson Street), Newton Lane (Oldham Road), and Livesey Street. Scene of numerous protest meetings in the early 1800s, especially by the many spinners and weavers who lived around the New Cross area. Housing had begun to encroach in the 1820s, but the building of Oldham Road railway station in 1836-9, with its accompanying sidings, took up fully half of the field. The rest disappeared, along with the original church, in the 1870s, when the railway extended its sidings, built a line across Rochdale Road to Gould Street gasworks and erected new warehouses for produce, mainly to serve the nearby Smithfield Market. Oldham Road goods depot, as it had become, was closed in 1968 and the area is now occupied by a Royal Mail sorting office, a Chinese emporium and the central Fire Station.

St Peter's Field - area to the west of St Peter's church, this large open space was bisected by Peter Street (then little more than a narrow lane) and bounded roughly by Dickenson Street, Watson Street, Windmill Street and Lower Mosley Street, although parts of neighbouring streets protruded here and there, and a few small sections were laid out as formal gardens. Because of its relatively large size and central location, it became a favourite venue for political meetings of the early nineteenth century and easily accommodated the estimated 60,000 attendees on 16 August 1819, at which the infamous massacre took place. Following this, such large meetings were never repeated and, probably in part to expunge the notoriety of the location, the area was quickly sold off, piece by piece, until even by 1840 little remained. The northern side of Peter Street was developed first, with the building of offices and a chapel, while Manchester's first Natural History Museum (long since gone) was located on the south side, together with the Free Trade Hall, which today roughly marks the centre of the southern half.

Palace Inn

Formerly the home of one John Dickenson, this early eighteenth century building stood in Palace Square, off Market Street, a little to the north-west of the junction with High Street. Prince Charles Edward Stuart stayed at the house in November 1745 and was proclaimed King James III while in Manchester. He left for the south on 1 December, but was back a week or so later, in retreat. By the 1820s the house had been converted to an inn and the square in front of it became one of many gathering places for political and other meetings, rooms inside also being occasionally hired. The original building was demolished in 1839 and a replacement built on Market Street itself, the new 'Palace Buildings' surviving into the early twentieth century. Today the whole area has been obliterated by the Arndale Centre.

Appendix 3

Currency and Imperial Units

To avoid burdening the text with old currency and unit conversions, all references to money, weights and measures have been given in the British imperial, pre-decimal units used in Elijah's lifetime. Anyone unfamiliar with these might find the following notes useful:-

Currency

Pre-decimal British currency consisted of the pound, divided into twenty shillings, each of which consisted of twelve pennies (pence), thus there were 240 pence to one pound. The abbreviations for these (taken from late Roman coinage) were 'l' (librae), 's' (solidi) and 'd' (denarii). So, for example, a price of 2 pounds, 4 shillings and 6 pence would be written 2l 4s 6d. In the latter half of the nineteenth century, the 'l' became a stylised capital 'L' (the '£' sign still used) and was written before the amount, so the above example would become £2 4s 6d. Amounts under a pound would simply gives shillings and pence, eg. 2s 11d, and anything under a shilling, just the pence, eg. 9d. The only time a zero would be used was for amounts over a pound, but with a number of pence less than a shilling, so for instance three pounds and six pence would be written 3l 0s 6d. In later years, the 's' would sometimes be omitted and an oblique symbol (solidus) used to separate shillings and pence, so six shillings and eightpence (6s 8d) could be written 6/8d, or just 6/8 (spoken as 'six and eight'). In this shorthand, a hyphen was often used for zero, eg. 1/- (one shilling exactly, ie. no pence).

Weights and measures

Some common standard imperial units, with their abbreviations, divisions and approximate metric equivalents, are given in the table below:-

	Imperial unit	Abbrev	Divided into	Metric equivalent
Length:	1 mile	ml	1760 yards	1.608 kilometres
	1 yard	yd	3 feet	0.914 metres
	1 foot	ft	12 inches	304.8 millimetres
	1 inch	in	-	25.4 millimetres
Area (land):	1 acre	a	4 roods	0.405 hectares
	1 rood	r	40 square perches	0.1 hectares
	1 square perch	p (or sq.p)	30.25 square yards	25.29 square metres
Weight:	1 ton	t	20 hundredweights	1016 kilograms
	1 hundredweight	cwt	4 quarters	50.8 kilograms
	1 quarter	q	2 stones	12.7 kilograms
	1 stone	st	14 pounds	6.350 kilograms
	1 pound	lb	16 ounces	0.454 kilograms
	1 ounce	oz	-	28.3 grams
Volume:	1 bushel	bu	2 pecks	0.036 cubic metres*
	1 peck	pk	2 gallons	0.009 cubic metres*
	1 gallon	gal	4 quarts	4.546 litres
	1 quart	qt	2 pints	1.137 litres
	1 pint	pt	20 fluid ounces	0.568 litres
	1 fluid ounce	fl.oz	-	28.4 millilitres

Table of weights and measures

* There was no distinction in the UK between liquid and dry volume measurements, but since the peck and bushel were almost always used for dry goods (cereals, spices, etc), cubic metres have been given here, rather than litres. Obviously, the *weight* of a bushel, say, would depend on the goods being measured, eg. wheat (60lb per bushel) is heavier than oats (32lb per bushel).

Appendix 4

Street Renumbering

Prior to 1830, the properties on most Manchester streets were numbered using the 'clockwise' system, in which the convention was to begin with the first property on the left, looking away from the town centre (or from the nearest main road) and calling this number one, then numbering consecutively in ascending order along the same side. At the end of the street, crossing over, the numbers would continue to ascend, but coming back toward the starting point, so the highest number would be opposite number one. Between about 1831 and 1838, the system was changed, street by street, to the now-familiar 'odd-and-even' system. Starting at the same point, properties on the left would be given ascending odd numbers, and those on the right, even numbers. A diagram might make this clearer:-

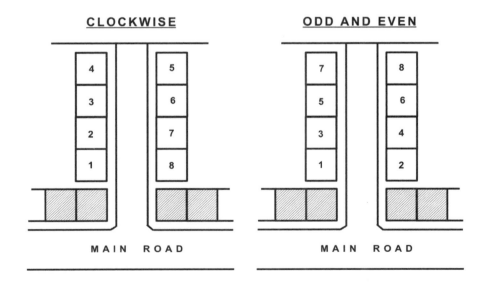

Street numbering examples

In either system, number one would remain the same, and there may be other properties that coincidentally retain the same number (as with number six, in the example above), but most numbers would change, sometimes quite dramatically so, especially on a long street.

Thus, Elijah's shop at 42, Great Ancoats Street became number 79 in 1832; similarly, 3, Dixon Street became number 5, around 1835. When James Wroe moved from 49, Great Ancoats Street to number 218, before renumbering, he was in fact only moving a short distance across the street, as those numbers became 91 and 92 respectively, on the odd-and-even system.

Note: some properties on the north side of Great Ancoats Street in fact suffered another minor renumbering in 1850, caused by new property construction and not by any system change. His former shop, first numbered 42 then 79, changed again to number 87. The south side was not affected by this, so number 92 remained the same.

Select Bibliography

ADAMS, G.B., *Constitutional History of England* (Jonathan Cape, revised edition, 1963).

ARMYTAGE, W.H.G., *Heaven's Below* (Routledge, 2006).

BOOKER, Rev J., *History of the Ancient Chapelry of Blackley* (Simms, 1854).

BURCHARDT, J., *Paradise Lost, Rural Idyll and Social Change Since 1800* (I.B. Tauris, 2002).

BUSH, M.L., *The Casualties of Peterloo* (Carnegie Publishing, 2005).

COOPER, G., *The Illustrated History of Manchester's Suburbs* (Manchester City Council/Breedon Books Publishing, 2002).

COURT RECORDS, *The Trial of Henry Hunt Esq and others* (T. Dolby,1820).

DERRY, J., *Cobbett's England, A Selection from the Writings of William Cobbett* (Parkgate Books, 1997).

DOHERTY, J., *Poor Man's Advocate, vols. 1-50* (Greenwood Reprints, 1988)

ENGELS, F., *The Condition of the Working Class in England* [1844] (edited by D. McClellan, Oxford Word Classics, 1993).

ENSOR, R.C.K., *England 1870-1914* (Oxford University Press, 1936).

FINER, S.E., *The Life and Times of Sir Edwin Chadwick* (Methuen, 1952).

FROW, E. & R., *Manchester and Salford Chartists* (Working Class Movement Library, 1996).

GIBSON, K., *Pennine Pioneer, the Story of the Rochdale Canal* (Tempus Publishing, 2004).

GREENALL, R.L., *The Making of Victorian Salford* (Carnegie Publishing, 2000).

HOBSBAWM, E., *Industry and Empire* (Pelican Economic History of Britain, 1968).

HOLYOAKE, G.J., *History of Co-operation Vols.1 & 2* (complete edition, Fisher Unwin, 1906).

HUISH, R., *A History of the Private and Political Life of Henry Hunt* (Saunders, 1835).

HYLTON, S., *A History of Manchester* (Phillimore, 2003).

LLOYD, R., *Farewell to Steam* (Geo Allen and Unwin, 1956).

MARR, A., *A History of Modern Britain* (Macmillan, 2007).

PARKINSON-BAILEY, J.J., *Manchester, An Architectural History* (Manchester University Press, 2000).

PICKERING, P.A., *Chartism and the Chartists in Manchester and Salford* (Palgrave Macmillan, 1995).

PRENTICE, A., *Historical Sketches and Personal Recollections of Manchester* (Parkes, 1851).

POOLE, R., *The Risings of 1817* (Luddite Memorial Lecture, University of Huddersfield, 2016).

PROCTOR, R.W., *Memorials of Manchester Streets* (Sutcliffe, 1874).

REACH, A.B., *Manchester and the Textile Districts in 1849* (edited by C. Aspin, Helmshore Local History Society, 1972).

RILEY, P., *Holmfirth, A Bygone Era* (P & D Riley, 2006).

SEALE, B., *The Moston Story* (St John Vianney's R.C. Church, 1983).

SLUGG, J.T., *Reminiscences of Manchester Fifty Years Ago* (Simpkin Marshall & Co, 1881).

THOMPSON, E.P., *The Making of the English Working Class* (Victor Gollancz, Pelican, 1963).

WILKES, S., *Regency Spies, Secret Histories of Britain's Rebels and Revolutionaries* (Pen and Sword History, 2015).

WILSON, A.N., *The Victorians* (Arrow Books, 2003).

WOODWARD, E.L., *The Age of Reform 1815-1870* (Oxford University Press, 2ed., 1962).

Index